MOOBLI

by the same author

THE BIG MAN
IT SURE BEATS WORKING
ALONE IN THE WILDERNESS
MY WILDERNESS WILD CATS
LIANE, A CAT FROM THE WILD
BETWEEN EARTH AND PARADISE
GOLDEN EAGLE YEARS
A LAST WILD PLACE
OUT OF THE WILD
ON WING AND WILD WATER
WILDCAT HAVEN

MOOBLI

Mike Tomkies

JONATHAN CAPE
THIRTY-TWO BEDFORD SQUARE LONDON

First published 1988
Text and photographs copyright © 1988 Mike Tomkies
Jonathan Cape Ltd, 32 Bedford Square, London WC1B 3EL

A CIP catalogue record for this book
is available from the British Library.

ISBN 0 224 02406 6

Phototypeset by Falcon Graphic Art Ltd
Wallington, Surrey
Text printed in Great Britain by
Butler & Tanner Ltd, Frome and London
Colour printed in Great Britain by
Chorley and Pickersgill Ltd, Leeds

Contents

For Shirley Bellwood

1 · A Preposterous Pup

The breeder placed upon her kennel courtyard the pup I had hoped would become my powerful, amiable and faithful companion in the wilds. My first reaction was to laugh out loud. He was droopy, fat as a piglet, and he stood square, knock-kneed, his four huge paws out of all proportion to his size. He looked as knobbly as a piano stool from the Gothic era. His coat was black from the top of his head, down his back and along the flanks to the end of his tail. The creamy tan of his underside stretched up the chest, ending in a pair of inverted question marks on his forehead, which gave a comically doleful look to his brown eyes. Two great ears flopped out sideways like a pair of wings. When he moved his huge front paws unfolded clumsily, *flub dub*, *flub dub*, upon the ground, so that romantic names like 'King' and 'Dancer' vanished from my mind and all that remained was the phrase 'Flubby Dub Dubs.'

I looked at the pedigree with unbelieving eyes – seventeen international, national and grand champions in just four generations. With an effort I gathered the floppy lump of a pup up into my arms. Immediately he thrust his wet black muzzle – as big as a bear cub's – into my neck and took a playful slobbery bite of my whole ear. He seemed affectionate anyway.

I told the breeder that I would fetch him in a week, by which time he would have received all the necessary inoculations. I would probably ring up with some excuse long before then and post her a cheque for her trouble. How could an ungainly young animal like this ever fit into my hard life in the wilds of the Scottish Highlands? These neat kennels in svelte rolling Sussex downs above elegant Eastbourne were a far cry from the old stone cottage where I lived more than six miles from my nearest neighbour in a cleft in the dark mountains of south Inverness-shire.

As I drove away from Hadlow Down I felt it might have been a mistake to look for so young a pup. Maybe my judgement had been clouded by a spell of consuming loneliness as the dark weeks of winter closed in along the 15 miles of roadless loch shore. Certainly I wanted an Alsatian, the breed most often used by the police and mountain rescue teams for their tracking skill, obedience, physical power and endurance. But maybe I ought to get an older and sturdier animal.

Perhaps all the last few years had been a mistake, to give up my life as a travelling journalist in London, Paris, Madrid, Rome and Hollywood, for the sake of a much harsher dream. After a nature-loving boyhood, I had not given much thought to wildlife until I built the log cabin on the Pacific coast of Canada. There I found black bears in my backyard, bald eagles nesting on a nearby island, and had then trekked after the awesome grizzly and the elusive cougar. That was seven years ago, and since then I had made habitable the shattered wooden croft which I had found on the island of Shona, between Ardnamurchan and Skye, and had begun to write about Britain's rarest and most spectacular wild creatures.

It had seemed inevitable that I should move to my present home in the most isolated spot I had ever discovered in the western Highlands. I called it Wildernesse. Here, halfway up the deserted shore of a long freshwater loch, on which the rare black-throated diver breeds in summer and ferocious storms often prevent navigation in winter, I had spent the last four months settling down to a spartan existence without electricity, piped gas, telephone, television or postal delivery of any sort. The only 'mod con' was icy water piped from a waterfall pool in the east wood burn. The nearest town lay 44 miles away, but I was surrounded by some of the richest wildlife in Europe. Golden eagles soared over the high crags upon which the mighty red deer stags roared in the autumn rut. In the lochside woods I was trying to track badgers, otters, foxes, rare pine martens and Scottish wildcats. I needed not only a loyal companion to alleviate the loneliness but also an intelligent and obedient tracking

2

dog, one that would not chase sheep or deer and would warn of intruders. On the advice of Gwen Cooper (wife of the comedian Tommy Cooper, who owned two magnificent German Shepherds) I had written to Molly Thomson.

Her next litter of German Shepherds was due in November, she said in reply, promising to reserve for me the best of the dog pups. It would be ready to leave for Scotland in January, after it had been inoculated and cleared for hardpad and distemper. She gave me the address of a firm in Lincolnshire which could despatch 28lb boxes of sterilised meat sausage that would keep for six weeks without refrigeration – ideal for supplementing the diet of a big animal in my primitive circumstances, where I could run only a small cold box off bottled calor gas.

> All my pups have superb temperament, and as far as I know none have ever worried sheep, but of course this would depend on the training. Their natural instinct is to protect their owners and property, and warn if intruders are about by barking only, so it really depends if you have the time to take on a pup . . . The sire of this litter is wanted in Australia by the Sydney police force but the owner has refused £2,000 for him.

She named a reasonable price and I sent off the deposit. In heavy snow blizzards I drove south in early January, and so first set eyes on the preposterous pup.

When I returned to Hadlow Down on January 17, he was leading the troupe of pups leaping up enthusiastically at the gate of their heated pen.

'There, I'm sure he recognises you,' Miss Thomson said.

I was doubtful. His eyes seemed more droopy, and his ears bigger and floppier than those of the others, and I wondered if I should take one of them instead.

'Nonsense,' she laughed. 'You wanted a big dog. He's the best of the litter, probably the biggest pup we've ever had here. You look after him right and you'll have a dog you can be proud of.'

I paid the rest of the fee, then carried the pup out to my Land Rover. Despite the strangeness he showed no animation, excitement or fear, and just sat on the seat next to me. He was friendly but solemn, his tan spectacles giving him an oddly old and dignified look. Molly Thomson told me he had been born on November 3, which made him not quite 11 weeks old. She handed me the pup's diet sheet, one glance at which made me realise that my own daily rations were meagre in comparison, and started me worrying about my diminishing bank balance.

I drove to the nearby town and left the pup in the car park while I had coffee with a friend before the 600-mile drive back to the Highlands. When we returned to the Land Rover the pup had a woebegone look.

'Heck, I hope he doesn't do that too often,' I said, as we swabbed down the fouled blankets.

My friend (a mother of three) just laughed. 'Well, you've never had kids or nappies to worry about. It will do you good!'

The Land Rover was heavily laden, the bed in the rear raised to twice its normal height by a sea chest filled with files and books. The pup whined briefly at the unaccustomed movement as I drove away. He cowered back from the noise of trucks whizzing past the windows on the motorway, and then slept fitfully with his head between his flubby-dub paws on my lap. At service stations he relieved himself on grass verges. He was so scared of rumbling truck monsters that he kept diving between my legs for protection and tripping me up. I was glad of our full load when gales and rain buffeted the Land Rover which, despite the extra stability, made slow progress against the strong winds. It was the worst journey home I had ever endured.

Four hours after dark I turned off the main road towards one of my favourite dormitories in a wood near St Anne's. Imagine my surprise when I saw that the entire forest had been felled. Wearily I drove on to another fir wood within 20 miles of Glasgow. Once settled there, I walked ostentatiously away from the vehicle to demonstrate to the pup that bodily waste functions were best performed out of doors. We whined to each other as he showed great interest in the human anatomy and performance, which I was glad to see him begin to copy. Later, while I cooked our suppers on the Rover's stove, he became perplexed by the reflection of our rear quarters in the dark windscreen. He kept trying to scramble into the room he could plainly see on the other side. He snored raucously all night on the front seat without trying to invade my bed, and remained clean and dry. It was astonishing for a pup that had never slept alone before.

4

After breakfast amid the sombre fallen firs in that icy cold glade, we drove on through more rain and gales. At times the pup sighed and pushed a big paw into my leg, as if he wanted to get out. As we passed through Glasgow I tapped the windscreen, to show him a town. He looked out intelligently and stopped cowering away from heavy trucks and buses. He began whining distractedly as we passed Loch Lomond, so I let him out. He learns fast, I thought gratefully. I was now racing against time: I needed to sign some documents at my lawyer's office and to get my boat back before dark from a local shipwright who had promised to repair a crack between the twin hulls.

'Flat tyre!' yelled a voice at the first sea ferry.

Cajolery and some bribery at a nearby garage produced a lad with a hydraulic jack who was prepared to delay his dinner, and we had the offside rear wheel changed in minutes. The lawyer turned out to be ill in bed, but a hasty phone call from his office straightened everything out and I signed the documents before hurrying on the last 40 miles to collect the boat. That was not ready either. Gales had disrupted the work, but I was promised it would be finished that night and ready at the lochside next morning. There was nothing for it, the pup and I would have to camp out for one more bitter cold night.

This time I let him sleep beside me, though outside the covers, and was grateful for his warm body heat. Again he did not disgrace himself, but whined early to be let out.

'You learn fast, my pedigree pup,' I muttered sleepily before snuggling back under the covers.

The pup attracted a good deal of attention as I finished my shopping in the local village.

'Look at those great knee caps and paws. He's going to be a monster!'

'Is the wee thing a cross between a dachshund and a St Bernard?'

At the post office a man I had never met before looked at him sourly. 'He'll no be a sheep chaser, will he?'

I apprised him of the fact that the Alsatian was the German shepherd dog and, because of its tractability and innate gentleness, was originally used for *herding* sheep. I assured him that my pup would certainly be trained not to chase sheep, and that in the life of tracking wild creatures I intended for him, he would probably not be interested in sheep anyway.

5

'Och, that's just as well,' said the stranger, 'for if he chases sheep we'll be shootin' him.'

Faced with such an abrasive remark from a stranger I repeated the writer T.H. White's words upon taking one of his dogs to help rout a troublesome fox with folk whose marksmanship he did not trust; he was afraid one of them might shoot his pet.

'Shot one will be the dog dead. Shot two will be the man who did it dead.' I fired at his astonished face with my fingers. 'Bang, bang, just like that!'

I winked at the post mistress, and withdrew.

The loch was churned up when I reached the shore. The shipwright had trailered the boat to within 50 yards of the turbulent water but half a mile away from where I usually parked the Land Rover in a pine wood. I pulled up short and unloaded the heavy 20 horse-power engine and its fuel tank amid a herd of cows that had surrounded the boat. As I dragged out the engine, the pup leaped down on to the ground beside me and, to my surprise, was instantly menaced by two of the cows which lowered their heads and lumbered towards him. He took one look at these strange giants and dodged with a high yelp beneath the Land Rover. After carrying the engine and tank to the shore, I returned to extricate the terrified pup.

It was not easy. A truculent cow can be as dangerous as a bull, and while bent down in an attempt at retrieval I would present an appealing target. Just a hard bunt could severely bruise or break my back-bone. I managed to shoo the cows away a few yards before enticing out the pup with encouraging words. As I bent to lift him clear, my gaze fell upon what looked like the foot of a rhinoceros, only a yard or two from my own feet. My eyes travelled up to take in the form of a huge Charolais bull, complete with copper-coloured ring through its nose. Twice I had been chased by bulls when I was a boy in Sussex, and roaming close to wild grizzlies in the forests of Canada produced nothing like the fear I experienced at this moment, face to face with this beast. I did not wait to see if it was friendly but leaped into the driving seat and hurtled off at unnecessary speed to my usual parking place, with the herd trotting behind. Then it dawned on me that they associated my Land Rover with the farmer's and were expecting a bundle of choice hay. When they saw that I had none they wandered away to graze.

I returned to the boat with an armful of loose pine branches to prevent the shore stones from damaging the hull. After man-hauling its 500lbs weight over them to the water's edge, I clamped on the engine and lurched through the waves back to calmer water below the parked Land Rover.

'Come on, Pups,' I said as I carried him down and tied him aboard under the canopy of the half-cabin. 'We don't want the cows to have another go at you.'

To my surprise he showed no agitation. He just squatted, his thick forelegs and great semi-webbed feet braced against the surging movements of the boat and stared at me with solemn sad eyes along the length of his black muzzle. He looks more like a duck-billed platypus than a dog, I thought.

There was no way I could carry the big sea chest full of books, so I emptied it out into piles on the ground. Immediately it began to rain. Covering the piles hastily with plastic sheeting, I dumped the empty chest into the boat and loaded the books into it in manage-able bagfuls. Then we set off.

We had gone only a few hundred yards into the stormy follow-ing waves when the engine gave out. It also failed to restart. Frantically I leaped to the oars as we wallowed dangerously and flailed as best I could into the lee of a small promontory. I took the fuel hose apart and blew through it, petrol spurting over the deck, then re-assembled it. The pup shook his little head and yiped, moving his feet up and down as the petrol stung his toes. He hated its smell.

I lifted him on to a dry sack and felt the whole body quivering. I held him up to see the towering mountains that were to be his home, but he was frightened now, ears down and whining, and sought the safety of the cabin. As the boat surged in the troughs, climbing slowly up a wave before crashing down its far side into the next, I looked at him shivering and thought of what he had endured since leaving his cosy protected home in Sussex – the long drives, two nights camped out in winter, and now this cold, rough, six-mile boat journey. I was afraid it might all have overtaxed his young strength, and that he might even die.

A wharf to the south had been broken up by the storm and I found many of its timbers scattered along my stretch of shore, so that I had to land on a small beach 200 yards away. The boat bay was being pounded by waves. I put the little pup out first, but he tried to leap back, missed, and fell into three feet of water. He swam to the bank, shook himself and leaped about wagging his tail. Far from dying, he seemed full of life and happy to be at Wildernesse. He plodded close behind me up the muddy path, sniffing at everything and peering into every room. At night he sat quietly by my desk while I wrote letters by the light of a paraffin lamp, as if he had been born to it.

During those first days, training him seemed easy. As I showed him the garden and woods, he soon learned not to entangle himself in my legs. Although he kept back naturally, he sometimes walked slightly to one side of me, so that he could see where he was going, which was sensible. He traipsed happily through marsh (usually the muddiest parts) and clambered gamely over rocks and small tree trunks that lay on the ground. He stared at the rushing waters of the burn and barked loudly, but on seeing me wade through he floundered after me. When I heard that extraordinarily loud and comically low-pitched bark coming from so young a pup I knew for sure I could never call him 'King' or 'Dancer' and rather absurdly hit upon 'Beowulf'.

When he whined to go outside at night to perform his major business, without any training, it seemed too good to be true. Apart from the first transgression in the Sussex car park, he had not disgraced himself once.

'There's a good boy, *and* a nice boy,' I said as he came in.

Suddenly I realised that this was a phrase I had used with my wild stray dog Booto in Canada, that unconsciously I said several things to Beowulf in the same words as I had spoken to my old compadre. I stopped doing it: those phrases belonged to Booto, to that life, and it seemed an odd kind of insult to employ them second-hand on my new young friend.

Beowulf was clearly a tough little chap and he loved to play. He shoved his nose into one of my shoes and chuffed it round the floor as if playing trains. He played with a conker like a cat, kicking and scooping it over the ground, throwing it up into the air with both paws and catching it with his teeth after the first bounce. I teased him with the broom and he instantly tried to bite it. I swung it round in circles. Pup or not, he looked quite frightening as he chased it with an intent stare, his small sharp puppy teeth clashing loudly. Once he got hold of the brush, his already powerful neck muscles enabled him to cling on against my tugs. This game made me dizzy, but it did not affect him at all.

Then I devised a game that required no participation on my part but could exhaust him. I tied an old shoe on to elastic suspended from the kitchen ceiling and he would grab it and run. The moment he let go briefly so as to take a firmer grip, the elastic whipped the shoe up into the air. Down it would come again, hit the ground, and then fly up again. Often the flying shoe would hit him up the behind after he had lost interest. He would then go after it again, swiping out with heavy paws, like a bear cub. When tired of this, he would chew an old deer antler he had unearthed, as if to strengthen his teeth, then suddenly flop down and snore raucously.

It was his snoring in my bedroom that made me decide he should sleep on his own in the kitchen. But after those first euphoric days I was so pleased with him that I wrote an enthusiastic letter to Molly Thomson, telling her of all the incidents. I said I thought it astonishing that he would ask to go outside to dispose of his wastes without any training, that he had learned to 'come here' after just a few calls, to keep to heel after one day, and that while he preferred to sleep in my room he whimpered for only a short time when left in the kitchen. Was I being cruel here? I was a little concerned about how gamely he struggled over woodland obstacles: could he break a leg at this stage? 'At any rate,' I concluded, 'I don't know much about pups but I feel he is a most extraordinary animal to have weathered and learned so much so fast.'

Miss Thomson was obviously pleased, but in her reply suggested that I should avoid taking the pup 'where there are trees to jump, as one is always told not to let a pup even go upstairs for several months as it is putting too much strain on it. Personally, I never take a pup for any walk until it is about five months old, and then only for about a quarter of an hour. Before that, they just play around here.' But I was right to shut him in the kitchen, if that was where I wanted him to sleep, for he would then get used to being separated from me.

Beowulf ate as if trying to engulf the whole world's food supply. Miss Thomson's diet sheet for the pup read like that of a heavyweight training for a title fight:

8 a.m. – Half pint of milk and cereal.
1 p.m. – 8 ozs meat or fish, 1 to 2 ozs puppy meal, with a

9

dessertspoonful of bone meal and a little gravy. (Gravy? I had not made gravy for myself in ten years!)

6 p.m. – 8 ozs meat or fish, 1 to 2 ozs puppy meal, with a teaspoonful of cod liver oil and calcium phosphate. Also a little green vegetable and gravy.

10.30 p.m. – Same as at 8 p.m. but with raw egg beaten in, followed by a few dog biscuits.

MAIN MEALS: Mince, liver, tripe, herrings, sprats, rock salmon, and 'Luda' meat fed dry.

I struggled valiantly to supply these gastronomic delights, far more varied than my own diet had been for the past seven years, augmenting them with venison from newly dead deer I found on treks. As I gloomily watched him chomp and slurp his way through it all like a noisy vacuum cleaner, I toyed with the idea of buying a special shovel with which to feed him.

2 · *Anything but a Sheepdog*

It was at the end of our first week together when my initial euphoria began to fade. Apart from Booto, who had come and gone as he liked, I had never owned a dog. I had certainly never brought up a pup, nor had anything to do with Alsatians. Looking back, I can now see that many of the problems which ensued were more my fault than his.

Quite suddenly, in contrast to the first days, Beowulf began to behave like a juvenile delinquent. He started leaving his droppings in the kitchen, even though I showed him his misdemeanour each time, said 'Badog!' loudly, and shoved him outside. I tried leaving the back door open (while shielding his bed from draughts) and walking him late at night. It made no difference: there was the pile of shit each morning, slap in the middle of the carpet. Even with scoldings he persisted. If I shut him out, he lay morosely looking at me through the window. Only when I let him in again would he urinate. He began delving into the vegetable waste box, throwing peelings, cabbage leaves and orange skins over the floor. He tugged down drying clothes, gnawed holes in the carpet (though he had bones and playthings to chew) and ripped the plum twigs off the bird table. What bothered me was that he went on doing these things even when he *knew* they were wrong.

He kicked up an awful fuss at not being allowed to stay in my room at night. He knocked down empty bottles, whined and hurled himself at the kitchen door. The constant thumpings and scratchings sounded like some monster trying to get through to me and made sleep impossible. I heated the kitchen with a paraffin stove and went in every hour or so to cuddle him, explaining that he had to be alone sometimes, but the second I left the bangings would start again.

Although he had retrieved sticks and balls in the first few days, he lost interest quickly and started following some scent, deaf to calls he now knew, like 'Come here' and 'Fetch the ball'. He would respond to 'Come here' only when there was food involved. He also became irritated if I lay down and put my head near him, or rested it upon him in an affectionate gesture. He made peevish grunts and whines, and put his head over the cushioned edge of his fishbox bed with an exasperated air, looking away from me. He did not like me fooling around or using silly dog language, for he would groan and twist his chin on the floor, eyes half closed in what seemed like contempt. I wrote in my diary: 'Well, he *is* a German Shepherd and has an aristocratic Teutonic sense of humour – about nil!' Once he flatly refused to go into the kitchen at night – so I smacked him. Instantly he snarled and whipped his head round, and would have bitten had I not withdrawn my hand fast. If he acted like this now, what on earth would he be like when he was mature and powerful? A little scared, as well as annoyed, I tried to quell the rebellion with a hard clout. Then I suffered mental anguish in bed at the unusual silence emanating from the kitchen.

I could see that what was going wrong might in some way be my fault, but I could not figure out why. I tried being soft. I forgave the morning poops in the kitchen and congratulated and petted him when he went in the garden. I let him back in my room at night, but he performed in the open-doored kitchen yet again. 'Badog!' I said several times before putting him outside. When I went to call him in half an hour later he had disappeared. I found him 200 yards away in the east wood. He had come upon a dead deer and had eaten half its thigh- and shin-bones, the big knee-joint and all – and he was supposed to be still on soft meats and puppy meal! Fortunately he suffered no ill-effects.

He became recalcitrant in other ways. He disliked being picked up and immediately whined to be put down again. If I whistled tunes, he would scratch at the door to get out. He seldom wagged his tail, even when about to be fed. Instead he jumped up at the bench where I prepared his food and seemed annoyed I had not put it down quicker. He never licked my hand, as I thought pups normally did with their owners. One night he hauled a venison haunch from the top of the calor gas fridge. I smacked his rump, but he went straight at it again. Often when I stroked him he walked off and sat down with a thump and a groan. He was, I decided, an aristocratic wretch who was determined to have things all his own way, an aristocratic wretch in fact who regarded me as an owner and Wildernesse as a home of decidedly inferior standard. When I found him with the hind's second thigh-bone, and took it away, he snapped at my hand. After a slap for that, he growled at me when I spoke to him, and it was hard to make friends again.

Although the favoured canines in my Highland area were sheep-dogs and terriers, I met one man who claimed some experience of Alsatians. He told me that if you treated them too kindly they would take advantage; if you were too tough they would finally turn on you. While I knew that an individual dog's personality had to be taken into account, I did not want one I had to pander to all the time just to gain simple obedience or pleasantness, especially when it cost so much to feed. It seemed that Beowulf and I were not right for each other.

Feeling foolish, I wrote again to Molly Thomson, listing my problems. I admitted that buying Beowulf was my mistake, suggested that maybe he needed a whole family in order to be happy, and that I would probably be better off with a bitch, or else a less independent breed, in such an isolated place.

Strangely, on the day I boated out to post the letter, things began to improve. I was in the store, having left Beowulf tied to the steps outside, when I heard a loud yiping. A male black Labrador had taken a fancy to him, had straddled him, and the perplexed pup was venting his fear. I shoved the Labrador away, told it to push off, and carried young Beowulf back to the Land Rover. As I set him on the seat, he suddenly licked my hand in apparent gratitude.

When we returned to the boat it was almost dark, and a south-east gale was flinging squalls of rain through a gap in the mountains. The boat pranced like a rodeo horse, banging through the waves as angry water lashed around us, shooting white spray overhead. For the first mile I thought we might not make it. Beowulf, feet braced against the bags of supplies, never took his eyes off my face. As I fought to keep the bows steady to the wind, I was sure he had

13

worked out in his young head that only the helmsman could ensure we did not go down!

Once we reached the first bend to the north east and were in the lee of the hills, the loch calmed and we arrived home in the dim light of a new moon shining fitfully through the clouds. As soon as we landed Beowulf, grateful to be back on firm ground, wagged his tail and came to lick my hand again, as if he thought I had saved his life. That night he was so hungry that it was easy to teach him to 'shake hands' for his meal. Even at that tender age I could not close my hand round his thick paw, which left a print almost 3½ inches wide.

A few days later, while cooking my own meal after he had been fed, I heard a violent choking noise. I grabbed his jaw as he yiped and saw half a biro pen stuck across the roof at the back of his mouth. I reached in fast and carefully but swiftly eased it out. Instantly there came a look of wonder and gratitude on his face.

It seemed important at this time for Beowulf to learn to like retrieving thrown objects. A growing pup needed a great deal of exercise. I would take him out and hurl sticks and stones as far as I could while he ran after them until he grew tired. Now when he lost interest I found that, instead of scolding him, I could achieve results by making a sound of disgust and leaving him alone. He then became oddly anxious to please, for he did not like being totally ignored.

He still raided the waste bucket, so I tied it to his collar. In that way it would inconvenience him and remind him that I did not want him rummaging in it. Far from biting it off, he regarded it for a few seconds as if it were some kind of decoration or medal, and then cheerfully lugged it around while he dug up bones, sniffed at deer trails, or watched the tits feeding on the bird table. Everywhere he lay down the blue bucket beamed his presence like a personal flag. Result? The bucket had become not a reminder of wrong-doing but an *authorised* plaything.

Each morning now he would leave the kitchen, rear up and put his huge flubby paws on my window sill before 4 a.m., squeak with annoyance at finding me still abed, drop back with a thud that seemed to shake the foundations, then gallop away sounding like a horse. New games evolved that helped to unify us, but they were not always ones that *I* cared to play. I had noted that he liked to kick balls about as much as fetching and destroying them with

14

his teeth, and as a result devised a game that would give him exercise on rainy days without us both being soaked outside. Kitchen football!

I have never liked football, probably because I was not much good at it, and all ball games soon bore me. I liked it no better when I found I was being beaten by a dog. He had more of the ball, one might say, due to being that much closer to the ground, and he either charged about with it in his teeth or dropped it down to dribble it with his front paws. He feinted me out of position by pretending he had lost it, only to cheat by pushing it forward with his rear feet. I fouled him a few times, scoop-kicking his feet away, but he still won. Four legs were better than two, not to mention a big mouth that kept ahead of the ball at all times. I managed to get some of the play by bouncing the ball (a large plastic fishnet float) which flummoxed him somewhat. It bounced as high as it fell, and in the excitement one day I lost a teapot. If this kept up, he might have to go on the transfer list.

On our next supply trip I collected Molly Thomson's answer to my pathetically querulous letter, composed (I now realised) in a mood of despondency to do with my writing rather than the dog. Her reply was indignant and soon put me in my place. Experienced though I was with wild animals, when it came to a pedigree Alsatian pup I was a mere novice it seemed.

I was horrified to hear your tales of woe with my super pup, and if you would like me to have him back of course I will . . . I am not surprised, and would not expect him to be clean in the house with the weather we have had, as no pup should stay out in the rain for more than a few minutes at his young age, and *never* at this stage without his owner to give confidence! . . . Yes, you are expecting too much, much too soon. No real training takes place until six months old, only the barest necessities . . . I am astounded about his not having a sociable friendly outlook, as he certainly had when he was here and was exceptionally affectionate. I can only think he has lost confidence in you, as you seem to have forgotten he is a real baby! Obviously, you having told him to stay in the kitchen, when he comes in to your room he is very confused and does not know whether you want him or not, hence the hesitation to come near you. The instinct is to be close always, my pup

15

follows me everywhere and gets attention always, is NEVER left or ignored at this stage.

She went on to say she felt that the pup and I had not reached a proper understanding, and that if she were to take him back I should think of getting a much older dog.

I was glad to reply that she was quite right to tell me off, that her letter convinced me she really believed him to be a super pup (for I too had come to believe he was), that he was now sleeping happily alone in the kitchen, had not messed the house once since my last letter, and had after all settled down well. I also told her about the latest unifying influence in our lives – the arrival of a large and aggressive ram.

It first appeared in the west wood at the end of January, and he was certainly the biggest ram I had ever seen in Scotland. He had somehow dodged the winter gathering after the tupping season and was now wintering alone out on the hills. I told my neighbouring farmer about it, and he was concerned that the ram would not find enough food on the bleak ground. He gave me half a sack of sheep nuts to feed to it now and again.

Next day, Beowulf at my side, I went to feed the ram. The nearer we approached the bigger he looked. I threw some nuts on the ground. Ram regarded the puppy with fearless disdain. Beowulf, however, took one look at Ram and fled for the house.

Later, we saw Ram with three ewes, then he disappeared and I found the cunning beast sheltering from the rain in a large hide I had erected in the west wood in order to watch the red deer. I dropped some nuts for him. Next morning, after feeding Ram in the rear garden, I went to inspect the deer hide and found the place where I normally crouched covered with dung and twigs. The sacking sides of the hide were completely demolished. Maybe just by turning round Ram's huge horns had torn everything down. It would have to be rebuilt.

When Ram spotted me putting nuts down a few days later, he came charging down the north hill. He stamped his foot at the puppy and shook his head up and down. Beowulf fled once again. Had I a coward for a dog? Sometimes I would find Ram standing near the workshop door, from which I always carried the sack of nuts. On the first occasion he stamped twice at Beowulf and advanced threateningly a few steps; on the second he stamped, lowered his head and actually charged a few yards. By now Beowulf had worked it out that Ram would not *keep* coming forward. Instead of running away, this time he danced about, barking loudly. Ram just turned slowly and walked away once he had finished eating all the nuts.

I was at my desk the next day when there was a loud bang, followed by barking. Ram, looking for his daily ration, had become impatient and banged his way through the half-open door into the workshop in search of the nut sack. Apart from lowering his horns towards the scared and noisy pup, Ram took little notice of him. I shouted and waved my arms, but Ram just stared belligerently back at me. Only by grabbing the nut sack and scattering a few nuts outside could I lure him out of the house.

Perhaps Ram was turning the young pup into a sheep-hater. The farmer told me that one tried and tested method of making sure a dog did not chase sheep, or of curing a sheep-worrier, was to shut it in a pen with a big ram. Being butted by a ram turned a dog off sheep-chasing for good. I was not so sure. It might work with sheepdogs or similar canines, but Alsatians were powerful, and when adult might well attack rams out of revenge. The farmer promised to come up the loch when he had less work to do and boat the ram back to the farm. Meanwhile, I could try to rope the ram on my own, but it would be a hard task without a sheepdog.

'The collie lies in front of it, distracting its attention,' the farmer explained. 'Otherwise a big ram in the open is a difficult proposition for one man.'

At this time I was starting a vegetable garden, and had sliced the marshy rush-filled turf off a 21-foot square patch. I was digging the first trench and had just broken a pickaxe handle on contact with a submerged rock, when Beowulf decided to join in. He came from nowhere, dived into the trench and started digging with his paws right by my flashing spade.

'Get out of it, you fool!' I gasped. 'You'll get your paws chopped off. Go and dig the other end.'

Suddenly Beowulf gave a short '*whuff*' and ran off in a tight circle. Ram, seeing me in the garden, had run down the hill for more nuts, and now stationed himself between the pup and me.

Every time Beowulf barked or tried dutifully to protect me, Ram made menacing short charges at him. Obviously Ram deduced he was just a pup – all animals know the young

17

of others – and wanted him out of the way, at least until he got his nuts.

For a moment I wondered if angry Ram would charge *me*. I grabbed the crowbar and warily walked up to the cottage to fetch the nuts, which I then set out in the woods. As Ram dogged my steps, Beowulf, now annoyed by Ram's constant aggression, started to sneak in towards Ram's rear. He was met by that great lowered head and fearsome horns. I was glad to see young Beowulf had some courage in him. As I entered the porch, Ram banged into the bird-table post and down crashed the top, the nest box breaking off and losing its roof. My philanthropic desire to help Ram through the winter waned right then. He had busted the deer hide and fouled the ground inside it, had shattered the bird-table, and for all I knew was turning the pup into a sheep-hater.

For two days Ram kept away. Then, on February 15, I heard a rumpus in the garden and saw Ram chasing the pup around. He even stamped his foot at me when I went out to investigate. But the young pup was no longer afraid of him, for he had realised he was faster on his feet. Now it was fun! Beowulf went rushing past Ram with great abandon, deliberately missing his horns by a foot as Ram darted sideways and forwards, whirling to face the frisky pup. It was no good. Ram had become a nuisance. Ram had to go.

An attempt to noose him with thick rope strung between two old posts failed when he neatly side-stepped the noose before guzzling up all the nuts and then sauntering away with what looked like a sneer on his avuncular old face. An hour later he came down the north hill to a broken fence where I often fed him. Again he chased the pup a few steps. He glared at me from a mere five feet and stamped his foot, impatient for more food. This time I really thought he was going to charge me.

I felt angry now and went to the cottage to put on my heaviest wellingtons, three sweaters and thick gloves. To hell with him! I returned with the rope noose and some more nuts. He looked even bigger now that I was set on catching him. His horns and bow-shaped convex head looked tough enough to knock down a tree. I dropped the nuts near an old fence post and talked to him in soothing tones while he ate. Beowulf did as I instructed and watched from a distance.

Carefully I draped the noose over Ram's great head and, bracing my feet when he was not prepared, gave an almighty heave. Ram stumbled into the fence post and fought back. I leaped over, tightening the rope round the post for increased friction. Then I grabbed the thick wool on his back with the hand that held the rope, reached down to his hind hoof with the other and, with a heaving jerk, put down his rear. Grabbing his horns, I twisted him over on to his side. That was it. Once down, he stayed there after his first few kicks failed to get him up again. His great amber eyes, like giant marbles, looked confused, like those of a hooked carp. Lying sprawled across him, I tied his legs one by one, not too tight, so he could walk a little. Slowly I manoeuvred him down to the boat. When I finally shut the dog in the cottage, I think he knew I was removing his enemy.

On the way down the loch to the farm, Ram sat on the boat deck munching more nuts as if he had been a sailor all his life!

I found the farmer in the cowsheds. A bit of ram-wrestling was something he was used to and he laughed at my boastful sense of achievement. Together we got Ram out of the boat and into a van. As we released him into a field with other tups, the farmer admitted he was their biggest and fiercest ram. The old beast often charged *his* sheepdogs!

3 · Games Pups Play

I tried to follow the breeder's advice to avoid extending puppy Beowulf too far, but he was so full of energy that I could not leave him locked up in the cottage. When he was 3½ months old I took him on short treks, and to prepare him for these I let him come on some early morning walks round the two woods and back along the loch shore.

We set off down the path between rhododendron bushes, ablaze with crimson and purple flowers in early summer, passed through my log gate arch and turned right above the shore where the waves either lapped or crashed upon the grey granite rocks. After a few high tussocks we moved across the long flat rock with which I had bridged a small run-off burn that fed a marshy pool where frogs were already mating. I had never bothered to position this rock bridge perfectly, so it always went *clonk clonk* as our weights passed over it. Passing below the scaly red-barked Scots pines that fringe its southern edge, I looked up into the shady gloom of the three-acre west wood.

Small though it was, it contained an extraordinary variety of terrain. In its centre, above a marsh where greening fallen trunks of huge dead trees lay across each other, like an obstacle course for commando training, rose a rocky 30-foot escarpment. From its ledges sprang rowans, birches and small twisted oaks. Red deer use these sheltered ledges as dormitories in winter, some of the weaker ones dying there when they are not strong enough to follow the small herds up into the hills to graze on heather. I used this rocky cliff for climbing practice, scrambling up, over, down and along the narrow ledges, but today I took Beowulf the easier route round its western edge only 150 yards away. We climbed up the steep little path I had made between slender larches and Douglas and silver firs, some of which reared 100 feet into the sky. The needles from the conifers provided a rich brown carpet between the jagged protruding rocks and made the going easier. At the top, 80 feet up, we passed through a more open, softly undulating area where the deer used the pines and larches as rubbing posts – to get the insecticidal resin into their coats and make them more glossy.

We sploshed through a low marsh before turning right and climbing another 20 feet on to a short hard path along the lower rocky brows. Above them hung the first 500-foot ridges, while still higher I could see the cone-shaped tip of the 1,000-foot crest which appears to be the highest hill when seen from the cottage for it rears up against the sky. I knew well that it was not, of course, for behind it lay almost 60 square miles of roadless wild land, a kingdom of yawning glens, misty ravines, rushing burns, rivers, vast sheer rockfaces and mountain peaks, one of which reared to almost 3,000 feet. Sixty square miles sounds a lot, but this wild tract was only one fifth of the terrain I was to cover over the years, much of it on foot with the dog when the eagle studies began in earnest.

I always stopped at this point to scan the hills, and we were not disappointed on this day. A pair of hooded crows cavorted in a small birch on a high cliff, ravens soared, a buzzard was wheeling near the long wood to the west, then I saw the nearest pair of eagles, sailing over the cone-shaped crest to the north. The female was leading, broad-winged like a flying door. The smaller male banked, then dived down on her. As he got close, she performed a sideways somersault, almost on to her back, and seemed to touch his talons with hers. Within seconds they had vanished over the crests again. After this awe-inspiring sight we turned down from the hard path and wended our way through more deep tussocks, where the first purple moor grasses were sprouting from the tops. Soon the small grassy plateau to our right would be host to a swaying choir of tall purple foxgloves. In late May this windless area behind the wood became a haven for butterflies, such as dark green and pearl-bordered fritillaries, blues, and the orange and brown specks of rare little checkered skippers.

Soon we were crossing the hundred-yard strip of grassy marshland that lies above my rear fence, the site of the finest display of wild orchids I have ever seen in Britain. The lilac and cream colours of the heath-spotted orchids dominate the scene, but there are also early purples, fragrants, and a few pale yellow spires of lesser butterfly orchids too. When the orchids have had their season, out come the tiny dark blue milkworts, the pink louseworts, the cheerful yellow suns of tormentil and blazing golds of bird's-foot trefoil. These too are superseded in late summer by a vast carpet of the yellow and orange spikes of bog asphodel, the flower that is said to have blossomed over the Elysian fields of paradise.

We came to the most magical place at Wildernesse, the spectacular gorge of the burn which is the main vein of the mountains for eight miles. Through the belt of trees up to the north ran the deer path I used to reach the higher slopes unseen by animals I was stalking. One false step here and one would fall 40 feet on to the granite bed of the burn. Near us, the waters flowed over four broad and deep-stepped pools, down a 10-foot waterfall into the pool from which I piped my water, then shot through three rocky channels and over a sheer 30-foot cliff, to splatter over a tangle of huge weirdly-shaped rocks that looked as if they had been placed singly by the hand of a capricious giant. It was never silent here, for the waters were always talking, tinkling, gurgling or whispering through the fissures and crannies in dry weather, splashing into myriad rainbows in the sunlight after moderate rains, or gushing, gouting and roaring in torrents after a major storm, when they became as dark as beer from the peaty debris they carried down, and the wind they created was so full of ions it tasted as salty as the sea.

We turned south, wended our steep way down beside the cliff and entered the large triangular east wood. Unlike the west wood, it held mainly deciduous trees, such as oak, ash, holly, rowan, birch and nut-bearing hazel bushes which grew right up to the side of the cottage. In its centre towered a huge Norway spruce, which created its own shady grove and was 15 feet round the butt. East of the spruce grew a broad belt of tall larches which ran right down to the shore 250 yards away, and these merged with a line of stately beeches which lined the banks of the lower reaches of the burn.

While this walk was familiar to me, it was a complete novelty to puppy Beowulf. He often paused to gaze around him with wide eyes and a look that showed he had never seen terrain like this before. He plodded upwards with determination on his over-sized feet and hauled himself through dead bracken on the steep slopes. When I crossed the burn at a flat part, he plunged gamely into the torrent behind me, his hind legs flailing to avoid being swept away as his front feet scrabbled with outstretched claws to grip rocks. He seemed as clumsy as a drunk; when he ran his huge ears flopped up and down, so that his head looked like a hairy winged bat trying to take off, and I wondered if he would become too heavy and so be useless for hill work.

We continued down between the beeches, crunching through the thick drifts of twigs, the bronze leaves from last year's fall, and the few mast nuts that had not been eaten or taken away to store by the pair of red squirrels that lived in the woods. On the south-eastern land spit we stopped and looked at the nearest pine-covered islet where the black-throated divers nested, then turned west again to walk below the fringe of ash and alder trees which lined the rocky shore. The shimmering waters of the loch opened out before us, a beautiful vista that stretched nearly four miles before the first bend below the highest mountain to the south. We carried on below the 1½-acre front pasture I was creating by hacking back the engulfing bracken, past the two boats, then back up the path to the cottage again. I was sure Beowulf had enjoyed his first walk round what I called 'the rough kilometre'. Of one thing I was sure: at least he was a trier.

Slowly he learned to leave his large droppings away from the house. He still tried to dig near my flashing spade in the vegetable patch. To keep him away I hurled the big stones out to the side. He chased and brought them back, dropping them at the edges. These, together with those I threw there, finally formed two small 'windbreak' walls!

One March day, with the first songs of chaffinches and great tits sounding in the woods, I hurled his ball far out into the loch, to see if he would swim for it. He did not, and a current from between the islets took the ball further off shore. I had to drag the small boat down and row out. As we came near the ball, Beowulf could stand the tantalising sight of it no longer and leaped overboard for his first real swim. He trod water with astonishment at first, then

23

soon got the hang of it. His strong legs and huge semi-webbed feet (his middle toes were now 2½ inches long) surged him forward, so that his head, neck and chest were well out of the water. He hit the ball, found it bounced to his touch, and spent the next quarter of an hour irritatingly offshore, bashing it up and down in the water with his paws, deaf to my urgent calls. He had invented a new game – water polo. This became a favourite pastime. He seemed convinced he was a seal. To show how splendid this new element was, he would emerge like a small grizzly from a bout of fishing, station himself as close to me as possible and shake as much water over me as he could. He thought nothing of plunging into icy cold water as if he was not a warm blooded animal at all.

At four and a half months he had lost his puppy look and was sleeking down into a healthy young Alsatian. I was becoming very fond of him. Beowulf suddenly seemed too pretentious a name for such a lively good-natured dog. I started to call him Moobli.

He now made mock charges at me, just as Booto used to do, narrowly missing me, then whirling round twenty yards away and coming at me again. When I flapped a tea towel at my side, matador style, he went at it like a small bull, his teeth clashing as I whipped it away at the last second to cries of 'Olé!' He was eating far more than I, in three meals a day. If I was writing and had forgotten his lunch, he sometimes went to the grate and noisily crunched a lump of charcoal.

To give Moobli more exercise, I started dropping him off the boat on our way home from supply trips, so he could run along beside it. At first these runs were only about half a mile, and if it was slightly stormy I took the boat in close to shore so that his feet would touch the bottom without water getting into his ears. On the command 'Walkies!' he would jump out happily, then trot over the rocky shore, sploshing through marsh and scratchy bog myrtle bushes, trying to keep up. I had to rescue him at the end. Not until his third run did he work out that to reach Wildernesse itself he had to climb up and over the rocky headland below the west wood.

One Saturday in mid-March I decided to break in a pair of light-weight wellington boots I had bought for 99p in Woolworth's. With young Moobli at my side, camera and lenses packed on my back, we set off to the north west over the first 500-foot ridges, along the sloping tussocky marshes and peat bogs up to the 1,600-foot level. Moobli plugged along well, keeping to heel but

24

He looked too fat and floppy, but when I returned to the kennels he was the first of the pups to leap up with enthusiastic greeting.

He showed no excitement or fear, but just sat on the Land Rover seat, waiting to be driven away.

The pup sought the safety of the boat's cabin on the turbulent 6½-mile journey up the loch.

On his first day at Wildernesse, I could only think of calling him Flubby Dub Dubs.

slightly out to the side. We had just passed two small lochans, the damp wind coursing up from the west, when he came up, lifting his nose and scenting the air. He would have run on but for my hissed 'Get back!' Then I realised there may be something ahead. We rounded a small knoll and there, less than forty yards below, was a herd of red deer hinds, yearlings and calves – sixty-two animals in all. I took photos in the poor light. Oddly, it was a calf and not the usual leading hind which saw us first and gave the alarm by running, its mother warning the rest with a short sharp '*Haugh!*' bark. But it was Moobli's nose which had alerted me they were there. He was proving useful already.

Shortly afterwards, as we were crossing a deep rift in a chocolate brown peat hag, I put my foot on a tuffet that looked as firm as the others and was not; it was a 'floater', and in I went – up to the hips in icy black ooze. Young Moobli, who had made a sudden swing to the left, barely got his feet dirty! As I cussed, stamped, wiped the messy peat off and wrung out my socks, he sat with his tongue lolling, as if laughing at my foolishness. Wet and cold, I put on a spurt over the ridge and down into the deep glen below Guardian Mountain, then partly up the steep side to a raven's nest I wanted to check, set in a sheltered crevice of oddly green rock.

As I started to climb up the projecting heather-covered boulders to the side of the rockface, I assumed Moobli would wait below. To my surprise he doggedly climbed right behind me, and I saw with astonishment that his big puppy claws were almost as extendable as those of a cat. He somehow pushed them out, hooking his toes downwards, affording four grapnel hooks on each front foot with which to haul himself up.

I was just focussing my fieldglass on the nest when a raven flew over calling loudly, '*Krruk krruk*', and then I saw his mate sitting tight on the nest of dry old twigs. Quietly, not wanting to flush her from the eggs, I returned to the glen and began the long haul back up the first mountain. To make it easier, I traversed sideways to the south west, and we came out on the last peak of the long saddle. From here we could see right over the nearest sea loch and its islands. Moobli seemed as entranced by the glorious sight as I was, looking all over the scene with quick movements of his head, his ears cocked, still panting from exertion. We had now covered more than five hard miles, and I decided to head south to our own loch shore and home. Below a tall rockface we found a dead hind,

25

her right foreleg broken and blood on her nose and lips. It seemed possible that she had been weak from pneumonia and had fallen off, perhaps shattering her lungs. One eye had been taken out by crows or ravens, but this did not deter Moobli from licking her bloody lips. Horrid little wolf! Perhaps she had been driven off the cliff by golden eagles, for they have been known to do this when hungry in winter. Yet surely an eagle would have begun feasting immediately, making a hole below the lower ribs? There was no such damage.

We had gone less than a mile, round two lochans and a third that was unmapped, when a wall of white advanced towards us. Within seconds we were enveloped in thick mist. Dusk was falling. Unable to see anything beyond a 30-yard radius, I was dismayed to find the land rising again. Were we moving in a curve? Fool, I had left my compass behind and could no longer orientate myself. The light through the mist was uniform all round, so it was impossible to tell the direction of the sun. I tried to see if Moobli had a homing sense and said all the words he associated with home – 'meaties', 'fetch the ball', 'get in the boat' – but though he plodded off, he went upwards, then began to twist and turn. I was sure he was yet too young for such a task.

I felt a slight panic, for we were miles from home. The occasional radio news of hill walkers who get lost each winter, necessitating costly search parties for which they never have to pay a penny, had always irritated me. Now my own dictum – 'If you can't handle the Hill don't go on it' – was flung back in my face. I kept calm and sat on a rock to think carefully. I reckoned the wind had stayed the same, from the west, and could use it as a direction finder. Feeling sure we were still south of the two lochans, and not wanting to head into the bog around the third, I turned so that the wind was at our backs and headed what should have been east. I counted our steps for about a mile, then turned to keep the wind on our right, praying it had not changed, and began to head down.

It was almost dark. The land started rising again and I began to think only a fool would keep stumbling around like this, running out of energy. When we found an overhanging rock with a large inward fissure above what was clearly a winter deer bed, I decided to spend the night there. I put on the rubberised nylon rainsuit, which also formed a pad for the cameras in my pack, plucked a great deal of heather and old bracken to cover us, then lay down with young Moobli curled along my chest and stomach, my arms around him and my nose touching the thick ruff of his neck. Cold night though it was, he proved to be a fine heater. My wet feet felt like ice, however, and my back stiffened with cold. None the less, despite little shivering fits, I managed to keep tolerably warm and even to doze fitfully.

I woke to a grey light. Moobli had barely stirred, as if knowing we were in trouble and some self-discipline was called for. Thrusting the heather aside, thankful it was still dry, we set out again. The mist was less thick and I saw that the hill was but a large flattened knoll. Still keeping the wind to our right, we crossed a series of tussocky mounds and then came into that special lightness which, in mist, tells you a large expanse of water lies below. In less than an hour we were at the loch shore and nearing home.

Moobli was so unperturbed by the misadventure that he picked up his ball, wanting me to throw it, and pranced about hungrily once he smelled his food heating up. According to his breeder, he should not even have gone upstairs before he was five months old! I made a mental apology to Molly Thomson. At least the event united us further and the 11-mile trek produced no blisters from my cheap wellingtons.

As a pup Moobli was naturally mischievous. One day in early April, while I was trimming two iron-hard larch logs to renew the gate posts, I discovered that my metal tape measure had disappeared. No matter how I urged him, Moobli refused to 'Fetch the ball!' Had he forgotten where he had put or buried it? I kept an eye on him while I worked on the gate in the west wood and, sure enough, he started to prowl, following his own scent until he found the tape measure where he had buried it under a cherry tree. I impressed on him not to steal my tools. A few days later he took my shoe brushes from the workshop. I showed him the tins of polish, pointed to where the brushes had been, and demanded to know what he had done with them. Where were they? As usual, when he knew he had done wrong, his ears went down, he developed a 'bald' look and out he padded to track them down by scent. They were found half buried in the east wood.

Through play I discovered more of his qualities. When he was in another room, I would quietly run off up the hill and hide in

27

the woods. Within minutes I was missed and he would come out, searching anxiously. It was soon clear that while his eyes could discern the slightest movement at long distances, like those of a deer or a bear, he had difficulty making me out if I stood still by a tree. He located me with his nose, and *always* found me. Even when he was only a few yards away, he did not trust his eyes, but moved round until he had the scent, then leaped at me in the joy of discovery.

He developed his own codes in play too. If his ball became caught up a hazel or rhododendron bush, he would jump after it to a height of six feet, or even try to climb like a bear. But if it landed deep in a bramble thicket, he would endure only a few stabs on his nose before looking back, as if saying 'Hey. That's not playing the game!' A new variation was to play 'Fetch the ball' at night. I would hurl bones, stones, sticks, even potatoes into pitch darkness and he would find them by scent alone and bring them back as fast as during the day.

A new game had me as 'goalie' in the gap between the cottage and the blackberry bushes. With himself as the 'ball', he would come pounding towards me, looking fearsome, hackles raised, and then brake suddenly, with great toes spread out like stars, feinting this way and that until I was off-balance, before thundering through into the non-existent net. I was amazed by how quick he was for his size; he was over five feet long at six months. Seldom could I get a hand down fast enough to touch his tail as he flashed past.

He began to practise his speed on the colourful little chaffinches and tits hopping below the bird table. He would lie in wait below my window, and then suddenly I would hear a loud scrabbling and see him almost catch the quick-witted birds from a sitting start. Once he actally pinned a chaffinch down by its tail with his paw. He watched it struggle to escape with benign interest. I had to fling open the window and with a sharp 'Na!' make him desist. Later I heard from my desk fluttering noises coming from the kitchen: I knew the sound well – one of the birds had come indoors looking for food. With the sudden silence on this occasion I hurried in. Moobli was sitting on his bed with the cheekiest, bossy cock chaffinch in his mouth. I made him give it to me, and was surprised to find it completely unharmed. I told him off with a sharp slap, and he soon learned to treat the little birds as our friends, not to be molested. Indeed, after that, he often let the birds pick scraps from his bowl when he had finished his meal outside. He would lay with his head between his paws, his huge brown eyes switching this way and that as he watched their fidgety antics and squabbles with evident interest.

In late April the birds benefited by Moobli's presence. They began gathering his moulted hairs to line their nests. As they hopped about, chaffinches, great tits, coal and blue tits, crammed their beaks with these hairs so that they all looked like little Colonel Blimps with tan moustaches.

At this time my work received a setback. The outline for my Canadian wildlife book had been rejected by two publishers. One said that British readers would not be interested, it was all too far away; the other simply did not believe that an Englishman who had spent most of his life in big western cities would wander alone and unarmed, never mind sleep out, in trackless terrain where wild grizzly bears and cougar roamed at large. Well, I had, and this reaction both angered me and galvanised me into action. Somehow I would have to prove the book was true. I determined to go back to Canada in June, when grizzlies would be foraging in the tidal flats of the great inlets of British Columbia, and get photographs of them. I would also try to photograph bald eagles, black bears, caribou and even the elusive secretive cougar to enhance the book.

More important to me personally was the idea that I could see again my old companion of the Canadian wilds, stray dog Booto, once more before he died. He had come to my lonely cabin one stormy winter night when life had been at a very low ebb and had become a staunch ally and friend for three years. He had accompanied me on my first wild treks, and also on assignments to Hollywood; we had travelled round Mexico together in an old milk truck. He was a cross between an Alsatian and a Labrador, with (so some said) a little wolf blood in him. He was too old and wild to think of sentencing him to months of confinement in British quarantine kennels, and so sadly I had left him behind in the care of friends.

I wrote to Molly Thomson to ask if Moobli could spend a well-earned holiday in her Sussex kennels while I was away in Canada, and set about preparations for the trip.

In the early spring small bands of marauding sheep had come out of the surrounding hills and descended on Wildernesse. They got through the gaps left in the fencing of my 3½ acres so that red deer could have access to the woods for shelter in harsh winter weather. The sheep came for the new grasses springing up where I had hacked away the engulfing bracken. I was not encouraging these grasses for the sake of someone else's domestic animals but for the wild deer and the rare moths and butterflies that feed on them. Sheep nonetheless launched determined raids while grazing was at its scarcest in the hills, and then began the retreat up to summer grazing on the high tops in mid-May.

I allowed Moobli to herd the sheep out but always went with him to see that he did not chase after them into the hills. It was not difficult to impress upon him that he must not cross the boundaries unless I was with him. Sheep training was reinforced on calm days when I rowed to the village at the head of the loch. To save hauling his weight and to give him exercise, I let Moobli trot along the shore beside the boat, shouting a sharp 'Na!' when we came near to grazing sheep and taking him back on board until we were well past. He soon learnt the taboo.

Sometimes on these long hauls, Moobli would become bored with my slow rowing pace and attempt to swim out and catch the boat. Puffing loudly with every second kick of his rear legs, he could not understand why I would not break the rhythm and stop for him. He would paddle back to the shore and plunge in again. Finally he worked out that if he ran 200 yards ahead of me before entering the water, then he would be better placed to meet me. He wore such a look of hurt bewilderment and frustration when, arriving on time, the boat just swept past him. He did not realise that I did not want to haul aboard seven stone of dog, whose coat held over a large bucketful of water, just as I was nearing the end of my energies.

A few days later we went to explore a tree-covered islet three miles from home, where Moobli again exhibited his developing scenting powers. It was not an easy place to reconnoitre, for here and there it was covered with the huge fallen trunks of ancient pine trees which resembled the bleached bones of giant dinosaurs. After working our way over these and through thick twiggy bushes, Moobli stopped with one heavy paw upraised, tail in the air like a pointer, and sniffed towards a blunt knoll covered with bilberry leaves. I hissed him back and stole through the undergrowth. A brown mallard duck took off noisily from a down-filled nest containing eleven greeny-grey eggs and winged away over the loch. Mallards rely upon their superb camouflage and sit tight until you are about to tread on them. I had been passing on a line well below the level of the nest, and she would have just watched me go by if Moobli had not detected her presence. We swiftly left the islet and had boated only 300 yards when the duck flew back and pushed her way up to her eggs.

Next day we walked through the west wood and saw many voles dashing through their tunnels in the new grass. Moobli seemed to find their scent fascinating for he kept shoving his nose deep into the herbage with loud snuffling noises. Suddenly I heard shrill high-pitched squeaks. He had cornered a tiny common shrew. Gram for gram, the little shrew is the fiercest of our carnivores, and this one stood its ground and fought him back valiantly. It must have given his big black nose a sharp nip for Moobli quickly pulled it back with a muffled yipe, and the shrew disappeared down a hole between the mossy rocks. Moobli came away looking most shamefaced. One can never win by fighting a much smaller opponent, I thought. If you win you are a bully; if you lose you are a fool!

Time was drawing near for my return trip to Canada. I had managed to make contact with a leading cougar hunter, a Scots-Canadian by the name of Percy Dewar, who with his wife Penny was running a cougar radio-collaring project on Vancouver Island. They trekked on foot behind trained hounds until the pack scented a fresh cougar trail. Then they had to run, often for miles over rocky timbered terrain, until the hounds put the cougar up a tree. There, Percy fired a drugged dart into the cougar's flank and then put a radio collar round its neck. After that they tracked each cougar for weeks with radio telemetry equipment, working out territories, finding kills, and gathering all the evidence they could about cougar behaviour.

For a fee, Percy agreed that I could go with them, help with the collaring and take my photos when I could. I knew that I would have to be super fit for this, never mind the treks after grizzlies on mainland British Columbia, and I trained for it like a commando. Each morning, wearing a heavy pack, I picked the most difficult routes over the marshes, tussocks, tangled windfall trees and the 30-foot granite escarpment in the west wood. Then I took to charging over them as fast as I could while trying to avoid serious injury. Moobli saw this as a great game. On the first morning the six-month-old pup flung himself after me with great enthusiasm, but I decided he

31

was not yet ready for such hard stuff and shut him in the house before starting these training runs. He did not think much of that and sank down gloomily as I closed the door on him.

As the day of my departure approached, I had to decide what to do with Moobli, for his breeder had said that she could not take him before June 25, and even then would be short staffed. Could I possibly find someone else? I thought briefly of cancelling the trip, until I heard that the Reader's Digest Press in New York was interested in publishing my Canadian book. It was now essential to secure the photographs the book needed.

At the last moment, a saviour entered our lives in the person of Dave Sturrock, an enterprising young man who had started a much needed garage in the village at the end of the loch. Dave had once given me a young sparrowhawk, which I reared and successfully returned to the wild. He was the only other person to have spent a night at Wildernesse in the eight months since I had acquired the place. He loved Moobli, and Moobli liked him. Indeed, when I had voiced my doubts about keeping Moobli, Dave had offered to buy him. He now offered to look after him while I was away, and to take him for good exercise treks into the hills with his own two dogs, a golden retriever and a terrier.

In late May I boated out and took Moobli to Dave's garage. The pup understood precisely what was happening, and to my chagrin leaped into Dave's Land Rover without so much as a backward glance at me. I felt dismissed. Within days I was in Canada.

At 4½ months, he was sleeking down into a healthy young Alsatian, and I finally called him Moobli. His bouncing plastic ball broke pots indoors, so I taught him to retrieve it outside. He took to water like an otter, loved to play water polo, and stood guard in the rear boat when I went to fetch heavy loads.

I remembered wild stray dog Booto as he was, eagerly waiting for his food outside the isolated log cabin I built in Canada.

After taking me on a wild chase, Percy Dewar put a radio collar on the wild cougar which he had subdued with a drug dart.

4 · Cats and Dogs in Canada

All his life Booto had survived by cadging scraps from various cabin owners up on the wild coast of western Canada where he had lived with me many miles north of Vancouver. He was living now mostly at the Seven Isles Cafe, which was owned by a couple I knew, Stan and Julia Dimopulous. Stan had died recently, and Julia was trying to run the cafe alone. For two days my phone calls to the cafe had gone unanswered, so I borrowed a car, caught the ferry and drove up the little coast road.

When I reached the cafe it appeared deserted, the ground round it overgrown. The two side apartments were devoid of furniture. I climbed up the wooden verandah steps and saw that there were a few simple furnishings in the centre room, a table, two easy chairs, a sofa. Someone must be living there. I turned to look out over the rolling Pacific, the little tree-covered islets, the view that had once been mine from my own log cabin a mile down the coast. I felt lost in the past.

Then there came a scraping on the wooden steps and an ancient moth-eaten dog tottered towards me. That can't be Booto, I thought; it must be some old canine acquaintance of his, all power gone from once muscular rear quarters, the eyes dark, rheumy, filmy with age, peering at me with difficulty. The dog whuffed as it moved, slowly, tired. It lay down as if sure I meant no harm, whoever I was.

33

Perhaps it *could* be Booto. I took out an old picture of him, taken in the palmy days that seemed so long ago. I looked at the white boots on the feet, the chestnut ruff, the white patch on the chest – my god, it *was* Booto! All the past surged through my mind, how he had come out of a storm one February night when I had been wrestling with loneliness and the theme of a long novel I was writing which was never published; how I had let him in and fed him, and his tail had wagged so vigorously that he could hardly keep his balance. I remembered all the comical tricks he employed to get attention and food, how he had accompanied me on a hundred treks, had once lured a charging black bear with a cub away from me so that I could reach the cabin safely. I recalled our salad days in Hollywood, where he had been a favourite at the studios and learnt tricks so quickly that a magician had used him in his act at the famous Magic Castle Club. I remembered him on the set in Durango, where I had gone to interview Dean Martin and Robert Mitchum, and Booto had run across in front of a shoot-out. The director, Henry Hathaway, had declared him to be the star of the scene!

I lay down beside him and talked to the old sleeping head. After a while he looked at me, oddly, as if seeing me for the first time. Then slowly he raised his head, and his tongue, as pink as ever, licked my eye. There came a little moan of recognition, a slight wag of the tail. I broke down, sobbing bitterly, not for the past, not for the lonely years in Scotland without him before I found Moobli, but perhaps a little for the terror of old age. It was heartbreaking to see my companion, dear old Booto, reduced to such straits. The small sums of money I had sent to Julia Dimopulous to help feed him could not stem this onslaught of time. I had never felt so sad.

An hour or so later Julia returned from shopping and Booto jumped up, glad to see her, burying his head in her lap, then in mine. He stood back looking at us both, from one to the other, as if wondering what was going to happen now? Then, with an effort, he reared up and begged in his old inimitable way, one white paw comically folded over the other. I choked back my emotion and fed to him the pound of pure ground beef I had bought.

Booto had been a terror in his younger days, instantly attacking any male dog, irrespective of size, if he was with or after a bitch. Julia told me that he still went courting, but in March had lost a battle with a bigger, much younger male dog which tore his throat and lacerated his side. It had cost 56 dollars for the vet to patch him up. She said that she was also getting old and was putting the cafe up for sale. She hoped she could take Booto when she went to stay with her son in Vancouver, but she seemed unsure about it. I promised to give Booto's future some hard thought. With probably less than a year to live, it was no good thinking of taking him back to Scotland: he was at least 14, and battle-scarred into the bargain. The least I could do was to help Julia with more money for his keep.

Poor old warrior, I thought as I looked at him. Old age makes us all so feeble. Death *is* the final onslaught of fatigue. We must only live each day at a time, taking the most we can, giving the most we can; for as sure as death itself, we all become weak in the end and regret we did less than that. I stayed a while longer, gave Booto a clumsy hug, said goodbye and drove south to Vancouver.

As I crossed on the ferry to Vancouver Island to meet Percy Dewar, I wondered what the legendary cougar hunter would be like. His reputation was of the finest. Whereas most cougar hunting guides tracked the elusive mountain lions over rough terrain in snow, Percy and his specially trained pack of Blue Tick hounds could locate and track them in summer too, when there were no snow tracks to follow. Even before drug dart guns were invented, he had caught several cougars for his studies by simply roping them. When his hounds put the lion up a tree, he fixed a pulley low down on the trunk, passed the rope through it, ascended with climbing irons, used a forked stick to noose the animal, then hauled it down to the pulley and affixed ear tags. As female cougars weigh between 80 and 140 lbs and males 90 to 200 lbs, and adults in their prime can kill an elk or moose of 600 lbs, he had to be one hell of a man! At 46, I was worried about my ability even to keep up with him in the bush.

There was no one to greet me at Departure Bay. After a few minutes a battered pick-up truck came down the track, pulled up in a shower of gravel, and out stepped Percy Dewar to give me my first surprise. He was 56 years old, with crew-cut iron-grey hair, slim but well set, and only 5ft 9ins in height. He had a tired smile and a slow quiet way of talking. He seemed to shamble along, toes pointing in slightly, as if walking on flat ground was an effort. I felt more optimistic.

He took me to a primitive cedar board cabin with a plastic sheet roof in the wooded mountains near Parksville, and I had a second surprise when he introduced me to his wife, Penny. She was a tall brunette, only 27 years old with lovely large blue eyes, and while she was a serious and qualified biologist, she would have fared well in any beauty contest in the world. I was unable to restrain a surge of envy. Over a simple vegetarian supper they told me how they had met, and of their present method of catching and radio-collaring the big cats. After 30 years as a hunting guide, Percy had had enough of killing and instead started studying the rare beautiful animals to try and gain enough about their habits to help their legal conservation. After two years of roping and ear tagging cougars on his own, he tried to raise government finance for the study but found no interest. He had begun to feel it was all too much for one man when he heard about young Penny Brown, a graduate in marine biology, who was looking after two young orphaned cougar kits in a lone cabin 20 miles away. She was having trouble feeding her young lions on deer which she had to shoot.

'I was given a huge 30.06 rifle, like a cannon, and the experts told me the deer came down into the valleys in the snow,' Penny explained. 'But the valleys were mostly logged-off slash areas with no shelter and I couldn't find any deer.'

One New Year's Eve Percy paid her a visit. He showed her where to find the deer up in the high timber on the mountain slopes. He lent her a smaller rifle, kept calling by and helped her to rear the kits. United by their love for the sleek panthers, they married six months later and began their scientific studies in earnest.

For two and a half years, rising at dawn and carrying heavy packs, they had chased behind the hounds to put the cougars up trees. It sometimes took 12 miles of hurrying over rocky ridges, barricades of fallen trees, through marshy swamps and swollen rivers to tree a cat. If it climbed too high Percy dared not fire a dart, for the animal could fall and injure or kill itself. In open country, where trees were small, the cougar might come down or turn at bay on a rock to fight the hounds, so the hunt would be called off for the day. Whenever possible, the Dewars wanted neither the cats nor their hounds to be injured.

Once the cougars were in trees, Percy and Penny worked with lightning precision. The hounds were tied up to prevent them attacking a fallen cougar. Out from Percy's pack came the Cap Chur pistol, drug bottle, syringe, dart, weight scales and a radio collar. Penny produced a camera, notebook and heavy climbing irons.

Swiftly assessing the spitting cougar's weight and using 1 cc of drug to 20 lbs of estimated weight, Percy filled the dart and loaded it into the pistol. Then, if the cougar was hard to see through the branches, he strapped on the leg irons, climbed a nearby tree, aimed, and fired the dart into the animal's thick haunch. Within 20 seconds the cougar would be anaesthetised. Usually it jumped from the tree when hit, ran some 200 yards, then fell unconscious. If, however, it stayed in the tree, Percy had to climb up, rope its rear legs and lower it gently to the ground.

He had about 15 minutes in which to work. With Penny taking notes and photos, he weighed and measured the animal and strapped on the light radio collar. They assessed its age, condition and sex, Percy clipped on ear tags, then they stood back, waiting until the cougar recovered and ran off into the bush. The animals were tracked by means of the radio antennae, the couple taking it in turns to sleep in the radio van so that the work could continue at night.

Despite the strenuous trekking and obvious dangers (three hounds had been killed by cougars) the Dewars had so far put 61 up trees, tranquilised 18 and put collars on 14. They had found out a great deal that was hitherto unknown. For instance, the legend that cougars are strictly territorial and that males will fight to defend boundaries was wrong. At the time they had three females, all with kits, quite tolerant of each other in an area four miles by two. Unmated females sometimes helped their sisters to train their kits to hunt. Males could run for miles searching for females in heat. One covered 30 miles in a single night. Another, after six weeks of tracking, was shot by a hunter two and a half months later 100 miles to the north. They did not make their typical scratch piles of earth and urinate on them to warn other males to stay away but to advertise their own presence to females. Cougars hunt by day as much as by night, unless there were humans around. They did not avoid wet or marshy places, as was believed, but took their kits to them to learn to hunt on slow-moving beavers. They also ate mice, rabbits, hares, marmots, grouse, raccoons and occasional porcupines, but their favourite prey was deer; and they consumed up to 80 per cent of the deer kills. They rarely killed farm stock, and four times the Dewars had tracked adult cougars passing within 100 yards of flocks of sheep without harming a single one. The few kills recorded were mostly made by young transient males that had left their family too soon, either through human disturbance or the mother being

37

shot. Ten times as many sheep were killed by domestic dogs briefly
running wild. Females would leave unweaned kits for up to 11 hours
at a time and go as far as 2½ miles to kill and feed. After weaning,
they took the kits to new resting-places at each site of a kill. And so
on. Their findings were fascinating to me.

When Percy showed me to my bedroom, a small octagonal plastic
sheet cabin further away in the woods, and told me to put my
sleeping bag on a bunk covered with a deer skin, I felt so excited
about what might happen on the morrow I could hardly sleep.

I was woken from a doze at dawn by light flooding through the
plastic. Then I heard Percy's 'alarm' to wake me up – loud banging
on an old camp cookhouse triangle at 5 a.m. When I entered his and
Penny's cabin, Percy poured some warm water into a small mug
from a kettle on the wood-burning range and said I could shave in
it. I said that as I often shaved in cold water, thanks very much!

For the next day and a half I thought they were really having me
on. I spent the first long morning with Percy, driving up and down
horrendously rough and rocky logging tracks in the old pick-up
truck, gloomily staring up the backsides of two of the hounds
which lurched ahead on the verges. They were trying to pick up
cougar scent trails, Percy said. They found none. We bounced about
so much on the truck seats that I was glad I had not got false teeth.
This was cougar tracking?

In the afternoon Penny came with us on foot, following behind
the two most experienced hounds, Lou and Lyn, both 12 years
old! We tracked a few scents on Echo Mountain, and found many
scratch piles made by males to inform females of their status,
sex and whereabouts. With their jowls drooping the two hounds
plodded along slowly, blowing wet snorts to clear their noses,
burying their muzzles in green moss where scent was strongest,
and sniffing delicately along low branches to their tips. When we
came to a 3-foot high barrier of fallen logs between her and Percy,
Lyn looked up at me pathetically. I lifted her hindquarters on to
the logs and she dropped with a grateful grunt down the other
side. Hell, I thought, with just a little training my young Moobli
would probably do better than this. It was all so slow. Was this
really cougar hunting?

Next day I went out with Percy alone. We again plodded slowly
for miles behind the hounds and I had a nagging suspicion that
Percy might be taking a few rest days at my expense. Suddenly,

late in the afternoon, Lou got a strong scent. She let out a loud bell-like bay and – *Phfft* – she was gone.

Phfft – that was Lyn.

Phfft – that was Percy.

I was left staring at hemlock branches moving thirty yards away, with only some bark slipping from a windfall log showing where they had gone. The Dewar shamble had suddenly become the Dewar dance! I had spent eight years in the wilds of Canada and Scotland, trekking after animals in rough country for pictures, but I had never met a man as fast as 56-year-old Percy Dewar in the bush. I was glad then that I had done those mornings of hard training in my little west wood. When I caught them up, his feet were twinkling over rocks, through thick sallal scrub and over barkless windfalls, as sure footed as the big cats he had spent nearly forty years tracking. I do not know what he had on the soles of his boots but he danced across a slippery fallen trunk that bridged a 30-ft gorge. I could only cross it on my backside, frantically heaving myself forward with both hands. After a couple of miles, when the cougar had emerged from a swamp with de-scented wet feet and the hounds lost the trail, I was not too sorry.

That evening we tried out the 11-year-old male hound Tige, and I soon learned why Percy called him 'the hustler'. Bouncing along old log tracks in front of the truck with a long, lurching easy stride, Tige moved tirelessly, often running parallel to the track to pick up the best scent in the undergrowth.

'He's a great worker,' said Percy. 'Hard to keep up with, but he catches up to the cougar real fast.'

Tige suddenly bayed and dived into a thick wood. Leaving the truck, we crashed after him. After a mile we heard a rustling ahead – a black bear and her cub were vanishing into the foliage, while under a huge cedar we found their droppings, still warm. We followed Tige another two miles but as the scent was becoming fainter and it was getting dark, Percy called him back. We had a three mile hike back to the truck.

Three more similar days followed, with Penny backpacking as well as any man over the high tough ridges. We followed one transient male for four hours, until it ran for a mile along a bare dry logging road without leaving any scent in the bush that the dogs could pick up. It was exhausting work. I spent one almost sleepless night radio tracking Dodie, an 80 lb female with two kits which the

Dewars had been following regularly for well over a year. She had been lying up in a den with her kits for three days.

It was an eerie experience, standing outside in the lonely mountains miles from the nearest humans and holding up the antennae, while the 'beep beep' in the earphones told me that not far away in the moonlight a full grown cougar was resting with her youngsters. At 2.30 a.m. she started to move, the beeps getting louder. She was heading towards me! I tensed, holding the camera and flash unit with the other hand, wondering if I would see her cross the road. Alas, I had no such luck. Dodie turned south east and I had to follow her in the radio van until the signals again came to a halt. Next morning we found her kill, a 75 lb deer which she had dragged a hundred yards to a thick bush.

Not until the sixth day did we tree a cougar. The same slow start behind Lyn, then off she went with a deep baying, followed by Percy, while I crashed after them with my camera gear. The Dewar dance ended in a clearing half a mile away.

'There he is,' said Percy quietly, pointing upwards.

High in a small fir, the chestnut tawny form of a young male cougar hung, his elbows hooked over branches, his huge round paws, claws sheathed, sticking out like flippers. Disdainfully, not snarling or spitting at all, he gazed down at us with large lustrous green eyes. True wilderness eyes they were, full of wild dignity and character, looking at each of us in turn and stripping the human watcher of all pretence and conceit. I shot off a roll of film, frantically changed lenses and climbed a slanting windfall tree, balancing precariously, so I could get to within 15 feet of its head. Then Penny, holding the antennae high on a logging track, shouted that the mother cougar was returning.

'We'd better get out of here,' said Percy. 'She's liable to get nasty – unless you want a photo of yourself being torn to pieces!'

He was joking. His real concern was to avoid upsetting the mother too much. He would radio-collar the young cougar when she was much further away than she was now. We made a quiet but hasty retreat.

After that incredible week I felt I had earned my first pictures of a wild cougar. I would like to have stayed longer but I had an appointment further north with an Indian guide and I needed to conserve my dwindling energies for some hard treks after wild grizzly bears with him. Before that, however, I allowed myself a day off and visited the West Vancouver home of my best friend in Canada, an ex-logger called Geordie Tocher, with whom I had shared many wild adventures. He immediately handed me a letter from Reader's Digest Press in New York. I fortified myself with a slug of rye whisky and feverishly opened it. They asked me to telephone as soon as possible. Over a crackly line I spoke to editor Bruce Lee.

'Hallo Mike,' came his voice. 'Y'know, we want this book. Those last three chapters you sent us are marvellous, ring so true. Do you have an agent?'

'No. Not any more.'

I had written all three chapters in one barnstorming day, a slog of 14,000 words, a feat I never achieved before or since.

'Well Mike, here it is. We can offer an advance of fifteen.'

Fifteen hundred dollars, I thought. That's not too bad. I wouldn't have minded nothing at all in advance. I just wanted the book published, and whatever little it earned in royalties could come later.

'Now, come on Mike,' said Lee. 'Fifteen thousand dollars is not, as you say in the old country, a sum to be sneezed at!'

Fifteen *thousand* dollars? I almost collapsed with delighted shock, but somehow managed to recover my composure.

'Yes,' I said. 'That's about the amount I was thinking of.'

'Right. When you've finished chasing those bears we'll discuss the other chapters and contractual terms.'

I put down the phone and performed a furious jig round the room. I felt free, set up for life.

'Come on,' laughed Geordie. 'We better head out for the beer parlour.'

The adventures I had after that with grizzly bears were even more thrilling – and nerve-racking – than anything that I described for Bruce Lee in *Alone in the Wilderness*, but that is another story which I will keep for another book. One day I might return and attempt an in-depth study of these majestic and dangerous creatures.

Before leaving Canada after the most strenuous month I could remember, I visited Booto again. How I wished there was some way in which I could look after the old dog and Moobli together.

5 · *Proof of a Tender Heart*

Moobli was sitting patiently by the entrance to Dave's garage as I brought the Land Rover to a standstill and got out. He looked at me standing there for a few seconds before padding back into the dark interior. Well, that's it, I thought, he doesn't recognise me at all. Maybe I should go back and look after Booto. I went off to the shop and to collect my mail at the post office, and then returned to the garage.

This time it was different. Moobli came towards me, bushy tail lifted, crest of hairs standing up along the ridge of his back, and sniffed at my trousers. The moment he got my scent he looked into my eyes with an expression of disbelief and burst into a frenzied show of affection. He whined loudly and leaped up, frantically licking my face, tearing at my jacket with his front paws as if he meant to strip it from my shoulders. Dave took all this in good part. I told him that the next time we were in the village, Moobli would probably make as big a fuss of him – and indeed so it turned out.

As I opened the Land Rover door Moobli barged past me, leaped into the front seat and then on to the bed at the back. There he flopped down, as he had always done, his mouth open in a wide happy grin, his tongue lolling. It was clear that he wanted to be with me and to return to Wildernesse.

We reached the pine wood where I had pulled the 13ft 6ins Norwegian-style deep-keel boat out of the water. I turned it right way up and laid a track of branches over the rocky shore before setting it afloat. Moobli had never really liked getting into boats, but before I had finished loading up, he leaped in and stood in the bow, looking back at me with an eager but solemn expression, anxious to please.

We covered the first four miles at speed, biffing against waves that sent showers of spray over the boat. Then I throttled down and drifted near the shore. Again Moobli remembered – this was his exercise run. He peered into the water at the rising ground below the surface, and when he judged it shallow enough, jumped out with a big splash. Shaking himself on shore like a small bear, he set off alongside the moving boat. It thrilled me to see the way he could move. Heavily built though he was, his flesh was mostly fluid muscle. He hurled himself over the deep tussocks like a charging cougar, threaded his way between large boulders with his light tan chest and thrusting rear legs flashing like polished steel, and broke into a loping trot over the yielding gravel banks and marshes, his large semi-webbed paws spread out like those of a wolf, so that he just drifted over ground that would cause a man to stagger and flounder. Even at his tender age, he could cover that last two miles of difficult terrain in little more than ten minutes.

We arrived home to total peace, though bracken was again in control of the front pasture, some of it six feet high. For the next few days I slashed at the rampant growth and weeded the vegetable garden. Mice and voles had burrowed down to take all my carefully sown peas and beans. Clouds of little black biting midges reduced me to a self-swatting maniac, and many times I ran down to the shore and doused myself in the loch. I threw tree branches into the loch for Moobli to swim after and fetch back. He loved this game. I hurled out a huge chunk of dead alder which I could only just lift by whirling it round like a hammer thrower. Moobli swam powerfully after it like a tugboat, head and shoulders high above the surface, tail swirling in his 4-knot wake. He seized it in his teeth with a bite that sent slivers of bark flying, and steamed back with it, again reminding me of a bear.

It was clear after just a few days that he was happy to be back at Wildernesse and would soon settle down. How well he would take to the presence of two spitting wildcat kittens was my only concern.

Wildcats are said to be untameable. They may look superficially like giant specimens of the ordinary domestic tabby, but with bushy black-banded tails and vicious claws an inch and a half long, the true Scottish wildcat can be a ferocious creature. In centuries gone by the wildcat inhabited large areas of England and Wales, and kings in the Middle Ages granted licences for the hunting of wolves and wildcats. By 1881 the wildcat was recorded as extinct south of the Scottish border. Although still rare, and now not to be found south of a line from Edinburgh to Glasgow, there is evidence of a small increase in numbers in recent years. Even so, I had been extremely lucky on just one occasion to see a wildcat in its natural environment for long enough to be able to photograph it.

On my return from Canada a local tradesman friend had offered me a pair of wildcat kittens which he had found abandoned by their mother in a ditch. The prospect of studying wildcat behaviour, about which there existed so many contradictory scientific pronouncements, although the sum of our knowledge was small, seemed almost irresistible, yet two fierce spitting tigers that could grow to as much as 16lbs in weight was not a responsibility to be taken on lightly. There was certainly a burgeoning vole population on which they could feed, and I would not want to keep them penned for long, but I had to think about Moobli.

We boated down the loch to inspect the kittens. Perhaps they were only domestics gone wild. They flared, even at the tender age of about seven weeks, as I gazed down at them in their box. Three Highland experts had said they were convinced that these were pure Scottish wildcats, and judging by their bright blue eyes and thick black-ringed tails, not to mention their attacking stance, I thought they were right. The opportunity was too good to miss, and I have told the full story of what became of them and their three litters in my book *Wildcat Haven*. Their effect on Moobli was remarkable, and that is all I will touch on here.

I took the wildcat kittens home in a box with wire netting sides, which I set down in the kitchen. On the second day I let the two little spitfires go loose on the kitchen floor and then brought in Moobli. I was sure he would have to be trained to resist a natural instinct to chase after them. I sat with one arm tightly round him, so that he would not feel jealous, and to my surprise he accepted their presence quite easily. In fact, he was fascinated by them. As the 8-week-old kits tottered about, sniffed firewood logs, mistimed feeble leaps at one another and hissed if we made the slightest movement, Moobli stared at them with large brown

44

eyes beneath furrowed brows. He could sense their youth and weakness. When they fell over while climbing the fireplace fender, he kept looking from them to me, as if wanting assurance that they were all right. He showed no belligerence towards them. When he moved forward carefully to get their scent, and they spat and struck out with their claws, he looked hurt and retreated with a whine, disappointed that they did not wish to play with him.

I named the kits Cleo and Patra. Because of their wildness, I installed them in the woodshed behind the cottage where they ignored a hay-filled den made from a tea-chest and took to lying on some sacking high up on a stack of firewood logs. Every time I fed and watered them in the shed I took Moobli with me, so that they would get used to each other. Sometimes he went on his own to the shed and sat for long periods at a discreet distance, entertained by the kittens' antics.

During the hours I spent noisily replenishing the supply of logs in the shed, the wildcats evacuated it. When they were not back at feed time I became worried and held their bed sacking to Moobli's nose, urging him to track the cats. After briefly sniffing the bedding he put his nose to the ground and pushed his way through the tall bracken that grew on the north hill. In minutes he put up Cleo, and she dashed for the safety of the shed. Then he began to whine. He had found Patra too, but she felt cornered in the thick bracken and was at bay, growling like a high-pitched motor, tail fluffed out, ready to slash at him if he went too close. Moobli obeyed my command to 'get back' and, once we were further away, Patra too rushed for the shed.

This was fine progress. I called Moobli a 'good boy', patted him and rewarded him with a tasty meat titbit. His natural urge to track after them had to be cultivated, for if they ever strayed too far he would be able to locate them where I alone could not. When they began to use the timber pile west of the cottage as a play area, he soon learned not to go too close, or to make sudden movements near them. It was fortunate that Moobli had known no nasty experiences with town cats when he was a puppy, so there was no ingrained dislike. He seemed to regard them as *his* charges as much as mine. One chop from those powerful jaws would have finished off either kitten, so I made sure he had no cause to feel jealous of them.

On our next supply trip a local forester approached us, looking at Moobli for a minute before asking how old he was. I told him, eight months.

'Well,' he said. 'I have kept Alsatians and those ears should be up by now. They should have come up at about six months.'

It was true. Each of Moobli's ears matched his large head and measured four inches across at the base, but their tips were floppy and flapped like a pair of wings when he ran. The right ear was worse than the left, and when he moved his head he appeared to be waving goodbye with it. He would never be up to show standards, although I had no wish to show him. I decided to write to his breeder for advice on how to get his ears pricking up stiffly.

On the way home I dropped Moobli off for a three-mile run, then trolled a fishing fly behind the boat. Within minutes I had a good hard strike and after a brief tussle landed a fine 1½lb sea trout for supper. Suddenly a movement on shore caught my eye. Far ahead of Moobli, an otter was bounding sinuously over the rocks below the trees of the long wood that flanked the loch. It ran for 200 yards before diving into a rocky grotto below a large broken alder tree. A few moments later Moobli came into view between the trees. It was wonderful to see him stop short as he picked up the otter's scent. Then he padded along, nose close to the ground, tracking it perfectly. He followed the scent to the grotto and paused, looking into it, his tail wagging slightly. What a fine nose he had developed by now, just what I had hoped for when first buying him. I did not want him to frighten the rare otter, however, so I whistled him away. He quickly obeyed and continued his run.

While I was typing at my desk one morning a large herring gull landed on the bird-table. Moobli, who was lying by my side, stared at the big white bird with surprise and got to his feet. This creature was different from the little tits, robins and chaffinches that usually ate there, but he did not bark or try to rush out; he just looked at me for guidance. Such incidents were enforcing my realisation of his stoic and innately gentle nature – fortunate in an animal of his size and strength.

In early August he gave me further proof of his scenting powers. We were returning from a long trek to the west, zigzagging up and down the steep wooded slopes, looking for animal dens, when he stopped, forepaw raised, and sniffed upwards against the wind. I gave him the command 'Go on', and he climbed steadily until almost at the crest, where he found a fox family's playground.

On a soft grassy plateau between large sheltering rocks, screened in on one side by fallen birch, was the skeleton of a large ewe. The whitened bones were scattered all over the place where the foxes had carried them about as playthings. The ammoniac scent reached his nostrils long before mine, and for the first time he lifted his leg against a tree, something he always did after that when smelling fox.

I now began Moobli's more serious training, intensifying the earlier work. I realised I had made mistakes when he was a pup. It had been wrong of me to push his nose close to any mess he made in the cottage and then to shove him outside with a stern 'badog!' It required patience, and it was far better to watch and wait and then swiftly to carry him outside with 'good boy' when he completed his motions out there. Those I missed, I picked up in paper and took outside, carrying him with me. After disposing of the droppings well away from the house, I said 'poops there, poops there!' Every time I found any new droppings I would point to them and say 'poops', so that he learned what the word meant.

Teaching a dog to lie down, or 'stay', is also useful, for it enables you to take him anywhere and not leave him shut up in the house, which a loyal dog dislikes. He can be left outside someone else's house, or a store where there are no hooks to take a lead, or to guard an item of property while you go to fetch another, or to perform some other errand. If I wanted Moobli to lie down, I used the word 'down' while gently pressing on his rear and shoulders with both hands. He resisted at first, but a steady pressure and more use of the word 'down' made his legs bend, and once down I used the usual 'good boy' and a reassuring pat. When I wanted him just to 'sit' I pressed only his rear legs down.

To make him keep to heel when walking with me, or to get back when he had already gone ahead and too close to an animal or a wild den after tracking it by scent, I just used the command 'get back!' Later I accompanied this with a sharp hiss. Eventually, when we were out in the wild and I did not want to use loud human speech, he learned that the hiss alone meant he should keep back. Earlier, of course, I applied his lead during this training. A sharp jerk on the lead at the time the command was made also helped to get the idea. Within a few weeks the lead was not necessary, and I used it only when we were in a town, where it is actually illegal to let the dog off it.

When I wanted him to go ahead on a trek I used the command 'go on', accompanied by a slight push forward on the base of his tail. He was always willing to follow any wild animal's scent trail, and if I wanted him to do this I would use the command 'track the . . .' Thus, when he was scenting the wildcats I said 'track the pussy coots' (I do not know where that coy name for them came from!), if he was on a fox trail I said 'track the foxy', and so on. All these creatures had different scents, and I hoped he would know I wanted him to keep to the track of a particular species. It took him two more years to work this out fully, though he soon learned that 'fetch the ball' meant he had to retrieve *any* object I threw, whether stick, stone, rock, potato, chunk of tree.

There is a school of thought that says one should never hit a dog, but I did not go along with this, especially with one of Moobli's size and strength. A sharp slap can bring a rebuke home more forcefully. At first, when he ran off without command, and then finally obeyed my angry 'come here!', I would slap him on his return. I soon realised the mistake, for he associated the slap with the coming back and not the running away – exactly the opposite of what I had intended. Nevertheless, I used the slap if he disobeyed *knowing* that he was disobeying, but it was better kept for occasions when he showed signs of ignoring the command 'na!' or 'get back!', and preferably *before* he took off. A large healthy dog like Moobli is, in fact, almost impervious to pain delivered by the human hand.

I always wore an old jacket for robust play with him. He would bite the cloth and almost tug me over, hit me hard with his paws and hurl himself bodily at me. Quite hard punches, and even kicks from my wellingtons, he seemed not to feel at all, nor did he mind being thrown to the ground. All this simply allowed him to get rougher in return! On the other hand, if I was really angry and meant it, just a sharp slap stopped him in his tracks. Looking back, I know that I could have trained him at this stage to obey more commands, for in later life he learned many many more.

In mid-August Molly Thomson wrote to me on the subject of Moobli's floppy ears.

. . . it is very difficult to describe what to do, but go to the chemist and buy some THIN chiropodist felt. Take a template in cardboard of the inside of the ear down to the first protruding bits, and shape it a little away from the edge and almost to the tip. If you buy the small packets of felt at 14p each, this just fits one ear. When you are sure of the shape and the felt is cut correctly, wash the ear where the felt is going with soap and water, dry *very* thoroughly, then cut off any hair.

When the ear is absolutely dry, peel off the paper on the felt, warm the sticky side slightly and place in the ear, pressing well on. This should stay put for three weeks. If not, put a piece or two of ½-inch zinc oxide plaster right round the whole ear, not too tight. When you want to remove the felt buy some Zoff; it is a wonderful plaster remover and there will be no soreness where the felt stuck.

Hoping it is not too late, as ears are usually assisted at seven months old if necessary.

Two days later I drove the 44 miles to the nearest town to trade in my ancient Land Rover for a new one, and also to buy the chiropodist felt. No chemist seemed to stock any, and I had to telephone a friend in England to send some up to me. As we trailed from shop to shop, the tourist crowds made me step into the road, and Moobli, who was on a lead, swung out too, on my offside. There was a slight thwacking sound as he leaped back on to the pavement, though he did not cry out. A car had sped past and hit the side of his muzzle. As I gently lifted his lip to inspect the damage he held up his paw for me to shake, as if saying sorry, yet it had been entirely my fault. Luckily, there was no serious injury; just a little bleeding where his lip had been forced against his teeth.

On reaching home I sorted out my mail and saw there was a long letter from Julia Dimopulous, which I saved until last. When I opened it I received a terrible shock.

Booto was dead.

He had run across the road to investigate another dog and had been hit by a speeding car. Despite a broken back, he had managed to haul himself into the courtyard of the cafe before finally collapsing. The woman driver of the car had been most contrite and had taken Julia and Booto to a vet some miles down the coast. The injuries proved beyond relief, and to end his suffering Booto had been put down. I held my head between my hands, unable to prevent tears. The strange thing was that as I read this news Moobli kicked out and whuffed in his sleep, something he had never done before. It was as if the shock in my own mind had somehow communicated itself to his. I went out into the oak and spruce grove and said my goodbyes to my old Canadian partner.

One morning soon afterwards I took Moobli up the loch to fetch some golden sand which had been excavated by badgers digging a new sett, so that I could cement the chimneys. Moobli was fascinated by their scent trails and followed them for many yards. He even found dung pits that had been dug a long way from the sett. I had not known badgers to dig these holes for their droppings away from the sett itself. On the way back I decided to row. Bored by my slow pace, which did not allow him to gallop, Moobli plunged into the loch and swam the full two miles home with ease. With his broad head high, he looked like a small grizzly swimming along. He shook himself on shore then bounced about, wanting me to throw sticks.

When the chiropodist felt arrived, I spent time following Molly Thomson's instructions and finally had two wedge-shaped pieces stuck to the insides of his ears, so that both stood bolt upright. He must have realised that this was for his own good for he never tried to scratch off the felt. Alas, the treatment did not work properly. Although the left ear came up well, the tip of the right continued to droop for the rest of his life.

When, in heavy rain, I next boated down the loch I dropped Moobli off early in the return journey for his first full three-mile run home, to make up for his lack of exercise that week. It was already getting dark, but I felt that after the first mile he would know the route well enough. I sped home in order to have all the supplies carried up to the cottage before he arrived, panting and hungry for his supper. That done, I waited half an hour and still he did not appear. I was worried now lest he had picked up some old poison left out for a fox, or perhaps had broken his leg charging over the rocky, tussocky terrain. I put my sodden rainsuit on again, hauled out the boat and went all the way back to the Land Rover, six miles away, whistling, calling and shining a torch at the shore. There was no sign of him. I would have to search again at dawn. Upbraiding myself for having made him run so far in the dark, I switched on the torch as I went to check the wildcat kittens on my return.

Moobli was standing by the woodshed door, tongue out, grinning. He had probably reached home while I was still picking the third load of supplies out of the boat, and had gone to see the kittens – *his* charges – before I did. I was too relieved to be angry, but he could not work out why I made such a fuss of him, what all the sudden hugs were for. It was then I realised that I truly loved him, especially now that Booto was gone.

One evening, when I was at my desk, Moobli – who was outside – gave a loud bark while staring at the hill above the cottage. He looked in at me, and as our eyes met, stared back at the hill and barked again. I dashed out and scanned the terrain with the fieldglass, but I could see nothing. Had he barked because he was bored and wanted me to come out and play? I told him off. I did not want him barking unnecessarily, frightening away the deer.

A few days later I discovered that he had probably barked for a very good reason. I took him for his hardest trek so far, right up to the peak of a 3,000-foot mountain. At the top we were enveloped in thick mist and had to cover a lot more ground than usual to find our way out of it. As we plodded back to the boat Moobli hung back, almost dragging his feet. For once, it seemed, I had tired him out. On arriving home I found Patra high on the logs in the shed, looking badly scared; Cleo was missing. This was odd at feed time, when both wildcats should have heard us coming. Suddenly Moobli gave a low growl and shot off to the top edge of the west wood. Far from being tired, he kept leaping high, like a gigantic springbok, so that he could see over the tall bracken. My nostrils caught the acrid ammoniac scent of fox. In the wood Moobli bayed deeper and louder than a bloodhound, a sound I had never heard him make before. It made the hairs rise on my neck, and would have scared off a cougar, never mind a fox. We soon located Cleo, spitting below a tree stump, and shepherded her back to the shed.

With a big fox prowling round, hoping to nab one of the kittens, I left the back door open at nights for a fortnight so that Moobli could go out and keep it away. This seemed to work, for the fox did not return. By then the wildcats could scoot up trees out of danger. The only trouble with leaving the door open was that the kittens came into the workshop, especially on stormy nights, in search of warmth, shelter and even the company of the huge soft-hearted creature that never harmed them. Perhaps he had even brought them in. They raided his carton of sterilised meat sausages and cleaned out his food bowl. Moobli established a special rapport with the soft and plumper Patra. One morning I managed to pick her up with gloves and carried her unprotesting on to my bed. She felt the softness of the coverlet and settled down. Moobli padded in behind us and spent the next 20 minutes with his chin resting on the bed, gazing at her in blind adoration. The moment I moved at the desk, however, she leaped down and defecated below the bed. I quickly transferred her back to the shed.

Proof of his tender heart came when an Australian friend of mine sent him an artificial steak that squeaked. It looked like a real slab of meat, but whenever he picked it up and his teeth compressed the sides, air was forced through the squeaker and it emitted a sound like a puppy in distress. He would drop it, paw at it, when it would squeak again, then whine in a worried way as if he was hurting it. In the end he buried the steak in the garden.

Even after nine-mile wildlife treks, Moobli would still be full of energy. On the way back, the wind behind us so that we could not stalk anyway, I would let him relax. I gave the command 'Go on!', and he knew he was off the mental leash. Off he would go in play, zooming about in circles through the bogs and swamps, his huge pads splayed out like those of a wolf on snow, sounding '*kerlupp, kerlupp*' as he slooshed past at great speed. He dived in on my plodding form in diagonal dashes, feinting on close approach like Muhammed Ali, before dodging my playful swipes. Where he got the energy for this on a pound of mutton flank, a tin of dog meat and a few handfuls of biscuit meal a day, I did not know.

He hated my bath times on our return from these treks, when I stood on a rubber mat in the kitchen and doused myself down with hot soapy flannels from a bowl. It was as if my naked form offended his dignity. I did not think much of this prim attitude in a big dog – we should have been as matey and manly as players in a Rugby bath after a match. While he lay glowering on his bed I would toss my peeled garments one by one on to his head. He disliked this teasing even more but bore it with his usual patience, only emitting the occasional groan as he extracted his head from beneath shirt, vest, trousers, pants and socks, then rested his chin on each article until his head was on a pile of sweaty gear. He never thought of moving, possibly because he thought it might delay his supper which I warmed up on the camp stove as I towelled myself dry. I always fed him first. After all, I had eaten lunch.

In mid-September an autumn gale, heralding winter storms to come, whipped the loch into a frenzy of white water. First the leaves of shoreside alders, then hazel, then ash, were blown from the trees and clusters of crimson rowan berries hit the ground with little thuds. When I boated out for supplies, I trained Moobli to lie up in the prow as we beat against the crashing waves. His weight kept the front of the boat down, so preventing it blowing up and back on us and the boat turning turtle, possibly ending our lives.

We found a fresh traffic-killed rabbit on the road, and I brought it back for the wildcats which did not seem to be catching their own prey. I would use it to train them to hunt. I rigged up a complicated device with nylon line, a fishing reel and a pulley so that I could make the rabbit bounce realistically to and fro through the grasses. The wildcats chased it at first, but by the third day they had worked out that it was an artificial contrivance and lost interest.

I was working on the Canadian book on the second afternoon when I noticed that Moobli had disappeared. I went out quietly and found him sneakily sitting down low in the bracken, chewing the rabbit. He was being clever, trying not to remove it from the line, and had not seen me arrive on the scene. I gave a sharp whistle and he leaped up, stole away through the bracken and then came running round the far side of the cottage as if he had been a hundred yards in another direction. He had eaten half the rabbit, yet there was uneaten food in his bowl. I sniffed the smell of rabbit on his breath and muzzle, and clouted him.

'Na!' I said, twice, as I showed him the remains; I wanted him to know why he was being reprimanded.

Later he went back again to the rabbit. I yelled, and he instantly shot off low through the bracken and stayed away for half an hour. Then he came sneaking back from the east wood, as if nothing had happened. I took him to the rabbit and this time gave his flank two sharp switches from a hazel wand. This did not hurt him much, but the fact that I had taken a stick to him for the first time offended his dignity. He was off me for a whole day, but the effect was salutary for he did not touch the rabbit again. If he disobeyed when he *knew* he should not be doing something (as shown by his sneaky attitude) he needed to be punished and corrected.

Moobli was certainly more obedient over the next few days, which was just as well, for one of the most exciting periods for the Highland naturalist lay ahead, and to secure the best results from it I needed his disciplined help.

6 · A Fearsome Pastoral Symphony

In late September and early October the wild red deer of the Highlands stage their spectacular autumn rut. Down from the high tops, where they have grazed all summer in their bachelor herds, come the big master stags. They cover many miles in search of hinds, as many hinds as possible, to round up into harems which they then defend from the attentions of rival stags. With swelled necks and manes thickened with the onset of oestrus, each stag first takes up a proprietorial position among his chosen hinds. Then one stag roars a warning, echoing across the glens. Another, still seeking hinds, bellows his challenge, and within a few days the hills are filled with roarings. The sounds are loud, yet eerie, filled with lust, anger and frustration, and can be frightening to one hearing them for the first time. They alternate between the bellows of a despairing bull and, when a heated stag is rounding a wandering hind back into the harem, the short grunting blatting roars that resemble those of unseen lions.

In prime condition after their summer feeding, the stags are now at their most aggressive. While attacks on men are rare, they have occurred, and more than once when stalking them my heart has thudded with fear as a stag has trotted angrily towards my lying form. Twice, after taking my pictures, I have been scared enough to stand up and flap my jacket to frighten a stag away. Despite their size (a big stag can weigh 15 stone) they and the hinds are hard to see on the Hill, the russet and browns of their coats blend so perfectly with the autumn herbage. Often one first locates them by the large buff-white heart shaped alarm patches on their rumps.

Occasionally, hearing no roars ahead, I have walked over a knoll or up a gully to come upon a stag with hinds right below or in front of me. And off they would run, before I could take a single picture. This of course is bad stalking, and one of the reasons why I had acquired Moobli. As one always stalks against the wind, I expected his nose to locate deer ahead by scent long before I could actually see them.

After the year's first frosts under clear moonlit skies on September 29 I took Moobli on a long trek over the high undulating hills to the north west. We saw no stags, but after two miles he began his prancing gait, nose held high, a sure sign he had scented animals ahead. After hissing him back I went forward and peered round a small rockface. There were some hinds and calves lying down on a high ridge a quarter of a mile ahead. We stalked them for 300 yards before I gave him the commands 'Down' and 'Stay', and crawled to a large clump of screening heather. The hinds were lit by the sun into glowing autumnal colours and were placidly chewing the cud. I had taken two photographs when suddenly they all leaped to their feet and made off.

Moobli, grinning inanely, his long tongue lolling, had sneaked up and was standing right beside me, his light tan chest glowing in the light like white hot coals as he looked at their departing forms with avid interest. I'm afraid I clouted him, hard.

During the next few days I re-trained him to obey 'Down' and 'Stay' as I crawled away over the front pasture, trying to imitate the situation when I had been taking photographs up on the Hill. On October 6, after hearing the first stag roars coming across the loch, I waited until the sun was dying in the west in late afternoon before trekking with him towards an 1,800-foot peak to the east against a cold easterly breeze. We had got up to 1,600 feet when Moobli lifted his black muzzle and began his high-footed scenting gait. My ears were assaulted suddenly by a loud roar. It came from behind a small knoll up ahead. Hissing Moobli to keep back, I wriggled forward, snake-like, on belly and elbows, using tufts of heather as cover. Moobli seemed to sense the need for caution for he held his head low and put one paw in front of the other carefully like a huge prowling dog-eared cat.

I reached the top of the knoll and peered through the heather. There, only fifty yards ahead, was the stag, a fine young 10-pointer with seven hinds and two calves. The stalking situation was ideal. The golden sinking sun blazed into the eyes of the deer and the gusting east wind took away both our scent and any slight sound we made. With only hand movements I instructed Moobli to lie down by my pack. For half an hour I took photos of the stag roaring, trying to mount a hind which slipped away from beneath him, scratching one ear with an incredibly delicate movement of his right hindleg, trotting round his harem, then lying down and dozing peacefully in the grass.

Finally, I looked back. Moobli, still by the pack, sank his head down guiltily when he saw my gaze upon him. Although he was fascinated by the deer, it seemed he really did now understand that this was my *work*, for he had obeyed my command to stay. I felt a surge of gratitude that he had learned so fast, slid backwards and, once out of sight of the deer, made a great fuss of him, telling him what a good boy he had been. I then had to prevent him capering about with delight.

There were many days filled with rain or hailstorms in Moobli's first autumn, making stag treks difficult if not impossible. As I tapped away at my book he lay bored with his head between his paws, his great brown eyes willing me to get up, go out and throw sticks for him. It was annoying to hear the stags roaring on the hills above and to know it was useless to go up there with the poor light and incessant rain making photography impossible. Sometimes the wet and cold north-west winds drove the deer down to spend a night in the west wood.

I was at my desk in late October when I heard a stag roaring in the darkened garden. I went out with the torch to find a fine 10-pointer with four hinds in the front pasture. They pranced off haughtily to the edge of the wood, where the stag stopped and stood its ground, bellowing at me. So we just traded roars for a while! Stag-roaring is rough on the human throat, and while it will often make a stag stop and roar back, it usually reduced me to a coughing fit. There is no need for a rifle here if I ever want venison: a pistol would do!

Two days later, as hail showers and spindrift whirlwinds swept across the loch, we trekked up and down the steep woodland cliffs to the east, Moobli trying to track a fox that was visiting our woods at night. We found no den. A male buzzard soared over the trees. As I watched, a peregrine falcon came arcing across the sky, dived briefly on the buzzard, dislodging a few of its feathers, and was away out of sight behind us before the buzzard knew what had happened. What speed, what control! The buzzard looked most put out, like a fat overfed school swot in a race when Victor Ludorum sweeps past.

A few minutes later I noticed Moobli had disappeared. A whistle produced him, his muzzle smelling awful. He had found a decomposing hind carcass lying in a small burn and had been helping himself to what for him must have been a delicacy. How he could enjoy meat that would poison a human being I did not know. On our return I threw a hefty waterlogged branch into the loch, where it promptly sank, leaving Moobli to swim around, constantly poking his bear-like muzzle and eyes (though not his ears) below the surface as he searched for it. Then he came out, all pristine and smelling clean again.

In early November I left a large supply of food, milk and water in the woodshed for the wildcats and drove down to London to collect a ferocious old wildcat tom from London Zoo, which I hoped to breed with one of my females. This time Moobli enjoyed the long drive, and when we camped on the first night in a pine wood near Douglas Water, he slept beside me on the Land Rover bed, his vast snoring form cramming me into the bulwarks.

To my surprise he took the big city in his stride, though he appeared not to hear the roar of the traffic and showed an alarming propensity to dash across busy roads if he saw another large dog on the far side. Little dogs he ignored. For the first three days I had to keep him strictly on the lead, which was a little irksome as he insisted on checking the doggy scents on every plane tree of the avenue where I had once lived, and cocking his own leg to establish his territory. But it did not take him long to learn that pavements were for both canine and human walkers, and that the black and white stripes were for crossing the road. He happily accepted the carpeted luxury of the small Hampstead hotel as befitting his aris-tocratic pedigree, even relocated our ground-floor room after our first walk out of it. To keep him fit, I ran with him up to Hampstead Heath and hurled sticks down steep slopes for him to chase and retrieve. One stick landed behind some bushes, and I heard loud barks, growls, thrashing movements, and then a high-pitched yipe.

I hurried down in time to see a large black whimpering Labrador limping away on three legs, one front paw held high off the ground. I did not know if Moobli had actually broken its leg, but as the Labrador's plump owner staggered up the hill towards us, shouting and waving his stick, I decided that I ought to try and keep fit too. With Moobli alongside I galloped a discreet half mile through the trees in what must have been a creditable time. Moobli himself had not sustained a single scratch.

I was surprised by the number of pedestrians who, upon spotting an abnormally large Alsatian heading towards them, instantly stuffed their hands in their pockets or behind their backs, fear on their faces. Some even foolishly stamped and cried 'Go away!' – which only made Moobli bark at people he thought were going to attack. Patiently I tried to explain that badly behaved dogs, like children, were the result of poor upbringing. I told them that an Alsatian which enjoyed a good, disciplined, fully exercised life and knew its place, which was not tied up all day while its owner was at work, or ill treated, or spoilt to death, was the best-tempered of dogs. Seen so often as vicious guard dogs in films, or as police dogs savaging criminals, Alsatians have acquired a poor public image. When a small terrier bites someone, little is heard; it can even be treated as a joke. With an Alsatian, it makes the news. No doubt its wolf-like appearance also has something to do with it. Certainly a badly trained or untrained Alsatian can be a menace, but no more so than any other large breed of dog.

On Sunday morning I took Moobli to a Kensington drinking club I used to haunt in my showbiz years. Many of my old acquaintances, whose lives had not changed in fifteen years, were there. Moobli became the centre of attraction, and many wanted to pat him. He put up with these ministrations with dignity but did not really like them. I was at the bar when a lovely Chinese woman came up to me, laughing but indignant.

'Your dog,' she said, 'has just drunk my Bloody Mary! Would you mind buying me another?'

I looked at her empty glass on the table. It was still standing up.

'I'll buy another,' I replied. 'And if Moobli can drink it without knocking the glass over, I'll buy you one too. Otherwise, you stand me a double Scotch.'

One look at the wildcat tom when I went to collect him from the Zoo told me that, while Moobli had formed a slight rapport with the females, he would never do so with this animal. He was a ferocious old cuss, 3½ feet long and weighing 16 lbs. As soon as I bent my head down in a friendly way towards his den, he growled loudly, slammed down a foot and gave a blasting '*PAAAH!*' spit that sounded like a small charge of dynamite going off. Never during all his ten years of captivity had he allowed a single human hand to touch him. Indeed, he was so prone to attack his keepers they always trapped him in the rear den before cleaning out his cage. I named him Sylvesturr, and before driving him home, I shoved his den box under the Land Rover bed, to keep him and Moobli apart.

Back at Wildernesse I spent four days out in drizzly weather making a strong roofed enclosure for Sylvesturr. I set the wildcat out in a special box-cage live trap I had made, draping a beach towel over the sides to protect him from draughts. Once, as I worked, I saw Moobli nose near the cage out of curiosity. Instantly the tomcat went on the attack, spitting loudly and slamming one set of claws against the wire netting. Moobli withdrew his nose just in time. As I came up, Sylvesturr repeated the performance, and Moobli began bouncing about on his feet, barking loudly. This would not do at all. I did not want the dog upsetting the old cat, and if they ever met out in the open I was sure Sylvesturr would attack him. He showed no fear of humans, and that probably went for their dogs as well. I had to sort this out right now. I slapped Moobli for barking, hating myself for it since he was probably just trying to protect me, and spent some time explaining that Sylvesturr was now one of the family and had to be left alone. He did not go near the cage again.

Before I could get Sylvesturr settled in the new enclosure, however, he escaped overnight. Now I had to rely on Moobli. Putting his nose into the empty cage-trap, so he would get a good strong scent, I gave him the command – 'Track the pussy coots!' I felt sure my earlier scolding and his obvious dislike of the big tom would make him refuse, but to my delight he instantly put his nose down, zigzagged round the pens, through the front pasture to the shore, and headed past some hazel bushes into the west wood. When I caught up, he was whining and pacing over a huge cairn of tumbled boulders below the rock escarpment, and from a dark hole came unmistakable growls and flares. He had located Sylvesturr in mere minutes. I petted and congratulated him, and rewarded him with a tasty piece of meat. That night I set the cage-trap on a direct line between the rocky cairn and the new enclosure. But for

Moobli finding Sylvesturr I would not have known the best place to put it. Luckily the ruse worked and two mornings later I had him safely caught.

I told Moobli to sit by my feet while I released Sylvesturr into the enclosure. It was fortunate that I did so, for as I tried to shake the old cat out I failed to notice a gap between the bottom of the box part of the trap and the enclosure's fencing. As the tom landed, he spat loudly and launched an attack towards the gap, which was at the level of my groin. Then he saw Moobli and transferred his attack to the dog, growling and slamming his inch-and-a-half-long claws against the fencing. This gave me just enough time to extract the trap and fasten the fencing again before the cat could escape. Moobli did not bark but just bounced about, facing down the wildcat, which turned and finally fled into the rocky den I had made for him.

It would be nice to report that that was the end of any trouble between Moobli and Sylvesturr, but a few days later another altercation drew me from my desk to where Moobli was barking outside. Normally he barked only at the approach of humans, and lochside hikers were rare. Hurrying outside I saw that he was deliberately teasing the old tom. He was having a great game, bouncing to and fro in front of the pen, shaking his head waggishly so that his huge ears flapped, and barking right in the tomcat's face. The big wildcat was enraged, standing his ground, rearing up on his two long front legs to present a ferocious frontal aspect, spitting loud '*PAAAH*'s and slashing out with his claws. I scolded Moobli and gave him another hard slap. From that moment on, Moobli never again acknowledged Sylvesturr's presence. He looked right through the tom as if he was not there, yet his fascination for the two young females, especially Patra, remained constant.

Not long after that, when Moobli was running along the shore as I was wallowing home in the boat through stormy following waves, I saw him stop by the rocky lair to which he had tracked the otter. His tail was waving agitatedly, his head deep into the rocks. There was clearly something in the holt. Above the noise of the gales I heard two high-pitched screeches. I yelled to Moobli to come away. He looked towards me, there was a brown blur, and an otter shot out between his legs. Moobli gave a loud yipe as the otter vanished into the water, then turned to run home.

I had just hauled the boat on to its runway before the waves swamped it when Moobli came running up with his usual enthusiastic greeting. I saw that he was limping. There was a one-inch gash across the knee-joint of his left hindleg. I felt sure that the otter, on its way through Moobli's legs, had delivered a slashing bite. Between the parted flesh I could see white cartilage or bone showing. The wound was too large to heal naturally on a constantly-flexed part of the leg; it would have to be stitched up by a vet in the town 44 miles away.

We could not leave next day, however, for the first winter blizzard began falling. Moobli reacted comically to his first sight of snow. He went outside and stared in amazement at the world of white. As the wind and flakes hit him he blinked, cringed and came back indoors. Maybe he thought I intended taking him on a trek and, what with his wounded leg, the snow was the last straw. While the blizzard blew itself out over the next two days, I kept the wound as clean as possible. Then, as light drizzle melted the fallen snow, we boated out.

The young vet in charge that morning did not have a muzzle big enough, so he tied Moobli's jaws with a piece of cord tightly enough to make the dog whine. As I held him down on the bench with reassuring words, Moobli jerked at the pain of the needle. A single stitch was all that was necessary. On the way back he kept licking the wound and whining, but within a few days it was healing well.

Christmas Day dawned dark and drear, with a constant drizzle falling. I shoved a turkey and some home-made bread into the calor gas oven and set out with Moobli on a short two-mile trek to 1,500 feet. It was our first Christmas together, and although he still limped slightly, Moobli returned feeling better for the exhilarating exercise.

Four days later I took Moobli on a hard eight-mile trek to the high peak overlooking the lochan below Guardian mountain, hoping the snow clouds would refrain from dropping their loads. I was wrong. Up on the tops we were lashed by hurricane-force winds and blizzards of hail. Once I was blown right off my feet. Moobli, being much closer to the ground and having four feet instead of two, was easily able to retain his footing. His nose-scenting and obedience helped me to stalk four deer herds and I was able to take fine pictures of hinds in snow. Moobli now decided he *liked* snow, for on the way back he galloped about in it, like a small horse, made wild swerving turns like a speedway rider, and scooped up mouthfuls with his bottom jaw, swallowing as it melted.

I threw soft snowballs at him. The first hit him on the top of the head and he started back, blinking with surprise. The second splashed on his chest. He gave a sharp '*whuff*' and jumped backwards. When he saw me preparing a third, he started dancing about, as if determined not to stand there and be a target. I threw it but as it was about to whistle past his ear, he shot out his jaws, caught it, squashed it and dropped it. This was a great new game! He started jumping up and down like a football goalie, eager for more. No matter how I threw them, tossing them gently or hurling them as hard as I could, as long as they were within range he nearly always caught, crunched their freezing substance and dropped them. It set my teeth on edge just to watch him. If there was a carpet of snow on the ground, Moobli would recall the snowball game, reaching down and grabbing a mouthful to crunch up and then shake clear, leaping about to urge me to throw some at him.

On New Year's Eve I set out to fulfil my annual ritual of renewing close contact with nature, a habit I had adopted from an old Scots-Indian called Pappy Tihoni who had taken me on a wild grizzly trek in western Canada. I took a pup tent out into the woods, cooked supper over a smoky campfire and renewed my vows to the wilds, asking for the strength to carry on my studies for at least another year. I forced myself to go through Hogmanay without a single drink, gaining a perverse feeling of strength from the self-denial. But this time I had Moobli with me. He looked at his huge pan of food simmering atop a stout coat-hanger, cocked his head enquiringly at the tinny sound of Beethoven's Pastoral Symphony issuing faintly from the battery record-player, and accepted the new situation stoically. As I lay down to sleep in the tent he curled up on a folded blanket in the flyleaf and stayed there, on guard, all night. Every time I woke up I reached out to give his huge warm furry form a reassuring pat.

7 · Love's Labours Lost

It is after the winter solstice, when the short dark gloomy days are filled with rain or snow and every supply trip is a battle against lashing wet gales, that the libido of the lone wilderness dweller sinks to its lowest. Moobli was there not only to help track wildlife but as a friend and companion, even a protector if necessary, and during the eerie events that followed he seemed to be letting me down.

In January old Sylvesturr kicked down his heavy den door and forced an escape from his enclosure. Moobli had never liked the wild tom, and every time I set him to track the cat he either obstinately refused or was unable to get his scent. Instead he just followed the trails of the two females to the woodshed. There were large but messed-up tracks in the snow outside Sylvesturr's pen, which suggested that something large had scared him enough to make him escape. Moobli could not seem to find the scent of whatever it was either.

One morning I was woken up by the harsh croakings of ravens. The decomposing body of a large hind had been washed down into the pool of the burn that supplied my water pipe. I managed to drag it to a high ledge in the middle of the waterfall. Next day it had disappeared. I found it thirty yards away on the far side of the burn, reduced to a bloody skeleton. Whatever animal, or animals, had dragged it there must have been big and strong. Moobli whined and cocked his leg on tufts as he did for foxes, but again was unable to follow any scent track.

Later, when walking round the woods, I found a dead hind with shotgun pellets in her rear haunches and her dying calf lying in echelon right behind her. I was surprised that Moobli had not scented them, for if we had come upon them earlier I might have been able to save the calf by feeding it sheep's milk from a teated bottle. I took some meat for Moobli and the wildcats, used some in the box-cage trap which I was setting for Sylvesturr, and hung the hind's heavy wet skin over the windbreak logs in the porch.

It was while boating back in misty sunshine that I saw the long sinuous neck and head, with twin spikes on it, of some animal in the water ahead. It flopped up and down, and in the distorting mist it looked like some legendary monster. As I drew nearer, ready to gun the engine and steer away, I saw it was a big red deer hind which had tried to swim the loch and was now drowning before my eyes. The spikes were her ears. I slowed down, but was still going too fast and had to reverse back to the twitching form. As I lifted her head, water billowed from her nostrils. I had arrived seconds too late. I hauled the beast into the boat and took it home where I skinned it and hung the hide next to the first.

That night, as I sat at my desk in the lamp's glow, Moobli dozing on the floor, there came a loud banging and flapping sound in the open porch. I rushed out. The 5ft-long wet skin of one of the hinds had been wrenched off the high logs and the whole smelly tail section torn out of it. No fox or wildcat would have the strength to do that. There was an eerie atmosphere about Wildernesse and I began to feel fear then. Moobli showed no inclination to track or chase after whatever animal had done it. He looked scared too, and wanted only to get back into the warmth of the cottage. Had I a coward for a dog?

There had been rumours that some misguided conservationist had released two wolves into the hills in my area, but if that were so, surely their sheep kills would have been reported by now. Whistles and calls failed to produce Moobli next day after he had disappeared for an hour. When he finally returned, uninjured but hungry, I was too glad to have him back to give him more than a token telling off.

Soon afterwards Sylvesturr was caught by the trap. He was suffering from pneumonia and had to be nursed back to health

Although powerfully built at nine months old, Moobli needed chiropodist's felt to help his ears become erect. Summer or winter, he was always ready to cross the burn.

At just over a year, he had developed wonderful scenting powers. He led me to a newly dead hind and her calf.

Moobli scented out the wandering wildcat kittens and sent them up trees so that I could check their condition. His eagerness for tracking wildlife showed on his face.

He loved to lie upside down and watch me typing at the desk.

in the heated woodshed. After that the mysterious incidents ceased and life returned to normal. It was two more winters before I learned the likely causes, this time through Moobli's help, but that story comes later.

Meanwhile, difficulties with Moobli continued. It had not taken him long to learn that sheep were taboo, and by one year and two months old he had lost all interest in them. Deer, on the other hand, continued to fascinate him. While I was at my desk on January 23, he chased after some hinds in the west wood. I called him back, told him off and shut him in the kitchen for an hour to make the message felt. Two days later there was another incident. I missed Moobli while I was hauling the boats up after overnight rain, and my calls brought no response. I chased through the west wood and was confronted by several hinds and yearlings running towards me with Moobli at their heels. Like a wolf, he singled out one youngster and drove it away from the others back into the wood, while the main group turned down towards the loch shore and made their escape. When I called him off, the dog desisted immediately. Moobli well knew by this time of my interest in deer; perhaps he had been trying to head the yearling towards me. Whatever his intention, he had to learn not to chase any wild creature on his own initiative.

Training a large and powerful male Alsatian is not easy, but I noticed that, unlike a human male in adolescence, Moobli showed little tendency towards rebellion for its own sake. Discipline alone was not enough; a build-up of resentment could cause him to turn on me later. I tried to put the emphasis on education rather than hard training. Yet he had to be kept fully occupied and exercised.

Over the next two months I took Moobli on as many treks as possible, but instead of keeping him to heel I let him nose about naturally, only calling him back with a hiss if he went more than about seven yards in front. By letting him range more freely, the tracking education became as much mine as his, for he nosed out things I would never have found. When he sniffed out fox scats or their scented urine on mossy rocks or tussocky tufts, I urged him to 'Track the foxy!' and he scented along narrow trails and discovered many of their territorial marking-posts. While he found it difficult to pick up scent after they had traversed wet rock faces or crossed burns, I was able to work out over the years much about their territorial movements and came to the conclusion that there were a maximum of five fox families in an area nine miles by four. The local foxhound pack accounted for five foxes a year from this area yet the families never numbered less than three.

On February 15 he paused, one foreleg raised, scenting beyond a tumbled cairn of huge boulders. I readied my camera and peered round. There, standing by the rocks, was a weak ewe. Hampered by a 15ft length of heavy fence wire embedded in her wool, she had been unable to graze freely and was near to starvation. I freed her and she tottered away, clipping avidly at the vegetation.

A few days later, as we were coming over a high crest and were about to descend a killer 1,800-foot steep hill, again he paused, scenting ahead. I crept up to him. There was a large herd of 63 hinds, yearlings and calves, and what a magnificent sight they were as they straggled across the valley below us. Because of his warning, I was able to belly-stalk to within forty feet of the nearest group and take photos. On the way back, Moobli scented out a young tup (a year-old ram) with its wool so entangled in thick brambles that it cold not move. Its left horn was loose and it was very weak. I set it free, gashing my hands in the process, and it staggered towards our burn. When eventually it fell to its knees, I carried the sodden creature home and put it in the woodshed, where it feebly sucked down half a pint of reconstituted powdered sheep milk. By ten in the evening it was dead, yet another victim of a sheep-farming system which left the animals to roam untended on the Hill.

During a 12-mile hike through the lochside woods in late February, Moobli again got a strong scent and wanted to hurry ahead. As I hissed him back, I saw a fox taking a drink from the loch only fifty yards ahead. I took the camera out of the pack, but before I could focus the telephoto lens the fox swerved away and dived under a fallen birch. Moobli tracked it to a small burn, where it must have de-scented its feet in the rocky pools, for he could not follow it further. On the way home, he located the holt of the otter which I believed had slashed his leg in December. He swerved, nose down on a strong scent, following it over huge mossy shoreside boulders, then paused above a gap, his tail wagging as he looked down. I climbed over and actually saw the otter in the entrance chamber. It bared its teeth with a hiss, turned out of sight and, before I could exchange the telephoto for the standard lens emerged from the next tunnel on my right. It slipped silently into the water and dived to safety. Moobli was doing his job well, but I was missing fine opportunities that his skill had presented.

Unlike me, Moobli had no fear of heights and would happily prance right to the edge of a precipice and look over. He whined and stared back at me after gazing down into a deep gorge when he picked up another scent on March 10. His manner was so intent that I moved cautiously forward, keeping one foot well back as a brace, and peered over the 50-foot drop on to the black granite rocks of the burn's bed. There was a ewe, trapped on a small ledge some four feet down. She could not escape without help. With a few deep breaths and a muttered prayer, I scrambled down to the ledge and, after a struggle, managed to lift the ewe to safety – one more sheep that owed its life to Moobli's nose. On that trek he also located fox droppings at 1,600 feet, and a deer calf carcass that had been well chewed from the anus. We were then engulfed in a snowstorm and mist on a 2,200-foot peak and retraced our tracks until 600 feet lower, where the storm divided into two forks. From there we tramped home under a vault of indigo-blue sky.

All through spring and early summer our tracking continued. The first badger sett was again occupied, and by nosing about Moobli found a second old sett high above it. A fox scat lay on freshly dug earth outside one of the holes and from the musty scent it was clear foxes had moved in. On a long trek up a river valley to the east we located a herd of 11 stags, some of which had lost their antlers, and a tawny owl's nest in the hollow of an old oak snag. Moobli obediently kept back as I climbed up a piece of thick branch and photographed the female owl dozing fitfully on her three eggs.

Three days of blinding snow blizzards hit Wildernesse between April 7 and 9, and one of the corrugated iron sheets atop the wildcat pens was wrenched from its moorings and sailed past the study window to land 60 yards away in the east wood. The news over the radio that many homes were now without electricity seemed ironic to me for I had not had any in my remote homes for the last nine years. Moobli liked snow, but not the blizzards, when flakes settled over his eyes. He became bored with the lack of action when we could not trek.

At last the clouds peeled away, the sun treated the still bare trees to their first warmth, and we went out for some fine snow tracking. Slots of hinds and calves led us through the west wood until we found them gazing at us from the high ridges. Moobli

67

picked up a fox's trail along the snowless shore, indicated by the odd 'huff' grunts he made now and again and the cocking of his leg on tufts. Over the burn he picked it up again, but lost it where the fox had crossed some unavoidable snow after turning to the north west. Here I could follow by sight the tell-tale straight line of fox's tracks, and when the snow petered out under the trees near the burn, Moobli again picked up the scent where the animal had urinated on small grass tufts, never on the snow itself. He lost the trail at the burn and could not find any trace on the far side. The fox must have emerged with de-scented feet further upstream. We swung back to the shore, where Moobli again picked up its scent, this time heading westwards, and I called him off. His tracking was certainly improving.

On another April trek, long after the snow had gone, Moobli nosed out the remains of a barn owl (rare in the area) which had been attacked by a wildcat; he also found a hooded crow, killed by a fox, and a roebuck skeleton. Once he helped me to locate a well-hidden sparrowhawk's nest by scenting the white droppings below their tree.

At the end of the month we checked a badger sett near the shore, five miles from the first. It had been unoccupied for over a year, the two old dung pits outside it disused and filled with leaves. The entrance to the sett was under a huge slanting rock slab, and I had always been puzzled by a small depression in the soft earth near the entrance pits. I had assumed it to be the day bed of a wildcat, probably the one that had killed the barn owl. To my surprise, the sett was now reoccupied by badgers, the pits freshly dug out and filled with blackish droppings, some of them small. There was an area of flattened bracken near the loch shore, probably made by playing cubs. Moobli scented about and solved the riddle of the rounded day bed. He found a fresh fox scat atop a mossy rock a few yards east of the sett.

I could imagine the shock the fox must have had when, arriving to use his day bed, he found badgers in occupation – though I doubt that there would have been a fight. Badgers occasionally tolerate a fox using an unoccupied part of a big sett, where tunnels can extend to as much as 25 yards in length. But foxes are untidy in their habits and are possibly smelly to the clean badger. In a sett this size I would not have expected the fox to be tolerated, especially when the badgers had cubs. I knew a man with a house backing on to

Richmond Park (on the outskirts of London) who regularly put out the leavings of local restaurants at night where foxes and badgers would often feast within a few feet of each other without showing any sign of belligerence.

On May 25, with the woodland trees thrusting out leafy fans of varying greens, and the ground round Wildernesse a colourful carpet of bluebells, yellow tormentil, buttercup, speedwell, clover and white stitchwort flowers, wildcat Cleo gave birth to two fine kittens. I named the tom kit Freddy and the female Mia. While tending and guarding the wildcats, and revising the text for the Canadian wildlife book, I had little time for treks, but we neverthe-less maintained our weekly visit to the tawny owl's nest in the oak tree snag three miles away.

The owl hatched all three eggs, but when we reached the snag on May 29 there were only two owlets in the nest. The third had disappeared without any sign of a struggle. At first I was baffled and walked round in widening circles, urging Moobli to track. He soon located three downy wing feathers in thick grasses north-west of the snag. But for him I might not have found them. Probably the owlet had fallen from the nest and been taken by a fox or a wildcat while stunned, so that it did not struggle and lose more down or feathers. The other two young eventually flew safely.

One morning, when the wildcat kits were two weeks old, I saw that Cleo was prowling up and down her pen, clawing at the fencing. I let her out for a run in the open, thinking that she would surely return when she knew her kits would be hungry for milk. By tea time she was not back and I urged Moobli to track her. Nose down, he charged through the bracken and summer herbage and traced her to the west wood and back again. He found her in the huge rhododendron bush by the path. Both females were fairly tame towards us in the pen, and in the woodshed, but out in the open they were afraid of Moobli. Ears back, and growling, Cleo climbed up into the bush and, probably because of her fear of the dog crashing about below, let me catch her with heavy gloves, which she clawed viciously, and carry her back to the pens. She fed herself first, then began clatter-purring as she went into the den box to feed her kits. Neither female seemed to bear ill-will for long, whereas Sylvesturr's life was one long grudge.

By now Moobli was well into his summer moult, mists of his long hairs clinging to furniture and clogging under doors. While I was performing acrobatics with a paint pot on the iron roof, I was surprised to see a siskin still gathering up his hairs in its beak for a nest. One slip of a gym-shoed foot and, to my horror, I found myself sliding down the steep roof on my backside. I let out an impromptu yell as my legs went over the edge. With just enough presence of mind, I managed to push back with both hands so that my back would clear the stanchions of the guttering. I landed on both feet, took the rest of the fall on both hands and instinctively performed a breakfall roll, remembered from army parachute training. As I scrambled to my feet the pot of paint crashed to the ground beside me and splashed me with the green liquid. Moobli gave a playful bark and pranced up and down excitedly, as if urging me to do that trick again. He must have thought I was playing. In fact, I was lucky to have avoided a broken ankle, or worse.

For some weeks Moobli had been collecting a great many sheep ticks in his coat. Near the end of their three-year life cycle, the young adult ticks climb up foliage and latch on to the fur of any passing warm-blooded animal, just as they did in the larval and nymphal stages. There the females burrow down to the skin, affix their mouthparts and within five to fourteen days become engorged with the host's blood until they are grey blood globules up to half an inch long. They then drop off and lay up to 250 eggs apiece. They are not only pests which weaken an animal through blood-sucking, they also transmit the virus of dangerous louping-ill to cattle and sheep, as well as tick-borne fever, and to lambs tick pyaemis, causing abscesses to form in the skin, the internal organs and the joints. The ticks did not appear to affect Moobli much, probably because at least three times a week I burrowed through his coat with my fingers (in addition to combing out his moulting hairs) and became expert at plucking them off without leaving their mouthparts behind to fester and form scabs in his skin. One night I pulled 23 ticks off him. Sometimes Moobli would sniff at the little bags of blood, cheerfully getting his own back by crunching them up and re-absorbing his own lost blood.

The other great Highland pests, the little black biting midges, were having a field day on June 13, and my attempt to weed the vegetable garden in misty light drizzle was defeated after three minutes. The islet gulls shook their heads and shuffled their wings, the wildcats twitched and blinked, and even the kits learned to flick their heads. Moobli constantly scratched the midges from his ears and eyes with his great paws. He could not understand why every time he tried to come indoors I thwacked him all over with a towel to dislodge as many of these wretches as possible. Without such precautions his coat released hundreds of midges inside, all heading for the light of the study window, some stopping to bite me en route. Finally he realised it was for our own good, and when he saw the towel in my hand after that he screwed up his eyes and took this odd beating without protest.

A few days later I boated over to the islet to see how many young gulls had hatched – part of a ten-year study of breeding success. To my surprise, I could locate only four. They were expert at hiding, squeezing themselves into tiny crevices between the tussocks. That I missed some became obvious later when I counted nine brown-speckled youngsters flying round the islet with their parents.

On a bright, sunny Midsummer's Day I brought Cleo and the kits out in their den box, hoping to photograph them together in the open. After a minute, however, Cleo ran back to the pens, possibly to visit old Sylvesturr. For an hour I photographed the kits stumbling through the herbage, calling little '*mau*' sounds, sniffing the summer flowers and playfully swatting out at each other. When I took them back to the pens, Cleo had gone. She did not return at dusk. I had just changed into trekking gear to go and look for her when Moobli came to the front door, his legs and feet wet.

'Where's Cleo?' I said. 'Track the pussy coots.'

He bounded off and I tried to follow him. He found Cleo holed up in a natural earthy den near the burn some 250 yards away. I told him to stay there while I ran back for the thick gloves. He must have realised I was trying to catch her for when I returned there were scuffed up marks in the earth, as if he had pawed the entrance to get her out. This had scared her, and when I reached in she spat, growled, bit through the gloves. Her rear claws scraped blood from my arms. I gave up and let her go again. After dark, when still she had not returned, I took Moobli round the woods with a torch. Even this noise failed to send her back to the pens. She finally turned up next morning as if nothing had happened, and ate and drank her fill before going into the den box to feed her hungry kits. I resolved not to let them out of the pens again until their final release.

As it turned into a hot and sultry day, I decided to go swimming. The water in the loch was icy cold. I donned my black rubber wetsuit, face mask and flippers, to see if I could spot any fish.

71

Moobli stared at the strange dark apparition that had just been me with a perplexed look as I shuffled backwards into the water and then struck out for the islet 200 yards off shore. Halfway across I heard loud puffing snorts and felt two sharp objects clawing at my back. I was also whacked hard over the head. I looked round and saw Moobli swimming behind me. As if to assure himself that it was still really me under the black wetsuit, he started scratching at me with his great thick claws.

'Get away, you fool!' I gasped.

The more I tried to keep him off, the more he attempted to clamber on top of me. I could have been in trouble, but I formed my hand into a scoop and dashed water into his face until he gave up and swam back to the shore. On my return I decided to swim to the boat bay where it would be easier to climb out with the awkward flippers, now that I had cleared it of rocks. Moobli ran across the shore with loud barks, something he never did unless strangers arrived in a boat. It took half an hour to make him realise it was *me* in the black suit, and after that he just swam beside me.

A few days later I hurled a hefty branch forty yards out into the water. Moobli plunged in, and while he was still swimming away from me, I peeled off all my clothes to see if I could retrieve the branch before he did. I reached it while Moobli was still making a wide circle round it and began towing it back, using the side stroke. Moobli came behind me and again started whacking me on the back with his paws, as if trying to get on top of me. I let go the branch and made for the beach with my fastest, somewhat inefficient version of the crawl. To my great surprise, I once more heard his huffing snorts and again found him clawing at me. I cold understand him doing this while I was in the black wetsuit but not now that I was naked. Clearly he could swim faster than I could.

Instead of driving him off, I called him towards me and manoeuvred slightly, seizing his tail. He then felt insecure and immediately struck out for the shore – and safety. I held on, just twiddling my toes, watching the great muscles of his rear legs stretching and bulging as he kicked with steady strong strokes and towed me to the beach. Moobli's power and enormous stamina in the water (he thought nothing of a two-mile swim behind the rowing boat) might come in useful if ever I fell out of a boat in mid-loch. For the next hour, while I stood almost up to my neck in water, I encouraged him to come towards me and let me grab his tail. He did not like this new game at first because, being shorter legged, he was out of his depth. I was careful not to splash him or duck him, and finally he seemed to enjoy it too. After that I always made him come to me in the water, and to let me hold his tail. Having hauled me ashore, he always received a 'good boy' and encouraging pats.

It was some time before I worked out the reason for him swimming up to me and scratching at me with his claws. On land he normally walked to heel, a foot or two behind or to the side of me; in other words, a foot or two from the perpendicular line of my head. In the water, however, my body was not perpendicular but horizontal. In trying to get near my head, he had perhaps inadvertently clawed at my body, which he could not see under the surface. This did not explain his bashing me over the head on the first occasion, but then I had been wearing the black rubber suit and large face mask, so he could not be sure it *was* my head.

By July 14 the wildcat kittens were getting faster on their feet, ambushing each other amid the ferns and bracken of the pens, and chasing the black tip of Cleo's tail. It was a thundery rainy day and after I had returned from hauling both boats higher out of the water, I saw that Mia, the shyer kit, had vanished. I told Moobli to 'track the pussy coots', but for once he just stared at me obtusely, as if unable to understand what I meant. I went down on all fours and sniffed the ground as I moved, held his nose to the earth too, and again gave the command. But after a desultory sniff or two he stopped and again looked at me stupidly. I forgot myself, yelled at him, and gave him a hard clout. This upset his dignity and he stalked off into the kitchen in disgust.

Later, I heard a faint '*mau*' and Mia emerged from a crevice in the rocks behind the pen. She must have squeezed through the fencing and then been afraid to come out again until the thunder had stopped. Fortunately, Moobli was now with me, and he saw her emerge too. If it is right to scold a dog when it disobeys, it is also right to apologise to it if you have been in the wrong. Moobli had been unable to track her for there had been no scent to track. I explained the situation in simple language (it is surprising how any intelligent animal can get the sense from human words, even when they are not those of a well-known command) and made a fuss of him, apologising several times. His reaction was to assume a happy expression and bounce about playfully, wanting me to throw his sticks.

Next day, as I boated home after a supply trip, Moobli having covered a mile of his exercise run along the tussocky shore, he startled a group of hinds grazing behind a tree-covered ridge. He got their scent, saw them and gave chase. The boat was too far away to call him off. I was sure he would not catch up to fleet, full-grown red deer anyway. As they ascended the steep slope, he bounded upwards as powerfully as any cougar and, to my surprise, caught up to them within 200 yards. To my further astonishment, the hind in the rear stopped, faced him and lashed out viciously with her front hoof. Moobli stopped in his tracks, then with a look that seemed to say, 'Oh well, if you feel like that . . . ', turned and amiably trotted down to the shore again. It seemed he had no desire to *hurt* them, just to romp alongside in play. I pulled in the boat and reminded him with a sharp clout.

I was surprised that none of the hinds had calves, which are usually born in the first week of June. Perhaps this was a small group of yelds which had banded together – or had it been a bad calving year? When July 20 promised an unusually fine mistless day, I decided to take Moobli into the hills to find out.

Summer trekking is a sweaty affair, and the last thing you need when tracking sensitive-nosed mammals like deer is the smell of human perspiration. My old Canadian method of obliterating it was to boil up pine or spruce needles and dip my stalking clothes. I did the same with gloves when I was setting live traps. Deodorising was a tedious business, for one had to wait for the clothes to dry out enough for use. This time I decided to use the heavily scented boy myrtle, also known as sweet gale, which grew profusely in the boggy areas near the cottage. I gathered several handfuls, crushed it up and mixed the mush with a little hot water. Then I smeared it over my face, neck, hands, boots and the parts of my clothes most prone to perspiration. As I raised one arm after the other and rubbed it into my naked armpits, Moobli turned his head on one side with an expression of bemused contempt. Had his master gone off his head, or turned 'fruit'? For a dog, Moobli himself was exceptionally odourless. Even when I thrust my nose into his fur and took a deep breath, I could detect only a faint aroma resembling that of young sweet chestnuts. Nevertheless I rubbed myrtle over him too.

As we set off I noticed that the pignut flowers were turning brown, the orchids were dying off, hogweed seeds were dropping from the plants' flat heads, and wood garlic had begun to show its clean white flowers along the edges of the burn. At 200 feet we came across a new garden of golden chanterelle fungi (delicious when fried lightly in butter) and, as we would probably return by a different route, I gathered some into my pack. It was dangerous picking some of them for they grew over sheer 20-foot drops on to the rocky waterfalls of the gorge.

We plugged on upwards for nearly three miles yet saw no deer, nor was Moobli getting any scent in the south-west breeze. At last, just below a 1,500-foot peak, I spotted a hind lying down chewing the cud, her 7-week-old calf standing beside her. Hissing Moobli to keep back, I stalked her, got some pictures, then more of two other hinds which also had a calf each with them. I was about to try a semi-circular stalk, to get near again as they moved towards the ridge, when I saw a lone hind with two fawns at her rear come up the hill to our left. As there were no other hinds about, these had to be twin calves, a rare occurrence with red deer. Could I now get close pictures of the twins with their mother?

My heart started to pound. I hissed and motioned Moobli to lie down near the pack, which he did, then slid like a snake until I reached a large heather tuft near to the deer. Everything worked perfectly. Small and large clouds passed below the sun giving me shade, soft light, stark bright light, as the calves chased each other, had suck, butted heads together, the creamy juvenile spots glowing beautifully on their red-brown coats. One even tried to mount its mother as my camera clicked.

I was just nearing the end of the film when the hind stopped grazing, glared straight towards me, sunk down on her hindlegs and bolted into the wind and, followed by the leaping fawns, disappeared. Moobli, unable to bear the strain of not seeing what was going on, perhaps feeling lonely lying way off by the pack, had crept up to me and was sitting by my feet, bolt upright on his front legs, tan chest shining, ears cocked forward, his huge mouth open in a grin.

'Moobli,' I hissed. 'I told you to LIE DOWN.' I gave him a token smack on the rump.

Doubtless he had done his best to stalk as he came up to me, but it had not been good enough. Well, he had kept back for a good quarter of an hour, and it was only his second year. He could hardly be expected to remember all the lessons about stalking from last autumn. In fact, he had done quite well.

'Y'know, Moobli,' I said, 'a handsome dog who won't do as he's told is about as useful as a beautiful woman who hates domestic chores. Both are decorative but not much damn use.'

The trouble recurred on July 31, when I figured the young wild-cats would be strong enough to go free. I boated down to fetch two friends who wanted to see Wildernesse and witness the wildcats' release, but when we got back I found that Mia had escaped again into the rocks behind the pens. I could transfer only Cleo and Freddy in the den box to their new home in the west wood. I had erected a sloping sheet of corrugated iron over a dry spot between windfall trees and placed Cleo's den box there, near a large flat-topped rock on which I would regularly set out food for them. Patra would spend the rest of the summer on a tree-covered islet in the loch where a plague of voles had erupted. When, in a few weeks, the kits were strong enough to look after themselves and scoot up trees, then Sylvesturr himself could go free.

Patra '*mau*'d, scratched my gloves and fought like a fiend to escape from the box in which I was to take her to the islet, and hared off into the east wood. Before boating my friends back to their car, I told Moobli to stay and guard the house, as he had done before, in case Patra or Mia returned before I did.

We had gone only half a mile in the boat when I saw him running along the shore behind us. He kept it up for three miles before plunging into the undergrowth. I wondered if he was returning home.

I went slowly along the shore on my way back, whistling and calling, but did not see him. He was not at the cottage when I arrived home. He must have heard the boat returning and would surely soon appear. I saw Cleo come up to the pens and give several '*mau*' calls. Mia emerged from the rocks to rub noses with her mother, and then followed her back to their new home in the west wood. At least all the family were together again where they should be.

Moobli had still not returned at dusk. Worried now, I hauled the boat into the water again and went all the way back to the Land Rover in the pine wood, calling and whistling in the gathering darkness. There was no trace of him anywhere. Half-heartedly I ate a small supper and gazed at his bed and empty bowls on the kitchen floor. I felt suddenly lonely. I was missing him already. He had never stayed away overnight before.

I left the front door open and went to bed, but I could not sleep. I had awful visions of him picking up some old poison left out for foxes or crows, or of being shot by a trigger-happy poacher. I started imagining how I would deal with whoever shot him.

He was still not back at dawn as a drenching drizzle fell in a misty westerly breeze. I typed out a 'REWARD' notice for the local paper, put £25 in notes into an envelope, and wearily hauled the boat down yet again. This was the fourth return trip in 24 hours. My heart sank further when I saw no sign of him along the loch shore.

Moobli was standing guard by the Land Rover in the pine wood! His mouth was open, as if he had been running. As I climbed over the pine roots on the shore, he ran down wagging his huge bushy tail, whining anxiously as he jumped up to lick my face. I was too relieved to be angry with him. I hugged him close, tears in my eyes as I realised how much I loved him. There was no such sentiment on his part when we arrived home. All he wanted was his grub.

8 · *Close Encounters of a Strange Kind*

All the wildcats except Sylvesturr were now free and able to range anywhere they wished, but I could not leave it at that – just putting food on the mossy rock each evening and hoping for the best. However far they might venture, somehow I had to follow their movements to ensure that the kittens were surviving healthily and were being taught to hunt properly. It would have been an impossible task in the dense undergrowth in the woods, or among the 6ft-high bracken forests on the north hill, without live-trapping them every so often. Yet I did not want to allow them anything less than complete freedom.

I had learned some useful techniques when working with the cougar-hunter Percy Dewar on Vancouver Island the previous summer. We had run – on *foot* – behind his trained Blue Tick hounds in order to catch and radio-collar the mountain lions. The hounds put the fierce creatures up trees and Percy did the rest. Moobli had been trained to track the two female wildcats and I hoped he would do the same now with the kittens as well. To my delight he really came into his own. As soon as he located any of the cats in the undergrowth, they would shoot up the nearest tree, allowing me to take photos and to check their condition. The kits would clamber up small trees from which they could easily be shaken out, something no mature wildcat would do.

Patra remained at large in the woods near the cottage, and I put aside all thoughts of transferring her to the islet when I discovered that she would take over the training of the kits to forage and hunt when Cleo appeared tired and depleted from weaning them. I also found that the cats used separate temporary day dens while hunting on the far side of the burn, which they crossed at night over a fallen larch.

Although he was slow to sight them, Moobli could follow a fresh trail nose-high and at the run. We tracked the cats every two or three days, but in between he often scented out their scats, which helped me to establish their increasing ranges, and sometimes their kills. Once he located the remains of a poor racing pigeon – just a few wing feathers and the two feet, complete with numbered bands.

In late August Dr Michael Brambell, Curator of Mammals at London Zoo, who had given me Sylvesturr, brought his family on holiday to the area and wanted to see the kittens. We tracked round the woods and they were disappointed when Moobli seemed unable to find them. At last, near the south-east land spit, he got a strong scent, and put Freddy up a hazel tree, spitting like a small replica of his cussed old father. Without Moobli's tracking abilities they would not have seen the kitten at all.

It was on a supply trip at this time that I first witnessed Moobli have a fight with one of the local dogs. Two in particular seemed to have taken a great dislike to him. Whenever our Land Rover appeared they would run alongside, barking wildly. One was the big black Labrador that had straddled him as a pup, the other was a large white-faced male collie. Moobli never barked back, but stood on my bed looking calmly out of the window at their hysterical behaviour. I did not succumb to the temptation of letting him out to see if he would settle their hash once and for all. On one occasion the Labrador followed me into the local store, growling and snapping at my heels. I made my purchases and went back to the Land Rover. Moobli put both feet on the driving seat as I opened the door and jumped out with a deep growl. Instantly the Labrador's aggression vanished. It turned, walked away stiff-legged, urinated on a corner of the store and disappeared behind it. Moobli made no attempt to go after it, even though he had clearly seen it barking at me. In the previous week, while I stood talking to my estate manager friend, I had seen the white-faced collie advance on Moobli with his pal, a black and white terrier, and bark at him, but Moobli's only response had been to make a brief snap back before letting the two go on their way.

'You've got a soft dog there,' my friend had said. I wondered yet again if Moobli was a bit of a coward.

Later, after getting some petrol at the local pump and paying for it in the office, I saw the white-faced collie pass the Land Rover, growling. There was a sudden rumble inside the vehicle and out through the half open window shot Moobli. The collie whirled round and tried to bite, but was instantly faced with Moobli's gnashing teeth and bowled over by his powerful forelegs. In a trice, it was on its back and squealing with submission. Moobli broke away but stood there growling horribly. The collie got to its feet and fled, tail between its legs.

A passing tourist couple said I should keep my dog under control. I told them that they should control their tongues, for they did not know the full story of the two dogs – how Moobli had been settling an old score with a dog that had tried to terrorise him ever since he was a pup. I apologised to the owner of the collie: no sense in upsetting the locals when my vehicle stood defenceless in the woods six miles from my home. The petrol lady took my side when the others had gone.

'That collie thinks it's king of the walk,' she said. 'It chases many cars which have strange dogs in them. Now it's had its come-uppance.'

Certainly the collie never chased after us again, though the black Labrador often did so. Its turn to be silenced was still to come.

Moobli's first romantic tryst took place soon after that. A farmer some twenty miles down the coast had long admired Moobli and wanted his 5-year-old female Alsatian, Tania, to have pups by him. He had sent me a note to say that she was in season, and I took Moobli along to lose his virginity.

After dodging Tania's snaps at his head with good-humoured ease, he got her scent and began to show a healthy interest in her. We shut them together in the stable. From time to time, as I consumed the stud fee (a cup of tea and two cucumber sandwiches), we took a look through the stable window.

Moobli had clearly overcome Tania's initial hostility for he was going at it hammer and tongs, but he did not seem to make the right connections. It was Tania's first mating and none of us knew much about breeding Alsatians, though we had a vague idea that the couple should become locked together for a brief time following a successful copulation. After leaving them to it for a further half hour, we found the two dogs apart, and Moobli showing no more interest. On the way home Moobli went to sleep, red-eyed, in the well of the boat. Despite all his efforts Tania did not become pregnant.

We continued tracking the wildcats until September 7. It was then clear that Mia would be the first to leave Cleo's care and cut out on her own. I set Sylvesturr free before leaving for a trip south, with a good supply of food for all the cats scattered about. Our absence for a week or two would enable the ferocious old tom to settle down in the wilds without risk of an encounter with Moobli, which could cost the dog an eye or the cat its life.

Shortly after returning I received a cable from Reader's Digest Press saying that they needed the revisions to my Canadian book in ten days' time, or we would miss the possibility of spring publication. I worked frantically for a week and finished it, five years and four months after I had typed the first words. I had to post it on Monday September 29 come hell or high water, and that is precisely what I faced.

Three-foot waves were crashing directly on shore as I gave two powerful kicks to get the boat into the water. The engine started first pull, and we banged down the loch against a fierce gale, the boat rising and falling six feet from trough to trough, Moobli hunched miserably in the bows. I saw two local fishing buffs sheltering in a boathouse below the farm, waiting for the wind to subside. They never did go fishing that day. When I returned from the postal errand, I saw that they had driven half a mile to a vantage point to watch me go by, should I be so foolish as to risk a return voyage in that storm. In fact I felt elated by being free from the book at last, and as I passed their crouching forms I stood up in the boat, holding the bow ropes like the reins of a bucking bronco and yelling 'yippee' cowboy calls as we crashed along through the thundering waves. That would show them! Moobli looked up at me as if I had gone crazy. He was only too anxious to leap out and run home once we reached the lee of Sandy Point.

The rest of the solo passage in the boat was appalling. I crouched at the throttle, desperately trying to avoid plunging into the depths. It was impossible to beach the boat as usual on the grassy bank for the waves would have swept over the stern and scuttled it before I could haul it out. Instead, I swerved the starboard side to shore at the last second, leaped out with backpack and armfuls of supplies and then ran from end to end, lugging the boat's 600lb weight a few inches at a time up the bank until it was safe. In the process I succeeded in pulling a back muscle again. Moobli panted up, having covered three miles of that awful rocky, tussocky shore in fourteen minutes.

Some stag treks were unsuccessful in the early years until I learned to make a whole day of it, leaving home early in the morning and covering at least fifteen miles of hard terrain, sometimes taking a tent for an overnight camp. I remember once climbing up and down those steep hillsides for four hours before seeing a large 9-pointer stag with 18 hinds about a mile ahead. We stalked them carefully, only to see the sun disappear over a high mountain and plunge the hillside into near darkness. If I was obliged to stalk against the sun, or to scan the shadowed side of a hill ahead, I soon discovered that it was best to wait until a cloud obscured the sun. This not only prevented us from being lit up like lamps for the deer to spot easily, it gave a diffused light to the dark side of the hill so that we could make out the animals' movements.

Until we became more practised, I made other silly mistakes. We were going through a deep cleft in the ridges one day when a huge stag suddenly came running downwind, giving short roars as our forms blocked its restricted way. It seemed bent on charging us. Though rare, fatal attacks on men have occurred. I had a brief vision of trying to deflect it with my pack while I grabbed the tip of one antler, where I could have the most leverage, but having seen stags fighting I dismissed the idea. Against another stag, it would not stab or gouge with its antlers like a bull, but rather lock antlers forehead to forehead, and assert dominance by agility and strength. The forward-pointing first brow tines are the most dangerous, and these can inflict fearful wounds to the other's head or neck, or sometimes even take out an eye. Recently I had seen Moobli approach a young pet stag with a fence between them, not to be menaced with its antlers but by the sharp black hooves of both front feet, which it aimed with devastating force at the dog's head, only the fence preventing a strike. Two more pawing downward strokes had followed. Such blows would cut, perhaps disembowel, a man and would certainly knock the fight out of him.

I was scared as I saw this stag coming towards us, and flapped my jacket out to the side, but this had no deterrent effect. I shouted to Moobli –

'See him off!'

The dog took a great swerving leap to the side, as if to put him out of the stag's line of charge, gave two deep baying barks and bounced about, as if ready to have a go. The stag, maybe seeing us for the first time, wheeled sharply and shot over the ridge to our left. Moobli, growling horribly, would have gone after it if I had not called him off. We went to see where it had gone, but it doubled to the south way below us and ran out of sight.

One morning in early October, under a brindled sky with misty stripes of blue showing through the high cloud, I rowed the three miles to the point, trying to locate stags on the lochside ridges. I spotted one with four hinds, and a lone stag on a crest two miles away. It boded ill for our Sunday trek. I had decided to confine our stag trekking in the stalking season to Sundays, when the estate stalkers would not be working. One brush with a landowner's hunting party in country so wild that I had never seen anyone else there in five years put me off full-time rut-watching until the guns were put away at the end of the season on October 21.

While Moobli ran along the loch shore, I saw an otter dive into the water from a rock where it had been eating a fish. As he passed the spot, Moobli got a strong scent and started rubbing his jaws, cheeks and even the sides of his neck on the ground. I rowed over and found the otter spreint and some of its smelly fish remains. It is believed that some dogs, and wild canines too, will rub in such strong odours to improve their social status and to signal their presence over longer distances. This did not seem to make much sense when the only other dogs were many miles away.

That day Moobli was full of energy, ran the full six miles, swam out to the boat several times, and still wanted me to throw branches for him to chase when we got back. After his meal, he was very tired and slept, as he often did, with his nose bent down against a stanchion of my bed, which caused him to snore loudly. To stop this racket while I was typing I gave a sharp whistle. He raised his head, so that my bed quilt draped comically over his eyes, saw that I did not really want him for anything, groaned loudly, and flumped his head down again.

On Sunday a cold north-east breeze was blowing so we took the big boat over three miles to the west, then trekked across the hills in a wide semi-circle back to Wildernesse. Up and down, up to 1,600 feet, and all along the ridges south of Guardian mountain, we went for eight hard miles, seeing no more than 19 hinds in three separate groups. Not one damn stag! I then went in the small boat to fetch the big one. In the village next day the estate manager told me that stalkers had taken five stags so far from that area and were now working the deer further to the west. The animals thought little of a three mile move to safety if stalkers from two or three estates coincided in one region. They also congregated on westerly slopes to escape the cold north-easterly winds.

As we talked, I realised that Moobli had wandered away and disappeared. I completed my shopping, but still he was nowhere to be seen. I became worried and drove round searching for him. At the garage, Dave told me that a man with a Land Rover like mine and a young bitch golden Labrador was staying at some caravans up the road. I went there, only to be told the man was fishing down at the pier. I rushed to the pier, found the man and the bitch, but Moobli was not with them. At the hotel I was told Moobli had been seen running along the road with a collie bitch called Sheila, which was now on heat. Moobli had always been friendly with this bitch, so I dashed to the home of her owner and found no one there. I drove five miles along the road where the dogs had been seen running towards the next village: there was no sign of them.

I drove back in time to see Sheila's owner going into the store. She said that Sheila had also disappeared, and she was worried for she did not want the bitch to become pregnant. Just then the owner of the belligerent black Labrador dog arrived distraught having seen Moobli and Sheila on the hills above the council estate where she lived. She was afraid that her dog might try to attack Moobli and end up being killed. All three of us roared off in our respective vehicles to the council estate.

There, high in the hills, we could see Moobli and Sheila romping together, rearing up to wrestle with their forepaws and to bite playfully at each other's muzzles. There was no sign of the black Labrador. I cupped my hands together and yelled 'Come here!', and then gave several loud whistles. Moobli instantly stopped and looked at us before galloping down over the rough terrain to where we stood.

I was as surprised by his instant obedience as were the others, and so delighted by it that I did not chastise him for running off. He might have thought he was being admonished for coming back, and I could not blame him for showing interest in his favourite bitch when she was on heat. I just said 'Badog!', as I opened the Land Rover door and he leaped on to the bed at the back, panting like a steam engine and looking happy after the best romp so far in his young life. I left Sheila's owner to retrieve her errant dog as best she could.

Over the next few days I cut up windfall trees in the woods, stacked the logs in the woodshed, burned the stumps and roots, and took the resulting potash for the big compost bin. I was making clearings for the army of 150 young spruce, sweet chestnut, Douglas fir, Canadian hemlock and oak trees I wanted to plant among the trees already growing there, so as to turn the woods into an ideal wildlife habitat. On October 20, after the stalkers had finished their work, I took Moobli on a really long stag trek. It turned out to be our most successful stalking so far, but only because we covered a great deal of ground. Moobli disgraced himself.

Under bright sun we hiked with the south-east wind until we reached almost to the western peak above the long glen below Guardian mountain. There I turned east, ready to stalk all the ridges of the glen against the cross wind, instructing Moobli to lie down by my pack. He did so, and I crawled up to some rocky cover on the crest. A roaring young stag with four hinds stood on the far slopes to the north east, and below that group was a huge mature stag with 17 hinds. There was nothing between us but the deep valley, our side of which lay in dark shadow. The sun would dazzle the eyes of the deer on the far slopes. As I moved back to retrieve my pack, I heard a brushing sound behind me. Moobli had disobeyed and was there at my heels. I made him lie down, just in time, before his head appeared over the crest.

Moving sideways like a crab, so as to present the smallest possible view of myself, and keeping Moobli behind, I managed to reach a deep gully leading down to the north west. Slowly, hunching myself up, I worked my way down the gully, over the

85

soft blackness of a peat hag, until I was some 400 yards from the big stag and his harem. Moobli now seemed to understand the need for caution, and I let him lie beside me. He even kept his big ears down.

For nearly an hour I took pictures as we watched the stag chivvying his hinds, rounding up two that wanted to stray as they grazed, tearing up divots with his antlers and sending them flying into the air, and returning the bellowing challenges of the younger stag above him which gazed down at his harem with apparent envy. Again I told Moobli to lie down by the pack, then slithered painfully along on elbows and knees until I was only ninety yards away from the master stag's harem. I had taken only one photograph through the grasses on a small crest, when I saw some of the hinds running away.

Moobli came walking up to the crest, his light tan chest shining in sidelight of the sun, and the hinds had seen him. Angry, I hissed at him to lie down and grabbed his neck ruff hard, whereupon he gave a loud yipe. This made the other hinds bolt. The big stag, however, hung back, looking about for the cause of alarm, and I managed four more shots of him before he too trotted away in the wake of his fleeing hinds.

Moobli's movement had been partly my fault this time, for I had not turned after the first few yards and hissed the usual 'Stay there,' but I made him feel my disapproval all the same. Several times on the way home I made him lie by the pack, told him to stay until I called him forward again, and petted and congratulated him when he got it right. What had caused this sudden reversion to puppyhood behaviour I did not know. I am glad to say he never disturbed a stag stalk again.

Early November brought the first winter gales, with hail that sounded like buckets of gravel being emptied on to the iron roof. On November 3 I was woken by Moobli making his warning '*whoo, whoo*' barks outside. It was his second birthday, but he could not be barking because of that! I hoped he was not trying to scare off visiting Sylvesturr and shushed him through the window. Having dressed, I went outside where I soon found what had caused the barking: some red deer hinds, seeking to escape the overnight hail, had come down from the hills to shelter in our west wood. Moobli had been trained not to bark at deer in our woods but he could hardly be expected to remember his first lessons on this last winter.

Although I had left gaps in the fencing to allow the deer access to winter shelter and my pasture I did not want to see damage done to the newly planted and unprotected young trees.

I took Moobli round the woods, and this alone was enough to scare the deer out on to the open ridges. These first hail showers were of short duration, and the real storms and snow blizzards would not start until late December. When Moobli showed any desire to chase after them, I called him back. Some of the deer, looking down nervously with their big radar-scanner ears switched forward, seemed to understand why I was doing this, particularly one large hind with a calf which I came to call the Red Hind. They had, however, already eaten the tops of two of the young oak trees.

Moobli had a boring birthday, watching me put individual staked wire netting cages round many of the trees though I did throw some fallen branches for him to chase and fetch. While I caged trees over the next few days, I allowed Moobli to bark at the deer in the early mornings, though not to chase after them. This ploy failed to drive them out of the woods altogether but it kept them away from the trees I had not yet caged. Later I had to tell Moobli to refrain from barking at deer even in the mornings, and after a few days he never did so again.

He actually snarled at me during play one evening, though it was largely my fault. He had usually enjoyed 'boxing' when he was a pup, swiping back with his heavy paws while I aimed fast light buffs to his head and chest with soft sparring gloves. He was not allowed to use his teeth, and proved himself to be an artful dodger, which stood him in good stead when he cornered one of the wildcats and it swiped at him with its claws.

The moment I took the gloves out of the old sea chest on this particular evening he seemed to regard them with distaste. After the gloves had caught him a couple of times, he gave a high whining growl. He looked angry and snarled, even viciously snapping at my gloved fist.

'Na!' I said sharply. 'Na! Don't bite. All right, no more boxing.' I quickly put the gloves away.

It was a sign of his growing maturity, I realised. If he could not use his teeth, he knew it was a game he could not win. His toleration for being made a fool of had grown less, and he was right. It would have been stupid of me to push the 'pack leader' concept onto him in any such way.

Despite its wolf-like appearance, the Alsatian is generally believed to be descended from the jackal (*Canis aureus*), which early man first domesticated. In her book, *All About The German Shepherd Dog*, Madeleine Pickup, who has bred pedigree Alsatians for forty years, points out that the aureus breeds were lone hunters with strongly independent characters. The Alsatian 'is certainly an independent thinker, and likes nothing better than to be trained in a job where he can use his initiative and extraordinary reasoning power. On the whole they prefer to be the "one and only" in their family, and may resent additions to the pack.'

Dogs like Elkhounds, Samoyeds, Finnish Spitz, Eskimo dogs, Chow chows are thought to be related to the wolf (*Canis lupus*). These lupus-blooded dogs in the early days hunted in packs, their lives governed and bound up in their own pack. Konrad Lorenz says in his book, *Man Meets Dog*, that even these breeds are not *purely* wolf-blooded. He puts forward the idea that when early man advanced further north, he took with him his domesticated jackal-blooded dogs and these breeds came from repeated crossings with wolf-blooded dogs. It is possible that the Alsatian has a mixture of both aureus and lupus blood in his remote past. Despite all the theories that have been advanced, we do not know for sure. Lorenz gives many examples of how the lupus strain makes a dog show greater allegiance to one master, not in a slavish Oedipus manner, but more as a colleague. Over the years, this certainly seemed true of Moobli.

To clear up a question that is often asked I went to the well-known show dog judge, Tom Horner. He told me that there is no difference between the Alsatian and the German Shepherd dog. The powerful modern form of the breed is generally accepted to have begun with the German breeders, Herr Sparwasser and Captain von Stephanitiz. The British first saw the breed at work during the First World War, when it was being used by the French Army. Many were brought back at the end of the war, from France and Alsace – then French but previously German. Hence the name 'Alsatian'. There is an excellent passage in Madeleine Pickup's book on the breed:

. . . it is easy to see that this is not a dog for everyone who admires his handsome looks and service potential to own, and easier still to see that he is not a dog to keep in large numbers in kennels if his rare intelligence and boundless energy are to be properly used and perpetuated. His enormous reasoning power, his gift of affectionate companionship and his great physical strength must be given an outlet and channelled to useful ends as they were originally intended, or the dog will suffer, and in his unhappiness may become mischievous and even dangerous due to the combined frustrations of lack of exercise, solitary confinement in kennels or the restrictions of city life, which are death to his unique qualities.

Our lifestyle was such that most of these problems were avoided, though sometimes Moobli became bored, especially when I was writing at my desk for long periods.

As the weather grew colder he began to grow his thick winter coat and sometimes he lay near the larch post that held my small windmill generator and gazed in mournfully at my typing form. Although the wildcats were free, Cleo, Freddy and Patra often returned to the cottage area. Moobli loved to watch their antics from a safe distance. It was comical to see him dozing, his great head resting between his paws, while the cats sneaked past quietly with furtive looks at him, hoping he would not wake up until they were further away.

Patra was always his favourite. He would sit and gaze at her adoringly if she slipped into the cottage and helped herself from his food bowl. She sometimes allowed him to lick her while she guzzled away, and as a result he could never be trained to keep her off the bird table. She even took to teasing him. She would walk past him, just a few yards away, tail up like a flag, then race off to some safe place she had already worked out in her mind when he started after her. She had discovered that with fast side-to-side dodging she could outsprint him over a short distance. She scooted up trees to a height *just* out of his reach and teased him with growls and downward swipes of her paws, while he whined excitedly, leaped up and snapped off quite large branches with his teeth. If this continued I would have no rhododendrons left. She knew full well that he liked her, and that if he did catch up to her, a few snarls and swipes and spits would keep him at bay.

89

9 · *He Could Take an Arm Off*

It was at the end of November that I began the daily regime of a pre-breakfast walk with Moobli round the boundaries of our estate. I came to call it the 'rough walk' – exactly one kilometre in length, it took us to a height of no more than 100 feet, but it was hard going over tussocks, bogs and steep slopes. By carrying a heavy pack on my back, it kept my legs strong for the Hill. On it we would check the nightly rangings of the wildcats, and Moobli scented out the droppings of visiting foxes or spreints of a visiting otter. We found where badgers had scraped for grubs, beetles and bulbs, and I kept count of the numbers of red deer using the woods for nightly shelter. Our walk also had the effect of shifting the deer up on to the 500-foot ridges to the north west where they could forage naturally and avoid becoming too dependent on the hay I set out for them as supplementary feed in the harshest weather.

Although I had permission to use the west wood for my studies, and to act as conservator of its trees, it was not included in my lease. Occasionally the estate stalkers boated down to cull the hinds in the area. While they were perfectly entitled to shoot in the wood, I did not want them killing the deer that were eating my hay, particularly Red Hind, with calf at foot. I was becoming fond of her, and she grew more tame with each passing week. Relations with the estate remained cordial. I explained that I could not work at my desk with rifles firing off near the house, and they promised not to shoot

Sylvesturr or any of the wildcats should they come upon them. In all, they did not bother me too much.

One day a stalker and his guest landed near the boundary and began to labour up the far side of a long bluff that led to the top of the high ridges. The hinds and calves on our side of the bluff must have heard them for most of them galloped away to the north east and over the ridges. Red Hind behaved differently, showing considerable cunning. She moved closer to the bluff with her calf and stood there, hiding from the stalkers. Through my fieldglass, I could see her quivering nervously, ready to flee should a human head appear over the bluff, but the stalkers did not see her.

Later, when I was with Moobli in the east wood, I heard two shots from beyond the ridges. I went back to the cottage, changed into camouflage gear, shut Moobli in, and hurried to hide myself in the cold heather beyond the west wood. Snow began to fall. I waited long enough to photograph the stalker dragging a dead hind down the hill and beheading and de-hoofing the carcass on the beach before loading it into the boat. I could clearly see the grey muzzle and the tattered ears. He seemed to be doing his job well for he had at least taken an old yeld which would probably have died this winter anyway.

After two days of light snowfalls, Moobli and I had one of our most successful snow-tracking experiences – first to follow the overnight movements of the wildcats for a full quarter of a mile in both east and west woods, and then to retrace the steps of a huge deer leaving slots over four inches long. Making sure neither I nor Moobli trod in the prints, we tracked them fifty yards to where they ended at the edge of the big rhododendron bush by the path. There, in a large shallow depression of flattened grasses rimmed with slushy fawn-tinged snow, was the obvious 'bed' where the animal had spent some of the night.

Although Moobli sniffed eagerly at the area I could not use his scenting powers to deduce where the deer might be, nor on such a windless day could I see it through the trees. We lost the tracks in the snowless areas of the wood, where I had to trust Moobli's nose. He padded slowly about, switching on and off the scent trail, until he picked up the tracks again heading up towards the first ridges to the north west. Here the snow was broken up by the high tussocks. I had to be careful where I trod for small dried-out bramble leaders tore noisily at my trousers. When my feet pushed down slabs of snow between the tussocks they crunched loudly, a sound deer can hear from some distance and feel through ground vibration. Moobli kept picking up scent trapped between the mounds and I was sure we were on the trail of a stag.

After another quarter mile of steep slow winding progress, we rounded a sheer rock face and there, sure enough, only thirty yards ahead, stood a large 10-pointer stag. Beautifully framed in the snowy hills, its front feet up on a powdered rock, its muzzle dilating as it tried to get our wind, it regarded us nervously. I cursed then. Being so engrossed in trying to follow the tracks I had completely forgotten to go back for the camera. For several long seconds we all just looked at each other.

He was an old fellow. I was sure he knew what a gun was and that he could see I held nothing in my hands. Slowly he turned and just ambled off higher, wending his way between the whitened rocks. When they are old, cold, and food is harder to find in the snow; when they are weaker for all three reasons, red deer are more reluctant to run unless they are sure of danger and are forced to do so. I should have remembered this.

On our winter hill treks we often had to contend with snow. I soon learned to follow deer tracks when I could, for the animals seem to know the lie of the land below its white surface and I thus avoided floundering in deep drifts. Moobli's great semi-webbed paws, which left tracks nearly 5 ins across when he was running, enabled him to move over snow with the grace of a wolf. Only in exceptionally soft deep snow did he have to bound, humping himself through it like a giant hare.

The hills can be savage in winter and soon cut a man down to size. Once we came over a crest at 1,700 ft and were confronted by what seemed a solid wall of white heading towards us. In seconds we were engulfed in a blinding, whirling blizzard, with visibility down to a few yards. I dashed for the shelter of an overhanging fang of rock, the trekking heat quickly draining from my body. Moobli just sat out in it, whitening before my eyes, until he looked like an ancient bearded mariner. Bad weather did not bother him, for his winter coat was twice as thick as that in summer. He was happy just to be out on the Hill, whatever the weather. When the blizzard passed, I shook off the snow and started round the knoll. Moobli stopped, sniffing ahead, one paw upraised.

92

Right below me, sheltering from the snow in a cleft, was a large 6-pointer stag with five hinds. I could have jumped on to his back. The hinds took off first; the stag shot up into the air with shock like a gigantic antlered jack-in-the-box as I groped for the camera, then bounded away after them. All I could manage was a shot of their forms fleeing into the mist. I kept my ungloved hands on the bitter cold metal of the camera for the next quarter-mile. A grouse shot out from below a clump of snowy heather and whirred away with harsh '*gebback gebback*' calls, swerving so much that I did not get a good shot of it either.

After shooting hinds, the stalkers always left the grallochs (stomach and guts) on the Hill where they were a magnet 'bait' for predatory species such as crows, ravens, buzzards and foxes. Moobli located several by scent, but I hardly needed his help. Small flocks of ravens flying about, or leaping up and down at some distant point in the hills, told me they were at a gralloch, and I tried to stalk them for pictures. Ravens are, however, wary and sharp-sighted birds, and I had little luck at first. Fortunately some of them must have mistaken my long-barrelled camera lens for a gun, for they occasionally flew close, riding the air like great tattered black hawks, croaking harshly to each other. I learned that if I stayed bent over, pretending to be doing something in the heather with my hands, they came even closer and I could take good flight photos. They evidently thought I was gralloching a deer!

A few times they flew from behind us towards any deer we were stalking then dived over the animals' heads with harsh squawks. This alarmed the deer, which promptly looked around for danger, and saw us quicker than they would have done normally. I was sure the ravens did this for pure devilment, that they knew what I was trying to do.

One day when we were up on the tops, Moobli began to prance head high, sniffing the air ahead. Hissing him back, I stalked to a rocky ridge, camera at the ready, and peered over. A huge brown bird was ripping at a gralloch. An *eagle*! The shock of recognition slowed my reactions and the keen-sighted king of birds shot away with the speed of a giant woodcock towards the dark backdrop of the hills beyond.

I was surprised that an eagle would bother with such lowly fare as a gralloch. I had never known it before. But that day's humiliation was not yet over. We were heading down the side of a burn that led to the lochside when Moobli again began his scenting gait. I hissed him back, but could see nothing.

'Come on, you fool!' I said and set off again.

Instantly there was a thwack on the ground near my feet, and a real woodcock shot away, leaving a white squirt behind on the grasses. Although I had the camera in my hands it flew like a swerving brown rocket, and I could not get on to it at all before it vanished round a hump. Moobli had been right and I had been wrong. He had clearly scented the bird when it had been taking a drink from the burn. I had to apologise.

'Good boy!' I said with enthusiasm, stroking his thick, neck ruff. 'That's a good boy!' He clopped his great jaws together, then leaped up and pushed my jacket with a paw as if to tell me that he *did* know his business by now, and that I was the fool.

In the new year, I saw some hinds and calves running east over a deer-crossing in the burn. Suddenly a calf fell in a tangle of legs and snow. It got to its feet and chased weakly after the others. Moobli ran off downstream, along the edge of the gorge. I ran after him and there was the calf, being swept in and out of the pools by the torrent. I cross the burn and got to the calf just as it was about to be swept over the big falls. Without Moobli's scenting skill I would never have known it was passing below us.

For two days I nursed the calf indoors before it went back to its mother. It was extraordinary to see how the calf accepted the artificial situation in the workshop and the presence of Moobli and myself. It even trotted into the kitchen to stand by my side while I was preparing supper. Moobli was very gentle with the young creature, and the calf just sniffed him without ever knowing that it owed its life to Moobli's nose. When I released it back to the herd, he whined at the loss of his playmate.

Early February bestowed four days of gorgeous sunny weather upon the land and I took him on a high eight-mile trek. We tramped over a 1,600-foot ridge, down to a small frozen lochan nestling between the hills, where I found the rare 4-toed tracks of a wildcat, then up and along the near 2,200-foot peak of Guardian mountain. Up on the steeper slopes I could just stamp my own steps into the hard packed snow while Moobli's rough pads found enough friction on its textured icy surface to enable him to trot along without a slip. Along the burns icicles dangled from vegetation, banging together in the easterly breeze making a chiming music. From small rock faces huge icicles dangled like fangs, their tips melting in the sun so that falling droplets looked like saliva from the glassy teeth of monstrous heads.

We saw three hind herds, one containing 24 animals, and on our return found the first recently dead hind of the winter, just above the east wood. As we had run out of meat I removed a rear haunch, marinated it later in homemade wine and cloves. The venison tasted strongly of fir and pine resin. As the hinds sheltering in the woods overnight had stripped my few unprotected Douglas firs and hemlocks a few days back, it seemed a sort of poetic justice. I got my own trees back in a sense!

By February 16, when the hind season ends, the estate had taken twenty hinds, a few more than usual. Even so, we found 25 dead hinds and calves within a half-mile semi-circle of the cottage, as well as three hinds, three calves and two stags on treks within three miles. (This was the highest deer mortality in all my years at Wildernesse – due mainly to the herds outgrowing their ranges, dwindling in size due to forestry plantations, and the long cold, wet winter, which is worse for red deer than dry, frosty snowy ones.)

Moobli thrived on all the pure meat and the hard exercise he was getting. Coming up to his prime, he was already an exceptionally powerful animal. To hear him crunching up the rear thigh-bone of a large hind was frightening. Crunch, crack, crunch, SNAP – and in less than two minutes the whole haunch, meat, bones, skin and all had gone down his gullet. His rear teeth were over an inch across in width. The cracking of the bones was so loud it sounded like pistol shots in the kitchen. By this time he could use his paws almost as well as a bear, holding the haunches upright between his two front feet as he ate, claws extended like a cat's. He measured 6ft 4ins from the tip of his tail to his nose.

Because my water pipe was frozen up on one of these rare sunny mornings, I went out to break the ice in the burn and bring back two buckets of water for household use. Moobli, who had hoped I was taking him on a trek, saw me sit back at my desk and reared up on the window sill, whining with impatience. I went out to throw his sticks. Sticks? They were chunks of tree branches in fact! It may sound odd, but not until now did I realise that throwing one stick for him to fetch was not enough. It was only by fooling around that I stumbled upon the ideal exercise for him. With *two* heavy sticks I could double his running distance. I threw one as hard as I could in one direction. He chased after it, saw me juggling the other, ran back with the first stick, dropped it at my feet, then hared off after the second which I threw in the opposite direction.

We perfected this game so that I could stand still, hurl the alternate sticks 50 yards in different directions so that he pounded up and down at full gallop for a mile or more in mere minutes. Often I threw them over the cottage, and up the steep north hill, and back down over the low front pasture. His eager surgings after them, allied to our mountain treks together, bred endurance and thick-muscled power into his legs, shoulders and back over the next year that amazed me, and often struck awe into strangers seeing him for the first time.

This exercise also increased his sure-footedness, essential in a large heavy dog which has to work rough terrain. I took to throwing rocks for him to chase in the same way over the rocky beach. As they were rocks that lay in the path of the boats, such 'play' had a double use, for it enabled me to clear a fine gangway. He seemed to realise that this was a different game, for while he chased the stones, he merely 'pointed' them with his nose instead of bringing them back each time, as if concentrating more on his running.

I had always believed, mistakenly, that a fit strong man could handle a charging dog but as Moobli shot past each time, feet thundering like a horse, his breath coming regularly between leaps – '*aheh aheh aheh*' – I knew that if such an animal went at you intending to knock you down, just the sight of him coming, broad head, gnashing white teeth, big-knuckled clawed feet, and the sheer *speed*, would paralyse most people. You could not dodge, for he could turn faster than a man, and he would sense which way you were going, by your body signals, before you actually moved, so would time his leap to hit you anyway.

The way he cracked deer bones revealed the maturing power of his jaws. Two quick chops and a man's hands would be useless. He could have torn a human arm off without much difficulty, for he also had great pulling power. The only game in which he ever showed stubbornness, or slight aggression, was the one in which I held a branch out to him with a hand at each end. He would clamp his jaws on its middle and heave. Only by exerting all my strength and bracing my feet could I prevent myself being pulled over. Even if, feeling strong, I lifted the branch up until his hind feet were off the ground, he refused to let go; he just dangled there for the few

96

Moobli was usually more sure-footed when crossing raging burns than I was. (Photo: Patrick Thurston.)

At 2¼ years, he thought nothing of surging into the raging loch to retrieve his sticks.

In winter Moobli helped me to locate many weak and dying red deer, including this old hind stuck in a bog.

seconds I could hold his weight. The only means of getting the branch off him was the unfair method – using leverage, and twisting it right over to one side, so that he had to let go or have his neck broken. He never resented this. The moment he was forced to let go he just stood back, waiting for me to throw the branch for him to fetch back again. I marvelled at the fact that, even when he was a bit peeved with me over some matter, I could put my face near his shaggy head, growl and bite him in fun, without any show of resentment from him. He could have taken half my face off with one bite.

The few dogs that had victimised him as a small pup now reaped what they had sown the moment any of them tried to re-establish ascendancy by a bark or an aggressive approach on the local roads. A quick efficient thrashing, then at the first squeal of terrified submission, Moobli broke away in dignified contempt. For many weeks I had not dared to let him out of the Land Rover unless I was close to him. The black Labrador which had tried to mount him as a pup still occasionally chased beside the vehicle, barking loudly. Once I pulled up near the store and it remained barking by the driver's side. I moved to the other side where the window was half open. The Labrador moved round too, still barking. Suddenly I was thrust aside and Moobli's bulk shot out of the window and literally fell on the black dog. I saw it try to bite as it was turned over, but in a trice Moobli had it by the back of the neck and was shaking it as if it weighed no more than a hare. It gave two '*Ki ki*' screams, Moobli dropped it, and it ran off with its tail between its legs. It never gave us any more trouble. From then on the formerly belligerent dogs melted into the landscape when they saw him. Yet he was initially friendly to any dog, never started a fight until *it* showed aggression, and he remained tolerant of tiny yapping terriers as if their small size put them beneath notice. So far, he seemed to have an innately gentle nature.

When heavy rains fell for several days, causing the loch level to rise two feet overnight, I hauled the boats out beyond the water's reach. Moobli brought down one of his big sticks, urging me to throw it for him. I hurled it out into the gales, over the advancing rollers, thinking 'That'll settle his haggis!'. But he plunged straight into the foaming waves, churned steadily out to the branch, ears folded down to keep out the water which frequently broke over his

97

head, retrieved it with a snap of his jaws and surged back. Where-upon he dropped it, shook himself and bounced about, waiting for me to throw it again.

In mid-February we saw a lone weak hind calf standing near the west wood. It was looking pathetically up at us as we passed above, almost as if asking for our help. There were no hinds to be seen nearby, and I wondered if its mother had been shot by the stalkers. Already it had learnt to fear man and it stumbled away.

Next morning the calf shot up from one of the overnight deer beds and with fawn tail patch bobbing ran away. I whistled Moobli back, but when I saw the calf curving back towards me, let him go on, hoping I could grab the calf. At the last moment it saw me and swerved, plunging into the loch.

I grabbed Moobli and retreated behind a small ridge to keep watch. After thirty yards the calf turned in the water, saw the coast was clear and swam weakly in a crescent back to the beach. I knew it was too weak to go far. It staggered over the rocks and sank to its knees, waiting for its strength to return. Clearly, it needed treatment. We stalked behind some bushes until closer, then stood up. The calf got to its feet and started to move off.

'Go on Moobli. Don't hurt!'

He ran round to its far side, blocking its route, and held it there, as a sheepdog holds an errant ewe. The calf was small and breathed with odd rattlings in its throat, the sign of starting pneumonia. I carried it home in a fireman's lift and nursed it in the heated workshop for three days, then let it graze on a line until it too was strong enough to be released.

In late February and early March violence came among the wildcats, which I still sometimes fed in the pens. Both Freddy and Cleo began to attack Patra, driving her off food and sending her for shelter into one of the den boxes. It was likely that Cleo was coming into oestrus again, and Freddy was backing her up in her attempts to drive Patra away. Amicable sisterhood, which had lasted twenty-one months, was now at an end. When I let her out, Patra raided the bird table and went after Moobli's sterilised sausages in the kitchen, eating compulsively. Eventually I decided to release her in some riverside woods nine miles away, where there were many rabbits and a lone young tom wildcat had been sighted. I drove her there on March 10, and with a last '*mau*' she disappeared into the herbage. If I was sorry to see her go, Moobli seemed even sadder. All the way back in the boat he lay on the deck in forced half sleep, his eyes red. Patra had always been his favourite.

10 · Threat from an Eagle

We were on the highest mountain on the other side of the loch, looking for golden eagle eyries, and it was hard going all the way, the lower slopes covered with deep bulldozed trenches where scratchy Sitka spruces had been planted. Moobli and I had to leap from top to top on the treacherous sods of upturned peat. Above 1,000 feet the rock faces in which there could be eyries seemed innumerable. Often we were dwarfed by great jagged granite escarpments. There were stretches of steep frozen snow, and the only way to negotiate some of these was to slide down them. Above 2,000 feet the herbage grew sparser, giving way to lichens and moss between the short turf, where the short grasses had not yet begun to grow again. My heart pounded when an eagle drifted over the peak from the south but it was going to show me no eyrie for it just drifted on over the loch.

Suddenly a small row of what looked like snow-covered rocks shot off a ledge beside us, their white bodies and whirring wings in stark contrast to the triangles of dusky black formed by their outer tail feathers. It was a small flock of ptarmigan, and they made odd coughing noises as they flew, like the gruntings of young pigs. They all dropped over the ledge and flew down low, to keep it between us and so be out of our sight. If we had been moving slower I might have taken a photo of them.

Ptarmigan are the only British birds to grow all-white Arctic

100

plumage in winter, so camouflaging them against the snow. Chunky, 14 ins long, they are true 'high top' birds, disdaining the easier life of the red grouse on the lower slopes and moors. They seldom venture below 2,000 feet, and only in blizzards or early mornings do they descend to the tree line. But they can burrow down through snow, to get at the mosses, lichens and shoots of bilberry, crowberry, heather and other mountain plants which sustain them until the fruits and insects of summer.

Ptarmigan are hard to spot in all seasons. They have three moults and colour changes in the year, with only the wings remaining white. In summer, the head and upper parts become mottled yellowish brown and grey, and in autumn this changes to grey before winter's white plumage. When motionless, at any time of the year, they look like rocks or clumps of herbage. A ptarmigan is exceptionally fecund and can hatch as many as nine chicks, which fly after about ten days. They keep their numbers despite being frequently preyed upon by eagles.

We went right round the mountain, zigzagging up and down, but I found only one old eyrie site, a few sticks on a ledge below an overhang. Up near the peak the icy winds made my eyes water so much that it was hard to appreciate the spectacular view of the loch shimmering away to the north, matched by the narrow silver of a sea loch to the south. As we descended again I kept my eye on the long ledge from which the ptarmigan had flown and stalked it stealthily, hoping I could spot them. Now there was no need for such care.

Suddenly a cock ptarmigan, his black eye streak prominent, stepped from behind a clump of dead grasses and strutted in front of us, mere yards away. He did not seem to be afraid of Moobli, who was restraining himself with difficulty. The bird hopped on to a rock and regarded us jauntily. He was so close that I had to take a few steps backwards in order to get him into focus! Then he just walked over the turf as I clicked away and my film came to an end. Moobli was intrigued, and moved nearer to the bird. It was an hilarious sight, Moobli edging forward like a great cat, his nose extended in curiosity, while the ptarmigan ran a few inches in front of him on furry feet like a friendly farmyard chicken. Sometimes, I thought, a ptarmigan can be pterribly ptame!

In the wettest spring I had known in the Highlands, most treks for eyries had to be undertaken in pouring rain. I was sure I had found a good eyrie on March 21 when I saw a dark mass of vegetation on

101

a high ledge. To get near it I had to climb a long, almost sheer rock covered with thick moss. Rain was still falling as I reached the top, but the grey mass turned out to be just old heather. As I turned to climb down, the soggy moss gave way and I slithered down the rock in a sitting position, trying to keep the camera pack from harm and using the leather elbow pads of my camouflage jacket as impromptu brakes. When I hit the steep wet slope below the rock I had to make some fast knee-jarring jumps to prevent my headlong descent towards a sheer drop. Moobli just pranced down beside me, panting and grinning, as if I had been fooling around on purpose. I was not having much luck.

Desperate for a close photo of an eagle, I endured an icy night in a hide overlooking a hind carcass I had hauled up to 400 feet. The zip of my sleeping bag broke and I shivered with cold. An eagle landed nearby but, perhaps foolishly, I dared not risk moving the fixed long lens camera off the carcass in case the eagle saw the movement. It did not go to the bait. When I returned home next morning, Moobli banged out of the half opened door, whining and prancing with delight at seeing me again. It was the first time I had left him alone overnight.

By early June I had located only seven eyries, three of them with the help of others. One up an inaccessible 1,600-foot cliff contained two eggs but had been deserted by the adults early in the season. Another, 25 miles away, also had two eggs, but they were stolen before I could erect a hide. While boating back from one trek we were hit by a freak whirlwind which swept over from the south, against the north-east breeze, and forced the bow towards the rocks below the west wood. I could not turn, and only by reversing at the last second did I avert disaster. I swung the bow round to fight the gust, which promptly died down. It was as if the elements were saying, 'Your time here is up'. When we climbed up the path to the cottage, I found my windmill generator (which powered a 12-volt battery from which I ran the record player and desk light) had blown down, its pivot and three vanes smashed. It took some fixing. At least on these treks, Moobli had helped me locate three more badger setts; one at 600 feet contained young, for there were tiny droppings in one of the dung pits.

We made an 11-mile trek all round the western and southern faces of Eagle Rock mountain on June 5, exploring first a deep river gorge with high sheer walls. I found Eyrie 8, just an old site where the nest had been blown away, and a young keeper friend had told me where to find Eyrie 9. It too was defunct, having been gouged out by a rockfall. I boated home feeling depressed for it seemed I was facing defeat with the eagles. From habit I went up to the wild-cat pens, and what I saw there did more than revive my spirits.

Cleo, who had been running free in the wild and had returned to the pens of her own choice, had given birth to four more kittens. And I was just in time to see her licking the foetal sac of the last born. This kit, which I came to call Liane, was a runt, and I spent considerable time over the next few days ensuring she did not perish in the competition for milk, even if it meant slipping one of the bigger kits off a teat. Moobli took great interest in all this, standing outside the pens with brows as furrowed as those of a bloodhound. Perhaps he was really fixing in his mind that I really cared about the survival of these kittens which, as events turned out, was a very good thing.

Three days later he amazed me with his scenting skills. I was walking through a wood seven miles to the east, intent upon checking the glen above it for eyries, when he put his nose to the ground, began to zigzag about, and yawned noisily as he often did when on a wildcat scent. I urged him on and he hastened away on a fresh scent, tracking nose-high. When I caught up with him, he was making the high anguished sounds in his throat that meant he had something at bay. He had tracked down Patra, and she was 15 ft up a tree, straddling a broad branch, her striped tail twitching. She made a low curdling growl of protest. She was fat and clearly pregnant. I baited the area with some sausage meat before boating home for the box-cage trap. I installed her in the woodshed where, on June 11, she gave birth to three kits. They were small, had scrawny fused tails and big black stripes all over their bodies. Patra had not mated with the wildcat tom, as I had hoped, but with a black domestic tomcat known to be in the area where Moobli had found her so brilliantly.

I was still anxious to photograph nesting eagles and spent two days fashioning a hide of my own invention. I wanted it to be undetectable either by eagles or humans. I carried it over a rain-swollen river and up to the 1,600-ft eyrie ledge. There were two nests on this long ledge, the left hand one containing the two eggs, which were now further apart than before. I saw no eagles in the sky, and the whole ledge had a mournful deserted look. Sweating

103

and panting, I put down the hide and used the last two frames of a film on the lonely nest.

There I sat, looking out over the terrifying expanse of the eagle's glen below me, when I heard a scrabbling sound higher up. Moobli had gone even further than I had dared, and was balanced precariously on a narrow ledge just below the second nest, and was sniffing up towards it, doubtless smelling some carrion. He could climb better than I could. I cringed for the danger he was in but dared not distract him by whistling or calling. Instead, I wearily turned and slowly dragged the hide down the dangerous steeps. After a hundred yards I looked back; to my intense relief Moobli had worked his way off the ledge safely and was catching me up.

Near the bottom he began scenting downwind to our right, not far from a cairn of large tumbled rocks. I went over to it and found the ground well trodden between two large holes, and piles of white grasses laid out – badger bedding set out to dry.

Moobli was not at all interested in my words of praise for he was still scenting downwind. I looked to the right and saw what looked like four giant hedgehogs romping along a deer path towards us. As they came nearer I realised they were badgers. I hissed Moobli to keep quiet. There was no need; he had seen the badgers too and had sat down, not attempting to bark. With no film left in the camera, here we were watching four badgers – sow, a boar, and two well grown cubs – haring along in full daylight! I frantically reeled the film back to where I always click off the first two frames with the lens cap on. I took a photo of the two cubs wrestling, rolling over and mock-biting each other's necks, and one of the boar falling off the sow after what looked like an attempt to mate. Then they vanished into the sett.

A few minutes later, as I waited downwind, the two cubs emerged and started digging in the earth above the sett. I could only sit there, arm round Moobli's great neck, murmuring 'Ssh. Good boy', so emphasising yet again the need to keep quiet whenever we watched wild animals in the open. He was intensely interested in the cubs. He sat with ears cocked, his body quivering with pent up excitement. It was obvious that he would have run over and tried to play with the badgers if I had let him. Soon the cubs got our scent and vanished back into the cairn. Later, I found I had photographed the badgers, but the images were blurred and somehow light had got in, spotting and blurring the pictures with patches of yellow and orange.

At last I found a viable eagle eyrie, but only after meeting a fine young keeper called Greg Hunter, a tall dark bearded man of twenty-eight who had located a nest with a well-grown chick on his estate many miles from my home. Greg, also a photographer, was interested in my unusual ideas for a hide. On June 27 we set it up, all camouflaged with natural herbage, on the ground of a knoll and under the shelter of an overhanging rock. It was a relief not to have to put it on some high precarious cliff ledge, as I had feared. The hide overlooked the nest and its well-feathered 8-week-old eaglet on an open ledge in a smooth rounded rock face 35 yards away. On each return visit to it I had to boat 13 miles, drive 65 and hike 5.

Greg first walked me into the hide on July 1 while poor Moobli waited for seven hours on the plastic foam bed in the Land Rover. I felt this would be a problem for him on future visits, especially during longer stays, but I soon worked out a fair modus operandi. As we boated out I ran him for two or three miles along the shore to tire him, and left him with food and water in the vehicle, opening the two front 'desert' ventilators so that he would have fresh air. If I went into hides around dawn, I made him run a couple of miles behind the Land Rover, or gave him such a run the night before. The trouble then was that I found it hard to sleep, because for about an hour he would be panting so hard he shook the truck like a giant vibrator!

I will never forget my feelings on that July day when, after an hour and a half, the chick began to squeak and stare into the sky, and the great mother eagle came soaring into the eyrie on her 7-foot wing span, surrounded by shimmering heat waves, and began to feed her chick. It fuelled an already relentless fascination with the king of birds that has lasted with me to the time of writing, eleven years later.

I promised to walk Greg into the hide on my next visit, which meant that Moobli could come with us for, after seeing Greg safely installed, I would walk out again with him. I took him swimming in the sea off the Ardnamurchan peninsula, the most westerly point on Britain's mainland. The beaches were of gorgeous silver shell sand, and Moobli loved pounding up and down in it. The water was icy. Moobli swam round me like a huge otter and towed me into shore with his tail. The salt water clogged his thick coat up so badly that I had to give him a bath in a fresh water burn before we went to fetch Greg from the hide. That night I slept in Greg's cottage, the first time I had stayed in anyone else's home since I had come to Scotland seven years earlier.

Moobli not only accepted Greg as a friend, he had also taken a liking to his lurcher bitch, so when Greg and one of his falconer pals walked me into the hide next morning, we let Moobli come too. He could then trek out with them again, which was far better for him than waiting stoically in my Land Rover.

After eight and a half more wonderful hours in the hide, I began to wonder when Greg and his friend would come to pick me up. Then I heard loud panting outside the hide. I made a hole in the camouflage herbage and peered out. There was Moobli looking in at me!

When the two men turned up they told me an odd story. They had seen the eagle fly into the eyrie on their walk in, so had known I was getting more good pictures. About a mile from the hide, Moobli had put his nose to the ground and clearly had picked up my scent. He began haring off over the rough ground, intending to follow it until he found his master. They watched Moobli disappear into a dip, then saw the female eagle leave the nest and swoop down low over the running Alsatian. Moobli had dodged, looked at the eagle in surprise as it wheeled away to the north west, and had then turned and run all the way back to them. I was surprised that an eagle would dare to menace a powerful dog like Moobli.

Shortly after that the dog picked up my scent again, ignored their whistles and commands to return, and finished tracking me down to the hide. That was an astonishing feat on an eight-hour-old scent on a hot dry day. Both men said they were impressed with Moobli's fidelity towards me.

On July 9 we searched the western face of Eagle Rock mountain and found Eyrie 11. It was only 14 feet up a small rock face and many of its thick sticks lay on the ground below, as if thrown out by human hands. On the way to it I had to climb a tall forestry fence which Moobli seemed slow to tackle. I left him behind, walked on up the hill, ignoring his anguished whines, and hid behind a ridge to see what he would do on his own. At first he walked up and down several times on the far side of the fence, trying to snap the stout wires with his teeth. Then he attempted to jump the fence, did not make it, and was thrown to the ground by the taut wires. If he could not leap a 7ft fence, especially when he had to run up a steep hill towards it, there were other ways. He pushed his nose under the tight bottom wire and heaved it up with power of his neck muscles. He squeezed his head under sideways and scrambled with his great claws, forcing his 38-inch chest through a six-inch gap. Then he tracked me down by scent and leaped up in the joy of reunion.

I last went to the eagles on July 10 when the eaglet was almost ready to fly. I left Moobli at Wildernesse in the care of a young Australian friend called Stella, who was staying for two days. It was around midnight when I returned to find Moobli waiting at the boat bay, all alone in the dark. Stella told me that for two hours he had insisted on staying there, ignoring the rain, staring into the gathering dusk and waiting for the sound of my engine. During the day he had disappeared and she had gone anxiously to look for him. She had found him standing on the sandy land spit three miles away, gazing towards the west and where I was in the eagle hide. It was wonderful to witness such loyalty.

11 · Rebel with a Cause

Liane, the runt of Cleo's second litter, ate meat for the first time in mid-July. She was more amenable to being touched by me than the others, and I had grown very fond of her. I decided to try to tame her in the house. As far as I knew, no human being had ever tamed a wildcat before.

The problem here could have been Moobli, for I did not want to risk feelings of jealousy on his part. Despite his gentle nature, he was an unusually powerful animal who did not tolerate any dog that showed aggression towards him. If, out of fear, Liane should scratch him, one chop from those great jaws would end her life.

At six weeks old, I brought her into my study each day, spending time playing with and feeding her, but always keeping Moobli in the act. I had warned him to be gentle and quiet, but she flared when she saw him and reared on her forelegs and spat. But he just sat down and kept still a few yards away. She seemed to realise that this huge animal had never done her any harm before and slowly subsided. After each such play session I returned her to Cleo in the pens, for she still needed occasional suck and of course her mother's hunting training.

Whenever Moobli tried to scent towards her in the study over the next few days, the quiet order 'Sit' brought instant obedience from him. Before long it was clear he was as fascinated by the young

kitten as I was. His expression was one of intense interest, even kindness, but how he longed to lick her! He would lie on the floor, his
legs out straight, until Liane found the warm fluffy comfort of his
huge bushy tail. She put both front paws over it, her head between
them, and went to sleep!

I was amazed by his forbearance. I had restrained him verbally
only a few times in the first days before he realised that any sudden
movement on his part wold scare her. If she came sniffing nervously
towards his giant form he remained quite still.

I was even more astonished by the big dog's speed two days
later. I was coming up the path with a bowl of blackcurrants when
Moobli dropped the stick he had been carrying and dashed away
silently, vanishing behind the cottage. I called him back but there
was no response. Then I heard his deep bark coming from the burn.
I floundered over. He had cornered a fox in a deep pool ringed by
boulders. The fox was trying to snap back at him, but his great teeth
and fast dodging speed kept it there. As I scrambled to it, the fox
rolled in the water. Soaked like a skinned cat, it made odd guttural
sounds in its throat.

The fox snarled with open mouth as I dashed into the pool,
grabbed the end of its thick tail and carried it snapping at my legs to
a 12-ft pen which had been separated from that of Cleo and her kits.
I lifted the gate and gently swung the fox inside. I did not want to try
to tame the fox while I was looking after Liane, a consuming task.
I decided to feed it well and then release it some miles away. Two
days later, however, the fox died. It had twin puncture wounds on
an inner rear thigh from which maggots were falling. It had clearly
died from blood poisoning.

In late summer I released Cleo and Patra with their kits in good
prey areas. They were sad occasions but to have seven wildcats and
three hybrids roaming the immediate area would have upset the
balance of wildlife. I left a supply of long-lasting sterilised meat
sausages at each release point. Moobli could hardly believe what I
was doing. He put his head down and wanted to track after them, as
of old, but I called him back. As we boated home he lay on the deck
looking downcast, his eyes red and bloodshot as he forced himself
to sleep, something he always did when he was unhappy. How he
had loved running out ahead of me each morning to check that *his*
charges, *his* wildcats, were still there. I was glad for his sake as much
as mine that we still had little Liane.

109

There were times during August and early September when Moobli might have had second thoughts about my indulgence towards the kitten. She spent much of the time with me in the study. As she grew bigger and stronger, she also became more playful and invented a score of games. She performed wild Zorba dances over the carpet, swiped my pencil and pen container off the desk, burrowed through my files like a giant shrew, and batted about a cardboard ball on elastic for hours. She also gave Moobli a hard time. She danced back and forth delivering sheathed-claw lefts and rights to his muzzle, chased after his bushy tail and dived, bit, clutched and rolled over with it. He did not care for this treatment, though not once did he snap at her. She even threw herself on her back below his nose, lay flat with her legs splayed out, then whacked out at his chin. If his nose went too close, she flared – while still lying on her back – then clouted him again. Once, when Moobli had had enough of this, he woofed right in her ear. She shot under the bed so fast he did not see her go. She was still scared of him in the open but took to having snoozes right on top of his chest as he lay supine on the floor indoors.

In early September I took the pair of them with me on a short trip to London. Liane capered about inside the Land Rover, giving dignified Moobli's ears the occasional cuff as she shot past. They were both allowed to sleep in the Hampstead hotel bedroom with me, and they were good company for each other while waiting in the Land Rover in stifling London streets.

A strong north-east gale was blowing when we returned to the loch, but I took a chance and set off for home in the small boat with its 4 horse-power engine. Liane was on centre deck in the best den box. We banged along at half walking pace until the engine cut out. Nothing would make it re-start.

Cursing the fact that I had left my long newly varnished oars in the cottage, I grabbed a frying pan and paddled desperately to keep the bow to the waves. It was impossible. The laden boat swerved slowly broadside and was swamped by the crashing waters. Down it went. I grabbed the handle of Liane's box with one hand, a briefcase with my wildlife notes and photos in the other, and leaped as far as I could from the sinking boat towards the shore.

I was 25 yards from the beach and struggling in about 14 feet of water.

'Come here, Moobli! Come here!' I gasped.

Rebel with a Cause

He paddled round with his powerful web-footed trudgen strokes, snorting like a bear. Just before he swerved off again I grabbed the end of his tail with the hand that held the briefcase. Off he went, surging with the waves that sometimes swamped his head. I tried to hold Liane's box high with the other hand, madly kicking hard.

Gasping for air and spitting out water, my heart pounding as if it would break out of my chest, we reached the gravelly beach. I lay there for a few minutes regaining my breath and strength. Poor Liane was soaked to the skin and terrified. I tipped up her box to let the few inches of water drain out. Somehow the boat had nose-dived bow first towards the shore and its rope now lay snaked in only six feet of water. I took off my jacket, dived for it and heaved the water-filled boat as near to the beach as I could, stacking what was left in it high on the beach, then retrieving everything that had fallen out but floated to shore. What a fiasco, and it was not over yet.

I set out to carry my most valuable possessions the two miles home and to fetch a baler and fuel mix for the boat's engine. I could not lug Liane's awkward square box as well, so I put her sodden subdued form on dry clothes in my pack, strapped down its top and, with Moobli walking behind, set off over the rocky bogs and tussocks. Halfway home I set down the loads for a rest and to give Liane some air. She had disappeared from the pack!

'Didn't you see her?' I yelled furiously at Moobli.

I looked back at the empty landscape and '*mau*'d' loudly, but there was no answering call.

'Track her, Moobli!' I shouted to the shivering dog. 'Track the pussy coots!'

He seemed unable to find any scent. What a time to be obtuse! I shouted at him again and cuffed him round the head. I was shivering in the cold wind. There was nothing for it but to get home quickly, change into dry clothes and return for the boat.

Before starting to bale, I went in search of Liane. Moobli still could not track her as I wandered up and down through the lochside trees making loud wildcat calls. Eventually I found her up a thick dying alder 40 yards from the shore. I lifted her off with relief and put her back in the box.

After baling out the boat and getting the fuel mix exactly right, I set off again, but once more the engine cut out, and the gales blew me back a further quarter-mile from where I had beached. More exasperated than before, I paddled into a small bay, unloaded

111

everything again in the shelter of some trees, and plodded back to the cottage with another heavy load. This time I put Liane into a pillow case tied round my neck and carried her cradled in one arm.

She soon recovered her high spirits, playing with her toys and eating well. Moobli looked all in and depressed. As he lay on his bed while I prepared supper, the awful error of what I had done to him that day struck me for the first time. I should not have shouted at him for being unable to track Liane, or cuffed him. She had been soaked through and her wet feet would have been de-scented. I should have remembered that. In any case, what was I doing hitting a dog which had probably saved my life? I might never have made it to the beach without his help.

I felt really bad about it and knelt by his head. He had that red-eyed look of unhappiness.

'I'm sorry I hit you today, son,' I said, feeling like my father must have done when once he had cause to say much the same to me. 'I really am. You're a good boy, a wonderful boy.'

At first he just grunted and moved his head away from my caressing hand. But he soon forgave me and ate with relish the meal of mainly fresh meat that I made for him. He was not a dog to bear a grudge for long.

As the autumn wore on and we resumed our stag treks, Liane grew apace and her play sessions took on an air of ferocity. She would launch karate-style attacks on my bare hands, clutching, biting and kicking with her rear feet. Then she would roll on her back and flare before allowing me to stroke her. These playful assaults worried Moobli more than me, for she clearly did not intend to hurt and rarely drew blood. Nevertheless he would sometimes approach me with a concerned whine, as if asking me to allow him to stop her.

She played outside much more now, and also used the pens, but the early bedroom days were so indelibly printed on her that she considered the cottage her private domain, the place for conducting personal hygiene and receiving intimate fondling. She would remain outside for hours and then rush in to perform on the carpet, my bed, even Moobli's bed. Although I had hand-trained her, I totally failed to house-train her. I took to closing the study and kitchen doors at night, leaving Moobli to sleep on his bed in the hall with the front door open. Often the wildcat would sleep snuggled up to him, and he was pleased to accommodate her as a bed companion. Eventually she made her nightly quarters in the woodshed, though she still came often through the window for a cuddle before retiring.

Snow showers fell on December 9, some as blinding blizzards which made the sky so dark I was forced to light the paraffin lamp in the middle of the day. Between them there were bright patches in which the clouds rolled away and the low sun shone with fierce primaeval brilliance, bouncing off the snow into my eyes so that I wished I had kept one of the trappings of my former civilised life – sunglasses. I looked out during one such blazing interlude at Moobli lying on a bank of snow. He was behaving like a spectator at Wimbledon – eyes staring intently, head switching from side to side as if watching a fast-moving ball.

Quietly I went out. Liane was behaving like a mad March Hare. This was the thickest-lying snow she had ever seen and she clearly loved it as much as Moobli. She had left her woodshed hay box and dashed down to the vegetable garden, swerving wildly to run back up through the bramble banks towards her pen, then made another slithering turn and hared off back down to the garden again. When she saw me watching as well as Moobli she increased her effort, revelling in the performance before an audience. I tried to capture her unique snow display with my camera.

Sometimes she stopped her headlong flight abruptly, ears back, a crazy happy look in her golden eyes, and bit at the snow, shaking her head as its cold twinged her teeth. She scooped it up in her paws, batted out at the falling remnants, and even performed a couple of somersaults in it. Eventually she tired and stood by the pen, her thick ringed tail drooping, watching me as I photographed her galloping tracks, a full five feet apart. Then she surprised me even more by squatting daintily in a little hollow, where she performed a business, then carefully raked snow over it with each front paw. Finally, with both paws at once, she scooped wide curves of more snow over the first lot until she had accumulated a sizeable mound which she patted all over before sauntering back to the shed. All this time Moobli had lain quietly in the snow, watching me take pictures, as if my work with the camera made him restrain his natural instinct to chase after Liane in play. I thought what a good dog he had been disciplining himself like that without a word of command. It did not last.

When I went to fetch Liane in the late afternoon, he was standing by the front door. I watched the wildcat eat most of her food and then returned to find that he had disappeared. I whistled and called but there was no response. I went round the pasture, following his huge tracks in the snow. He had started to run near the west wood, but I lost the tracks in the snowless area beneath the trees. I searched round on the far side and picked them up again where he had run out of the wood towards the west. I climbed through the snow-covered heather to the top of a steep ridge and scanned the hills and lochside to the west with my fieldglass.

To my surprise, I saw a red deer hind and a calf in the icy water of the loch near a gravelly land spit a mile or more away. There could be only one cause for that in winter. Furious with Moobli for his disobedience, I hurried back to the cottage for the bung, hauled the big boat down to the loch, upsetting the whole wooden runway system, and boated along to where the deer stood in the water. Long before I got there I saw them clamber out on to the beach and walk away into the long wood on weak and shaky legs. Then I saw Moobli; he had heard the boat coming and was running along the shore back to Wildernesse. I shouted to him – '*Come here!*'

This was the kind of day I had been dreading. Despite his growing maturity, the big Alsatian had broken two cardinal rules – never to chase deer and never to leave the cottage area without word from me. He had disobeyed even while *knowing* what he was doing, proof of which lay in the guilty look on his face as he came towards the boat. I was angry at being made to haul the boat into and out of the water, which took three hours out of my short working winter day. I felt he needed a forcible reminder. As he climbed into the boat I yelled that he had been a '*Bad dog*' and gave both his flanks a good larruping with a slim hazel wand. He whimpered from the stinging pain.

I then scanned along the shore and lower slopes, following trails, to make sure no deer or calf was lying wounded. I found none. I did not know whether the lapse was due to a sudden reversion to the natural predator role or he had simply become bored and wanted nothing more than a playful chase. Whichever it was, it could not be tolerated and had to be nipped smartly in the bud. I got back into the boat and took him home without a further word. I left him tethered by collar and lead in the workshop. I intended to keep him there without food all night, but after two hours I relented and let him out again. He seemed very sorrowful but ate his food normally. He had bad dreams that night, whuffing and kicking in his sleep.

Next morning Moobli seemed anxious to please. I had been woken by a fox barking in the front pasture at 4 a.m., and had gone out to track its prints. Moobli, who had whined in the kitchen, knowing it was there, followed its scent in the snowless areas but lost it at the burn. He then followed a new scent through the east wood but did not perform his leg-liftings on tufts as he usually did for fox. Once we reached the snow again, I found he had been tracking the old tomcat Sylvesturr for there were his prints, one and a half inches across and three to four inches deep.

'Good boy. Good boy!' I murmured, giving him an encouraging pat.

We followed the prints and the scent across the pasture and into the spiky jumble of old bracken swathes near the west wood. There, where the snow had melted along a small burn below the trees, we lost them. I was delighted by proof that old Sylvesturr was still alive, and later set out meat for him in the wood, but Moobli was not finished yet. He soon located a badger's scent and took me back to the snow in the pasture, where I could see the big padded 5-toed tracks and places where the badger had stopped to scrape for worms and grubs or pupae below the soil, but he lost the scent again in the wet snowless areas filled with sodden autumn leaves in the east wood. I rewarded Moobli with a tasty titbit, hoping I would have no more trouble with him.

For the next week all went well, and when I was not putting in eleven-hour days at my desk I took him for woodland treks, during one of which he located new spreints of a young otter on the shoreside rocks to the east. On a supply trip in atrocious gales, he ran a full three miles home and a frightened hind I had not seen dashed into the loch ahead of him. I did not scold him for the animal had simply been in the line of his run: he had not chased it deliberately. One morning he barged out of the door in front of me, scaring away a roe deer family – buck, doe and their fawn browsing by the wildcat pens – before I could get my camera. But this was my fault, for I had long since learned that at this time of year, when deer come down low, I should always go out quietly and scan the terrain. I had forgotten to hiss him back.

On December 16 I had my worst day ever with him. It was dull, cold and snowy, and before starting work at my desk I threw sticks to give him exercise. Before lunch I went out to throw them again, only to find they had vanished. He had buried them somewhere and now looked at me as if wondering why I had nothing to throw. I told him several times to 'Fetch the ball' but he just looked obtuse, as though he did not understand. I shut him out, hoping to force him to find at least one of them before I indulged his wish to play games. He did not do so, and it seemed to me like a stubborn refusal.

After a whole day at the desk, I cut two more sticks and threw them up and down the hills while he pounded after them. This time I supervised right to the end and made sure I had the sticks back before returning indoors. These were no ordinary sticks, just bits of dead branches that could be found in the woods. I cut them from stout hazel bushes to a length of two and a half feet, peeling off the bark and spokeshaving the ends to a rounded shape so that they were streamlined and would travel farther through the air with each hard throw. They took time to make. Instead of leaving them on the kitchen floor, as I usually did, I hid the new pair on a shelf at the end of his exercise, out of sight and out of his reach. He watched me do this, whined, and wore a look of annoyance.

Next morning I threw them again for him, intending to keep an eye on his activities while I made breakfast. Somehow he evaded me, for when I went out again the new sticks were gone. He had buried them, as he had the others, and was now sneaking furtively through the fruit trees. I recalled then that he would never bury an old bone if I was watching him but would always wait until my back was turned. Well, he could be secretive with his bones if he liked but not with the sticks that cost me some trouble to perfect for him. All my efforts failed to induce him to find even one of them. He peered around, running here and there as though searching, but refused to dig one up.

Exasperated, I clouted him, hard. He then hid in the big rhododendron bush, mouth open, tongue out, smiling. I gave up and went back indoors. Half an hour later I made another attempt to persuade him to find the sticks. I tried being nice to him, took him round all the likely bushes and bramble clumps, and again he seemed to make a casual pretence of his search. I was determined not to give in this time for it appeared to have become a serious contest of wills. I gashed my leg badly on a bramble leader and lost my temper. I broke off a hazel wand and whacked him twice. He still flatly refused to fetch either of the sticks from where he had hidden them. Instead he ran up to the house and rushed into my study.

'I don't want you in here,' I yelled, 'you can stay out all day!'

He ran to the kitchen, but I chased him out of there too.

'You're no good,' I shouted, still angry. 'Disobedient bugger! Get out. Go away!'

He walked down to the bottom of the pasture and stepped into the water. I thought he was going to cross the loch. Instead he swam round in a half circle, climbed on to a flat rock below the west wood, and without looking back began to walk away to the west. He broke into a trot and disappeared over a ridge. I ran after him, but he was already a quarter of a mile away by the time I reached the ridge. He was really going, really leaving me. I felt distraught. I must have been crazy to make a fuss over such a matter. He had never buried his sticks until recently.

I ran for the boat, tore it down to the shore and roared after him. I caught up one and a half miles away and called desperately to him. He came to the boat looking sorrowful and confused. I threw my arms around his great neck and chest with profuse apologies and brought him home. I was so depressed as he walked by my side up the path, so utterly ashamed of myself, that I was near to breakdown. Was it all my fault, or partly his? Perhaps there was a sort of latch in his canine mind that made him forget where he had buried anything immediately after he buried it. This certainly seemed to be the case with bones. Perhaps this forgetting was part of the dog's survival system. When he had walked about with his tongue out, as if leering and playing a stubborn game, he had in fact been confused and bewildered by my anger.

Was I going mad? Was the constant isolation finally destroying my judgement, as I seemed to be destroying the only creature in the world that was close to me? Was I here, miles up this lonely, dark and storm-bound loch for no other real reason than that this was all I deserved? I sat on the bed looking at Moobli's sad face, the brown eyes that now showed nothing but faith and forgiveness, and was suddenly overwhelmed with an awful sense of loneliness. For more than ten years I had battled to survive in remote wild places, to write about them and photograph them well, and had ended up a lonely old fool on a hill with no one to turn to, drinking too much and destroying even the love of his dog. I hugged Moobli and wept like a child.

117

After a few minutes I felt him tugging himself free and he went to the door. He had a happier look on his face now and I thought he wanted to play. I went to the workshop and picked up the hand-saw. When he saw that he began to prance up and down, knowing that I was going to cut him a new stick. I cut the stick outside, peeled and shaped it and began to hurl it for him, down into the pasture and up the hill behind the cottage. It was in the delight of his running to retrieve his new 'ball' and drop it at my feet that I felt his forgiveness. The foolish crisis of which I had been the main cause was over. He seemed to forget it quickly but I never would. Before dusk he had found one of his old sticks, and when I went out to call him in I found he had laid it beside his new one.

12 · The Stag Fighter

Moobli and I saw in the New Year by camping in the woods below a stout oak which I had carefully eyed for dead spikes that might fall in the night. It was bitter cold as a north-west wind soughed through the trees, but overhead the stars were bright diamonds in a black velvet gown. As the camp fire crackled merrily near my tent and the stew bubbled in its pot, I felt a little smug. I had not had a single drink and had bought only two small bottles of beer to last me the coming week. Having recently glimpsed the great veteran eagle I had watched the previous spring wafting over the snowy mountains, I decided to get on even closer terms with the king of birds in the months ahead, and for that I would need to be fit. After supper, with Moobli snug on his bed in the fly leaf of the tent, I slept peacefully through the long night.

I woke at dawn from a dream in which a lion was stalking me in these woods! It had roared loudly and I sat bolt upright, my head hitting the frosty crackly sides of the tent where my breath had condensed into little icicles. Moobli was on his feet staring intently towards the west. Then I heard the roar again, followed by two loud '*hoff*' barks, the kind red deer hinds make when sounding the alarm to the rest of the group. What was going on? I slipped on boots and clothes and slid out of the tent.

Four hinds, two calves and a yearling were filing from their dormitory in the west wood up the steep slopes to start their day

119

grazing on short heather between the lying patches of snow. Maybe one of the hinds had made the roars. Usually the only roar a hind makes (more of a flat bellow really), is heard before or during the birth of a calf in early June. Maybe one of them had roared with the cold, for it was now well below freezing! A thick hoar frost clung to the remaining leaves on the bramble bushes, and skeins of dank mist were drifting across the loch. After breakfast, with the sun beginning to beam through a gap in the cloud battlements, I climbed up to the first 500-foot ridge to take photos of Wildernesse in the winter light, hoping also to find the hinds again and perhaps solve the mystery.

We had reached 400 feet, scaling rock faces and tussocky ravines, when I thought I heard another roar. Moobli started his deer prancing, his great black muzzle scenting ahead. We stalked round a heathery knoll to overlook a broad hollow in the hills 200 yards ahead. There, with eight hinds and three calves, was a stag! I judged him to be about six years old, with eight points on his antlers. This was most unusual, for after the autumn rut stags form bachelor herds and spend winter apart from the hinds. Yet here was a stag behaving as if in the last stages of the rut!

He walked slowly along, sometimes opening his mouth as if about to roar but now making no sound. He approached one hind and sniffed her rear. She let down her tail and skittered coyly out of the way. He stretched his neck over a clump of herbage, closed his eyes for a few seconds, then walked towards another hind, which also turned away. Suddenly, in the shifting breeze, they got our scent. A big yeld hind barked and off they went as I finished changing to a 300 mm lens. I got only one poor shot of their fleeing forms.

I was sure this was the odd stag I had seen with the hind groups in our area the previous winter, only then I had counted six points on his uneven tines. He was certainly behaving in an aberrant way. It was somehow comforting to think that the wild animal kingdom sometimes throws up its quirky individuals too.

Over the next two weeks, when not trying to reduce the workload at my desk, I took Moobli trekking. Our best stag stalking came on January 16. After a hard climb in snow up and down 1,800 feet, when my new boots gave my feet hell, we located no less than eighteen stags lit up by the sun on the far hill, about a mile away. We were already some three miles from home. As we approached,

I found that the only way to stalk them was to crawl up and down deep forestry drain trenches, my hands and knees wet and frozen. Moobli scanned the tight forestry fences until he spotted a six-inch gap, in front of which he threw himself down and hauled his massive bulk through sideways by using his strong claws.

After taking my best wintering stag pictures so far, we plodded back over the hill, my feet so cold in the new boots that I could hardly feel them. Next morning the flesh below the big toe ball of my right foot was still a pale yellow; I must have got something close to frostbite, and I could hardly bear to put the foot down for two days. Just carrying a bucket of water from the frozen burn was agony. Fortunately, after considerable massage, the flesh returned to its normal colour inside a week. I could not trek, and used the time for writing, for varnishing my oars and for sewing the loose twin hulls of my old sea-boat together with copper wire. The constant battering the boat received in rough water over the years had caused all the original rivets to snap.

On our next trek, for which I wore good old rubber wellies, we again saw the aberrant stag running with the hind group. Clearly, my seeing him with them earlier had not been mere coincidence.

One morning, as I was clearing large stones from the boat slipway for Moobli to chase after, the dog scented something in the west wood. Thinking it might be Sylvesturr, I urged him to track. As he moved up to the rocky escarpment, a large calf rose from one of the deer beds and, with buff tail-patch bobbing, ran away. I whistled to Moobli but then saw the calf curving back towards me. I tried to grab it as it swerved and charged down to the loch shore, where it sprang into the water. To my surprise, Moobli plunged in too, swam after it, overhauled it with ease and seized the back of its neck in his jaws. The calf gave a loud '*bleah*' cry, then gurgled as its head went under. I yelled loudly. Moobli immediately and obediently left the deer and swam back. Knowing the calf would soon swim out again once it saw the coast was clear, I hid with Moobli behind a rock. The calf collapsed when it reached the shore, but after a few seconds it got to its feet and started to totter weakly away. It would not survive without being dried and fed.

'Go on. Turn it. Don't hurt,' I said as I sent the Alsatian to perform his sheepdog act.

He ran off, and when the calf fell down again, stood over it until I got there. I carried the calf home, dried it, gave it warm lamb's milk from a bottle and fed it garden vegetables. In two days it was strong enough to be released. The odd thing was that it kept coming close to the cottage in the next few days, as if wanting another look at its helpful captors, but it quickly ran off again when it saw Moobli. Inside the cottage it had been quite tame towards the dog. Indeed, one morning I had found it curled up on the kitchen carpet beside him, and Moobli had looked up gently as if having a wild deer calf of almost his own size and weight sharing his bed was quite normal.

Soon after that I awoke at dawn one day and saw on the far side of the loch some poachers with a car frighten a big stag into the water. When they moved off, it tried to swim back to the far shore but then began to flop about weakly on the surface. I got the boat down and roared across, hoping to save its life, but I was too late for it had drowned by the time I reached it. I hauled its 230lb dead weight into the boat and was attempting to revive it with artificial respiration when I heard huffing snorts nearby. Anxious to take part, Moobli had swum almost half a mile at considerable speed in the icy water. I was touched by his bravado but also alarmed that he too might drown. I tried to get him aboard but failed, and he sank back beneath the surface briefly before deciding he would be safer making his own way home.

Once back on shore, I started to skin the stag while it was still warm. Moobli arrived and shook himself before settling down to watch the operation as if he had just returned from a short summer swim. I was conscious of an odd silence as inadvertently I punctured a small vein in the rear leg and blood ran out. Moobli was looking on with a sombre expression and he winced as I cut into the flesh. Anyone would think that his hunting instinct extended only to romping alongside deer in play, but if he did not like to see the blood flowing under my knife he certainly enjoyed the venison meals over the next ten days.

In late January I saw from my window another stag ensconced in the middle of my vegetable patch. It must have jumped the deer-proof fence and was eating my sprouts.

I was of course running Wildernesse as a wildlife sanctuary and was actively encouraging deer to use the whole area. For the sake of the deer, I had refrained from fencing off the woods, laboriously caging the little trees one by one instead. I had cut back the bracken in the front pasture for winter feed areas when deer were forced down from the hills in harsh weather, and had cut hay in summer for them. Yet establishing that vegetable garden had been a back-breaking job. I did not want deer breaking in and stealing my own produce after I had dug out two tons of rocks, hauled fertilising seaweed and manure down the loch, and hammered in posts for the fencing that was designed to keep the deer out.

I went outside and clapped loudly. The big stag jerked up its head and stared. Then, with graceful ease, it leaped from a standing position over a sagging part of the fence (which had been quite firm the day before) and trotted off into the west wood. It was the same aberrant stag, I noticed, that had run with the hinds for the last two winters. Moobli watched it go too, but growled softly.

I was annoyed to find a whole row of sprouts decimated. The stag had broken down the fence so hard it had uprooted a corner post and left it leaning inwards. I hauled the post upright and wedged it back in place by sledgehammering long rocks in beside its inner base.

That evening it was back in the twilight, stabbing at the fence netting with its antlers. Then it reared up and tried to strike down the fence with its forefeet. I dashed out with a light and scared the beast away. Next morning all remaining sprouts had gone, so had half a row of cabbages. That stag had become a determined marauder, and having tasted elixir now wanted the lot, no doubt my kale too. As many a crofter knows, such a deer, or group of deer, are difficult to discourage: they will return even after shots have been fired over their heads. Normally the crofter will shoot the invaders, or else ask the Red Deer Commission to send a professional stalker to do so. I have always frowned on this practice, especially where gardens are unfenced or merely a few roses are nibbled.

On the third morning I awoke at dawn to find the stag again steadily depriving me of my hard-grown food, and I got mad. Something had to be done. Thinking that it would frighten the stag away for good, and cure Moobli of any instinct he may still harbour for chasing after deer – for surely he would not be able to subdue a stag – I sent Moobli in.

'Go on. See him off!'

The dog needed no second bidding. With a deep-throated growl that sounded like a lion, he took off, his eyes fixed on the beast that was also usurping *his* territory. The stag heard me, saw Moobli coming and once again leaped the sagging enclosure fence. But before it could reach the lochside fence, Moobli was at its heels.

123

The stag turned at bay, head down, making sweeping curves with its long 8-point antlers to keep the dog back. Stags do not gore like a horned bull and then toss upwards; they sweep and poke, fence and push, and I was sure Moobli was smart enough to keep out of range.

The fight that followed was terrifying. I was astonished at the speed, power and resource of the dog against an antlered animal more than three times his size and weight, a beast that used not only those antlers but flailing forefeet as well. At first, when Moobli got in close, it shot both front feet out together, a combined blow which, if it had landed, would have staved in his chest. Twice I was worried enough to call Moobli off, but his blood was up and he was determined to teach the stag a lesson. Whirling about with incredible speed for so heavy an animal, he growled and snarled as if to subdue it with frightful noise alone. The stag was kept turning about in half circles, first one way then the other. As the minutes ticked by, it seemed to be tiring. Only once did the antlers catch Moobli, but on a back swing which bowled him over. The dog got up, gave a whoofing whine on a high perplexed note, then went in again, constantly feinting for position, swiftly and intelligently becoming used to the stag's style of fighting. He literally wore out the bigger beast.

Showing all his teeth like a wolf, he went in low, as if going for the rear legs, then turned for the throat, dodging back easily with each tired whirl of the stag. Twice he got close enough to throw himself at the stag's chest, seizing great bites of skin and hair from its lower throat and nearly hauling it off its feet. He was clearly trying to weaken the stag so he could get a fatal hold on the throat.

Suddenly the stag lost its nerve, wheeled round, ran through the gate archway and plunged into the loch. Moobli splashed in right behind it and swiftly began to overhaul it in the water. I had no doubt that he would have climbed on to the stag's back, hooked himself on with teeth and great claws and, by weight alone, drowned the beast had I not thrown a large stone near them with a loud splash. Only then did Moobli heed my yells to stop. He swam back, shook himself near me, panting with exertion and excitement, only too ready to plunge in again should I give the order.

The stag swam in a large half circle, gained land again just past the west wood, staggered out laboriously and made off to the west at a wobbly trot. Its days of feasting on my vegetables were over. It never returned, nor did it re-join the hinds. We had ended that unnatural practice. I also had the answer to an old suspicion – Moobli was certainly no coward.

I do not claim to have been infallible in my approach. I felt I had done a great deal for the deer around Wildernesse, and I was not having any of them destroy my own food supply. It was that stag or me. I rewarded Moobli with some tasty venison, thinking he would be tired for the rest of the day. Far from it; in the afternoon he wanted to trek, so we zigzagged up and down the steep wooded cliffs to the east. We found a woodpigeon that had been killed by a wildcat, near the spot where a wildcat had killed the rare barn owl two years earlier. Moobli even sniffed out one of its scats, bigger than Liane's but smaller than Sylvesturr's. I wondered idly if it was a tom, and if it would one day come for Liane.

Some days later Moobli twice ran to the study from the kitchen, whining. Anxious to finish a long slog at my typewriter, I told him to shut up: I would let him out later, after I had first gone to investigate. I finished the last sentence, then wandered into the kitchen.

The entire 14-foot square concrete floor was under an inch of water! The carpet and Moobli's bed were soaked through. My frozen-up water system had begun to thaw a little earlier, and I had run a pipe from the slow-dripping tap into a ten gallon container. Unfortunately, while I was working, the thaw had become complete, and for half an hour the pipe had filled the container and then flooded the kitchen. I manhandled the sodden carpet and his bed outside to dry in the sun, and then scooped 15 bucketfuls of water up with a dustpan before the room could dry out. I should have taken more notice of Moobli, who clearly had understood what was happening.

After I had dragged the remains of the drowned stag above the west wood, hoping to attract a buzzard or an eagle, I was woken one morning by the harsh 'kar' calls of hooded crows and the croaks of ravens. They had found the carcass. Suddenly there was a loud squawking, a few 'krock' calls, then silence. When it was light I took Moobli up to check. Next to the carcass, the flesh of which had been pecked, lay some wing and tail feathers of a raven. Something had killed it and borne the body away. Could the predator have been a wildcat? Liane had made a new bed in the bracken which I had stuffed behind the den to keep it warm, and I was curious at seeing the hole she had left at the side, as if she had wanted to be able to look out at all times. There were, however, no raven remains to be seen in or near the pens.

Two nights later she '*mau*'d at the window, wanting to come in. She had been in my arms only a few minutes before she began clawing and peering intently through the window, wanting to go out again. I let her.

Next morning we found that some animal had been chewing neatly at the stag remains. Moobli got a strong scent (not that of a fox, for he did not cock his leg on tufts) and led me 200 yards through the woods to a rocky den below a dwarf birch which old Sylvesturr had once used. It was empty now. Could it have been Sylvesturr's scent he had followed? I decided to make a thorough search, and with the sun shining the following afternoon, Moobli and I set off against a north wind to check all the rocky cairns on the steep slopes to the north west. We searched for hours among the leg-breaking rock falls. Just as I was about to give up, Moobli led me to an unmistakable wildcat lair – a long dry tunnel under a ten-foot slab – and there, in the brown dust, was one wildcat footprint, four-toed and a full one and a half inches across. Near it were raven feathers, and also those of a missel-thrush, together with a few bones. Without Moobli's expert help I would not have found this proof that old Sylvesturr was still alive. (I tell the full story in *Wildcat Haven*.) I wondered if he might even mate with Liane.

In late February I left ample food and drink for Liane in the woodshed and took Moobli to London to see my publisher and to do some complicated research in the British Museum on wildcat skins. This time Moobli did not have to sit patiently all the time in the Land Rover in the traffic-filled streets for we took time off to stay with friends in Worthing in Sussex. It was here that I grew up and saw my first glorious Peacock butterfly near the Sussex Downs. My friends were keen nature lovers, and had visited Wildernesse. Together we hiked from Cissbury Ring to Chanctonbury Ring and back, a trek that had seemed enormous when I was a boy at Steyning Grammar School. Now, after Canada and Scotland, it seemed a mere amble, though I had forgotten just how the Weald clay could clag up one's boots! Moobli loved the open Downs, saw his first brown hare and chased after it. I let him run for a bit, but when I saw him gaining on it, I whistled him back. The clay did not seem to slow *him* down much.

Shortly after our return home I had cause to regret Moobli's speed, his power, and his agility in water. It ended tragically, and was largely my fault. I was training him to track wild foxes, and when he showed a keener interest in a scent not far from our west wood, I gave the command –

'Go on!'

Instead of just walking faster along the scent trail, he shot off at speed. To my dismay, a roe doe and a buck which I had not seen grazing below a small sheer ridge were now in flight. Within seconds they were a hundred yards away and I felt sure the fleet roe would soon outdistance the heavy Alsatian. When I saw Moobli was actually gaining, I yelled and whistled him back. Perhaps he did not hear in the keen wind, for he did not stop.

Suddenly the roe buck, which for all its dainty appearance can be extremely aggressive, turned at bay and menaced the oncoming dog with its sharp lowered antlers. The stance had no deterrent effect whatever. Moobli charged in, swiping out with his paws. His right paw hooked into the inside of the buck's right antler and swept the creature right off its feet, as a grizzly would throw a weakened caribou.

The buck gave up all idea of fighting, sprang to its feet and, finding a burst of speed, shot into the wood. As I reached the trees I heard a great splash, then another. I saw the buck swimming out about two hundred yards from the shore, with Moobli after it and easily overhauling it in the water. I hurried through the rough ridgy corner of the wood, heard a loud '*braah!*' and came into the open again to see that Moobli had the buck by the back of the neck. I kept yelling for him to stop, but he seemed totally deaf, twisting the buck's head underwater as if forcibly drowning the animal. The odd thing was that he looked as if he did not *want* to, as if he was being directed by an outside force, as if a deep ancestral instinct from centuries of evolution had taken over from his real personality.

When he saw me coming he left off immediately, and then guiltily swam round the drifting dead buck. I yelled at him to fetch the buck into the shore, which he did. I cursed, but it was no good scolding him, for I had given him the word, thinking he was tracking a fox. Clearly he had thought I wanted him to chase what was ahead, though I had not given him the additional attack order of 'See him off!' – as I had when setting him at the marauding stag. With his blood up in the heat of the moment, he had not realised the difference.

Hell, I thought as I bled the buck and carried it back to the cottage. Poor little roes! They had enough trouble surviving the winter without this. The fact that there was in the area a spare lone buck (which I had photographed across the burn while Moobli watched calmly) did little to alleviate my annoyance. I sat the dog down by the corpse and talked to him firmly. I kept pointing to the inert roe and did all I could to make him realise that he should not have done what he did. He put on his bald, ears–down look and appeared to be sorry. He made up for it next morning by alerting me to a red deer calf that had got its head and front leg stuck in some fencing near the west wood. I set the animal free and watched it trot through the wood and up the slopes, looking this way and that for the hinds.

At the end of March I intensified the eagle treks and took Moobli on a hard 10-miler to check two glens beyond precipitous terrain to the north west. I located three perfect sites with nothing in them. In the west Highlands eagle numbers are limited by the available food rather than a lack of nesting sites. Up there, on a lonely mountainside, I paused for lunch. I ate a tomato sandwich, then pulled out a hard-boiled egg which did not crack when I banged it with my knuckles. Impulsively I reached out and cracked it on Moobli's pate as he sat patiently waiting for a titbit. All he did was blink, put his ears down, and then resume his solemn stare. For some reason this suddenly struck me as wildly funny and tomato and breadcrumbs from my mouth showered over him as I exploded with laughter. I found myself rolling hysterically down the hill, Moobli running after me, his face full of concern. Laughs are not easy to come by alone in the wilds, and when I recovered I threw my arms round his great neck and hugged him.

In April Moobli found a weak, thin stag deer calf of about ten months, lying in a hollow. It was frothing from the nose, which indicated both pneumonia and a severe infestation of nasal botfly grubs. It struggled to its feet, but was barely able to stand.

I knew from experience there was nothing we could do to save it. As we turned away, the calf suddenly staggered down to the loch and began to swim out weakly. I could not let it drown before my eyes. I boated over, caught it round the chest and hauled it aboard. Once ashore I carried it up to a sunny spot, dried it with an old towel and set garden vegetable leaves before it. Moobli was most

Among the autumn bracken on the south-east land spit.

He liked to sleep under the bedclothes!

Moobli enjoyed the snow and, while returning from treks on the high tops, liked to gallop about in it.

He would lie patiently inert while wildcat kitten Liane enjoyed the warmth of his furry body.

In April Moobli found a sick deer calf, over which he mounted tender guard while I went to fetch vegetable leaves for it to eat.

A month later he scared away a fox that was attacking a lamb, in which he took a parental interest after I had nursed her back to health indoors.

After every hot summer trek he loved to plunge into the cool loch, sometimes swimming almost out of sight.

Margot Wallis, a skilled outdoors woman, looked after Moobli when I had to go abroad.

Waiting patiently for his food when we camped out. (Photo: Patrick Thursto

concerned, lying on guard beside it, licking its nose as if trying to make it better. Although it seemed to know we wanted to help and it sniffed the leaves, it was too far gone to eat. In the morning it was dead. I heaved the carcass up into the hills for the eagles. A fox got to it first, at night, as he had done with the roe buck remains, before any eagle could put in an appearance.

A few days later we trekked up a long river valley to the east and saw eleven stags, some of which still retained their antlers. Moobli also nosed out three more dead deer calves, the last of which had three of its feet trapped in the wooden slats of a bridge. Later he scented out the year's final victim – a hind about thirteen years old, judging by her worn and missing teeth. She lay helpless in mud below a fallen silver fir, her neck twisted stiffly upwards as if she wanted to die gazing at the sky. She was a goner, but I moved her to dry ground so that she could at least die with more dignity. That brought the year's tally of dead deer to eight, which was a lot better than the previous year's thirty-two.

13 · It Shouldn't Happen to a Dog

Early one May morning, as I was working at my desk, I saw Moobli behaving oddly on the grass outside. Sitting bolt upright, ears cocked forward, he was staring towards the north edge of the west wood for a few seconds then turning his head to stare in at me. He no longer barked if he wanted to communicate – he just stared. Sooner or later I would feel that gaze, and when my eyes finally met his, he would switch his attention to what it was he wanted me to see, and then back again to me. He was becoming a master of silent telepathic communication.

I pushed back my chair and went outside.

'Show me,' I said. 'Good boy. Show me!'

Off he went into the north-west breeze. We worked our way up through the early fragile bracken spears, the boggy ground dotted with tussocks, then topped a small knoll above the wood. There, all tangled up in a bramble, lay an old ewe at her last gasp. Two thick tendrils were embedded in the wool round her neck, twisted tight by her constant circling to break away. She lay, hardly able to breathe, her nose resting against the stems. All she had to do to get free was to gnaw through them, but her intelligence did not stretch to that. I disentangled her and she wobbled shakily away to graze. That was the fifth sheep so far to owe its life to Moobli's nose: two he had located trapped on ledges in sheer-sided gorges.

On May 8 he improved on this figure. He was running beside

130

the boat for exercise when he first scented, then located, a lamb being attacked by a fox. He arrived just in time to scare the fox away, and I saw it run off into the woods. The fox's teeth had torn a deep hole in the lamb's throat so that the trachea was exposed. The lamb would not survive without treatment. I took it home, Moobli sitting proudly in the prow of the boat after my extravagant praise. I treated her wounds and fed her milk from a feeder bottle. Moobli seemed glad to have her company in the kitchen as she recovered. At first the wildcat Liane seemed scared of the lamb but finally accepted her too.

As the days passed the lamb grew stronger and kept wandering up the north hill to graze. I had to go out, spot her snow-white fleece, and carry her back down again to spend the night in the kitchen. I did not want the fox to have another go at her. Then she disappeared altogether. Oh well, she would probably be all right for just one night. I would make a big search for her in the morning. As it happened, there was no need. While I was still dressing next morning, Moobli reared up outside the window and whined. He led me into the kitchen. Sitting on the spot where her haybed had been was the lamb, calmly chewing the cud. She had obviously ambled past Moobli as he lay on the hall mat, and he had come to fetch me. It all seemed too good to be true. A few days later I had good cause for thinking that.

I was at my desk again when I saw Moobli trot past the window. He is just going to play with Liane, I thought, and carried on with my work. The two had evolved a chasing game in which the wild-cat would saunter cheekily past his dozing form until he spotted her, then scamper off at full speed, so arousing his instinct to give chase. Fast as he was, she could outsprint him in a short run, and she always made for the safety of the woodshed. She would then dance round the shed with her tail fluffed out, emerge from the gap between it and the cottage wall, and cuff him playfully round the muzzle, as if to say, 'You're just not fast enough, old man!'

Twenty minutes later I was conscious of a strange silence. I went out and saw Moobli's tan rear showing over the lip of a ridge above. He must have heard me climbing up, or got my scent on the south wind, for he came sidling down with what looked a sly and guilty leer on his face. On the other side of the ridge, I found the lamb (which I had begun to call Clarrie) lying on her side, head back in an unnatural position, the top and sides of her neck covered with

131

saliva. The almost-healed fox wound had been re-opened slightly, but it was not bleeding. She was breathing with difficulty. Just then Moobli came up beside me, and as I turned to him, his ears went down and again he assumed that guilty look.

In that instant the awful truth struck me. He must have been trying to kill this poor sick lamb, perhaps out of jealousy, for all the attention she had been getting, or perhaps from an upsurge of some deep ancestral instinct. I recalled then how he had drowned the roe buck when there had been no need, even though I had said 'Go on', thinking he was on a fox trail. There was a vicious streak in him after all. In sudden fury, I lashed out with fist and boot, sending him yiping down the hill.

I carried Clarrie down to the cottage and laid her on a rug, just as Moobli also came through the door. Now as he peered at the lamb, and back at me, his look was not one of guilt but more of concern. Only then did it cross my mind that he might not have been trying to kill the lamb, but to bring it back to the cottage! He had many times seen me go up the hill at dusk and carry her down, so that she would not risk another encounter with the fox. If he had really wanted to kill her he could, after all, have severed her head from her body in seconds. Hell! I would never know for sure.

Feeling doubtful and confused, I talked to him, trying to find out by tone of voice and choice of words whether he had tried to kill her or just to help her down. As he moved forward and licked gently at the lamb, I decided to give him the benefit of the doubt. I tried to impress upon him that he should never leave the cottage area or go up the hill without me, or without being told to by me – rules he well knew by now. If he went into the hills thinking he could carry lambs about by the neck, he could get shot. And I could go to jail for dealing summarily with whoever shot him.

By nightfall the contretemps was forgotten and Clarrie soon recovered her strength again.

In the days that followed, Moobli seemed to be trying to prove to me that he did not feel jealous, or wish to hurt the lamb. He often stood quietly beside her as she grazed, and sometimes I found him lying down, with the lamb asleep in the lower curve of his body between his legs. The fact that she showed no fear of him after the incident also impressed upon me that my first surmise had been wrong. I felt guilty that in sudden anger I had broken my vow never to hit the dog hard again. After that, I never did.

More treks followed, on which Moobli helped me to locate a huge new badger sett on the shore line. He also developed a liking for jumping. One morning when he was on the far side of the four-foot high windbreak of logs which I had made for the porch, I slapped the top log and said encouragingly:

'Come on boy. Jump. Over!'

He quickly realised what I wanted, gathered his legs and in one bound cleared the logs. It took only three more attempts before he had it fixed in his mind that the command 'Over!' meant he had to jump whatever I was touching, and he loved to do it.

Later, when I was digging in the vegetable garden, hurling out rocks which seemed to have crept in from the sides, I heard a loud baying shriek. One of the stones had hit Moobli in the eye, when I had thought that he was lying in the cool of the porch. He came running to me, tail between his legs, his left eye closed. Fortunately, the eye itself was not damaged. I bathed it, put on special eye ointment, and as soon as he knew I had not *meant* to do it, he was happy again. He really was the best-tempered dog I had ever known. Even on the few occasions I had hit him in the past, he had never once turned on me – which was just as well, for it would have been like fighting off a tiger. Sometimes if he felt annoyed when I playfully rolled him around on the floor, or fooled about when he did not feel like it, he would suddenly begin chewing his own leg rather than me, a sort of loyal displacement activity.

That summer the book about my experiences in Canada, *Alone in the Wilderness*, received many fine reviews in North America, though it was largely ignored by the British press. Encouraging letters began to arrive from readers, including words of praise from such distinguished American ecologists as Sigurd Olsen and Dr Victor H. Cahalane (author of the definitive *Mammals of North America*) who was director of the New York State Museum. With open invitations from them and from the editor of *International Wildlife* magazine, I made plans for a trip to visit them and friends in my old haunts in Vancouver.

At about this time I received a strange and alarming letter. It said that the village at the head of the loch, a place I had never visited and where I knew no one, required three 30-foot larch trees to build an access bridge for their forthcoming Highland Games, and they wanted to take the trees from the area around my cottage. It did not seem to me a genuine request for it would have been easy to find suitable trees in the Forestry Commission conifer woods which stretched along almost the whole length of the opposite loch shore. It may have been a touch of wilderness paranoia on my part, but I was sure that the letter represented nothing less than harassment by some faction that wanted me out of Wildernesse, now that I had smartened it up, so that it could be used as a profitable stalking and fishing lodge. Besides, I had bought a twenty-year lease on Wildernesse precisely because of its little woods, where the beautiful stand of larches was a major attraction. There were many young birds now flying in these woods, including a family of sparrowhawks, and I did not want them disturbed. I did not want any of my trees taken, nor the attendant racket and noise of their extraction. I resisted the idea from the start and wrote letters of polite explanation. I also telephoned various influential people, and in the end it seemed to be agreed that the trees could come from one of the other lochside woods instead of mine.

On July 25, two days before I was due to leave for Canada, an acquaintance who worked on the nearest farm agreed to boat down the loch at least once a week to feed Liane. He also took Clarrie to join five other orphan lambs on the farm. I thought then that all would be well while I was away.

Imagine my surprise and horror when I heard loud voices next day and a large boat pulled into my shore. It contained four men from the village where the Games were to be held, including the local priest. I grabbed my tape recorder and hurried down to the loch.

'Can I help you, gentlemen?'

There was a pause; then came a gruff announcement.

'We have been authorised by the estate office to take three trees from here.'

There was no politeness, no courteous request, just the bald statement.

The bitter harangue which followed, and which I recorded, is best forgotten. I told them they could get any trees they required from a wood round the sandy spit three miles away, where they could fell them straight into the water. Luckily, no one stepped out of the boat, and they departed with extremely hostile glares.

I was now very worried about the safety of Wildernesse in my

134

absence. When I heard the big boat coming back up the loch three hours later, I dashed out to try and make peace. I shouted across the water, and the man running the engine put his hands over his ears. I then saw that they were towing three pine trees behind them. As I turned away, I was treated to more menacing looks.

Next morning I loaded all my valuable possessions (mainly documents, diaries and photos) into the big boat and left it at the public pier below the farm, where it could be watched. I had left a large supply of food and drink in the woodshed for Liane. In London, where I was staying for a few days in a friend's flat in Regent's Park before taking the trans-Atlantic flight, I quickly engaged an Edinburgh lawyer to write to the Games' organisers and to take care of my legal interests at Wildernesse. I was still so upset about the incident over the trees that I found myself airing my troubles to various friends over the telephone and seeking their advice. I also consumed two bottles of wine.

It was gone midnight when I realised that Moobli had had no exercise that day. I reeled out, climbed the iron fence into the park, which he jumped easily, and gave him a good walk. On returning, I climbed the fence again and casually called 'Over!' before starting to walk across the road.

Suddenly I heard Moobli behind me making a terrible howling noise. He had jumped the fence badly and one sharp paling had penetrated through the right side of his belly. He was hanging by a one-inch strip of skin. I was appalled, and clumsily tried to lift him off. He sank his jaws into my thigh in agony. All I could do was to lift him a little and snap him off, tearing the skin even more. The poor dog limped the few yards back to the flat, trailing the strip of skin and hair. Mercifully the wound was hardly bleeding at all.

It was well past midnight. I made frantic telephone calls and located a vet called Trevor Farrell, who ran a clinic in Acton. He said I could bring Moobli in right away, though if he was not bleeding, or in great pain, it might be better to leave him to rest and bring him in early next morning.

I was grateful for this, for the truth was that I was in no fit state to drive across London to Acton and back. Besides, the Land Rover was behind private locked gates for the night. Moobli just whimpered a little and licked the wound. He howled when I went close or tried to take a look. I made a weak warm solution of water and Dettol and gently tipped it over the wound. Poor Moobli, and it was all my foolish fault. I sat up with him, dozing fitfully in a chair, as he lay panting heavily but making no further sound for the rest of the short night.

I took Moobli into the clinic as soon as it opened next morning. Trevor Farrell swiftly gave the Alsatian an injection in the thigh, but it took several minutes before the powerful heart slowed and the huge dog sank down in my arms. He went out with his eyes open but slightly crossed. We rolled him over a little and the vet lifted his leg. I was horrified to see that the paling had opened a deep gash between belly and the inner thigh, and I actually caught a glimpse of his intestines. I had not realised it had been so bad. How the dog had endured the pain through the hours of even that short night with nothing more than an occasional whimper I did not know. At least I had been right in believing the paling had not pierced any vital organs – the only good aspect of the whole appalling business. Farrell told me that Moobli would be unconscious for five or six hours and he would have to stitch up the whole wound. I could call back later in the morning to see how he was, and probably collect him in the evening.

Unwilling or unable to be alone with my feelings of guilt, I visited my friend, wildlife photographer Geoffrey Kinns, at his home in Kew, and took him out for lunch. Later I phoned the vet, who said the operation had gone very well and I could fetch the dog at 6 o'clock. When I drove back to the clinic, Moobli was still very groggy from the anaesthetic and could not walk. I had to lift him up and carry him like a huge baby bear to the Land Rover, ensuring I did not pull any of the forty stitches. The vet gave me some pain-killing tablets to put in his food and said Moobli was a lovely, docile and intelligent animal. Despite the severity of his wound, he had been easy to handle.

I drove him back to the flat and helped him on to his bed rugs, over which I spread a doubled clean sheet. As the anaesthetic wore off he whimpered; he must have been in great pain. He was very shaken by it all and clearly suffered from shock. He managed to eat some prime steak and to lap up some milk, and before going to bed I left open the front door so that he could go into the flat's private garden if he wished.

Early next morning he was gone. I found him down in the basement, hiding in a dark corner, as a sick wild animal would. I took him for a short walk in the afternoon. He was losing saliva, leaking from his penis, and did not seem able to see beyond a few yards. I was sure that he was going to pull through, but I would have to cancel the trip to North America.

I took Moobli back to Trevor Farrell four times, to check that the wound was healing satisfactorily. Fortunately, there were no major complications, and the final stitches were removed on August 13. He still had to take antibiotics and was not allowed to run, but after a week I was walking him in the park. One evening a large terrier burst out of the long grasses and started barking at him; then two huge Great Danes appeared and looked as if they would back up the terrier. Moobli could not fight with all those stitches in his belly. I am as scared of big aggressive dogs as the next man, yet if one of those Danes had attacked Moobli I would have sailed in with fists and boots flying. I told their owner that if he did not swiftly get his three dogs under control I would prosecute him.

After two weeks of town living, I began to feel out of condition and took to running round the three-mile outer perimeter of Regent's Park, which I managed in twenty-three minutes in mountain boots.

Then, just as I had given up all thought of going abroad, Margot Wallis, and her young son and daughter, who were approaching their teens, came to the rescue. Margot had escaped from East Germany at the age of 19 by hiding on a train. I first met her shortly after her arrival in London, when I had been a gad-about Fleet Street journalist, and after a couple of dates she decided that I was 'just a playboy' and wanted nothing more to do with me. Since then she had gained high qualifications in agriculture, hygiene and catering, and became head chef at a large school in Worthing. Her marriage had ended in divorce. When I appeared in a BBC television programme shortly after moving into Wildernesse, she wrote asking if I remembered her and expressing interest in my new wilderness life. Perhaps rather scoffingly, I told her that if she thought herself fit enough to walk in the extremely rough seven miles from the road where the bus would drop her off, she was welcome to try. One November morning, as I was preparing for a trek, Moobli had barked outside the cottage, and to my surprise, there stood Margot. She had not only walked in but had carried with her some forty pounds of gastronomic delights she had cooked – beef stews, chicken stews and heaven knows what else! She and her children visited Wildernesse several times after that and proved knowledgeable on

137

the Hill. She was an expert amateur botanist and could also climb rock faces better than I! We had all become firm friends. Moobli had already stayed with the family a couple of times on my visits south, and he liked them as much as they liked him.

'Of course you must go on your trip and about your business,' Margot said when she came to dinner and saw Moobli's condition. 'I have just cancelled a holiday anyway, so we will look after him.'

That was that. No one would look after the Alsatian better than efficient, animal-loving Margot. That night I rang my friend at the neighbouring farm who told me that he was boating to Wildernesse twice a week, and that Liane was eating the food he took. The whole place was unmolested and in good shape, he assured me. I felt much better then about going to the States. On August 14 I took Moobli to Margot's home in Worthing, and next morning he did not even come to the door to see me off! His wound was healing well. I drove back to London, left my few valuables in Geoffrey Kinn's home, the Land Rover in the street outside his door, and flew off to Chicago.

The trip was both memorable and exhausting. I bought an old milk truck in Milwaukee, slung in plastic foam for a bed, a spirit cooker and some food, and rattled away. In eight and a half days, often driving for sixteen hours a day, I covered 5,400 miles, the old truck's dual wheels thundering across the broiling deserts of Montana and battling through snow blizzards in the heights of the American Rockies. I visited everyone on my schedule and journeyed up through Seattle and Vancouver to my old log cabin and to meetings with all my old friends. I found Ed Louette, the log craftsman who had helped me to build my cabin, in an old folks' home, his money sequestrated by court order. I battled with the authorities to get him a better deal, then ground my way back through the Canadian Rockies and down to Chicago. There I sold the truck for fifty dollars more than I had paid for it and flew back to Britain on September 12.

From Geoffrey's flat I immediately telephoned Margot. Moobli was now in fine shape, she said, his wound almost completely healed. What a relief that was, for he had been much on my mind during the hectic trip, as also had wildcat Liane.

When I arrived at Margot's house Moobli did not seem to recognise me, but as he came close and got my scent, he gave a little whine and thrust his great head between my legs. There was no leaping about or loud barks of joy, just an affectionate boring-in with his head. He was such a stoic. His wound had healed well, Margot having bathed it daily with a herbal infusion, but it could be felt as a hard line along his stomach. Margot had found some good haunts for butterflies near Findon, and we spent an enjoyable two days hiking round them photographing Red Admirals, Painted Ladies, Tortoiseshells and Commas and Peacocks. Moobli ran up a steep hill chasing his sticks, as of old. Then I drove him home to Wildernesse.

It was wonderful to be back. No trees had been taken, but I learned that little Clarrie had died at the farm, apparently from eating over-rich foods. Looking after her seemed to have been for nothing. Liane was also missing, but after seeing Moobli on his exercise run three days later, or else getting his scent, she returned. She was thin, but glad to see us as she walked about with loud caterwauling cries before leaping into my arms. Though still tame, her wild streak had begun to assert itself, and now she sometimes spent several days away at a time.

All through the autumn I ranged the hills with Moobli on our usual stag treks. He also helped me to track the territorial movements of foxes and badgers, and to find their dens, setts and eating places. Our first stag trek, on October 2, was one of our best so far. We stalked three hind herds over four tough miles, but they had no stags with them and I thought it would be a duff day. Suddenly I noticed a huge whitish heart-shaped rump of a lone deer grazing in a fold in the ground. Then I saw the tips of antlers moving, like tree branches blown by the wind. It was the biggest stag I had ever seen, and while it had only ten points it had a huge barrel-like body. The sun was shining perfectly on him, only 40 yards away, and I dared not voice an order for Moobli to lie down and stay for the stag might have heard. Instead, I looked back, and when Moobli's eyes met mine, I just made little downward flicks behind my back with my right hand. To my surprise, Moobli understood what I wanted him to do and lay down, even lowering his head on to his paws. I completed the stalk and got perfect photos. Not until I stood up after the stag had ambled away and called him did Moobli move. After that I could control him on stalks by the hand signals alone.

In late October, Margot visited us for a few days' stalking. In capricious winds, but with the help of Moobli's nose, we followed

139

and photographed an old stag with seven hinds, a young stag with three, another roaring on the skyline, and one chivvying his harem about. A master stag, tired out after its rut, stood for long periods with drooping head. We were about to turn for home when we saw at about 2,000 feet on Guardian mountain a large herd of hinds lying down, and decided on one last stalk. We crawled behind a low flat rock above them and looked round its shady side. At first I thought there were no stags, but then a big beast came into view from below a crest and roared. I took two photos before it became aware that there was something behind our rock and trotted towards us to investigate. All the hinds stood up and he advanced even further. He looked old and fierce; two 'dewlaps', like those of a large blood-hound, hung from each side of his neck. I took two more pictures, then ran out of film. He seemed really angry and came on, giving short blatting roars, while Moobli whined behind us, ready to have a go if I gave the order. We stood up and flapped our camouflage jackets, and the stag finally turned and ran off towards the hinds. They turned with him and all vanished over the brow ahead.

On the next supply trip I found that Margot had sent a large soft brown-paper parcel, on which she had written 'Not to be opened until November 3'. I spent the rest of that day with a coal chisel and hammer, transforming a 44-gallon diesel drum into a cottage heater, having learned how to do so from an old Indian friend in Canada. I cut a rectangular hole in one end, in which to put logs, then hung the cut metal back on a zinc sheet. After fitting a curved asbestos pipe into a circular hole at the other end, I laid the barrel on its side over rocks and shoved the pipe up the chimney piece in my study. With just a few smouldering logs this free heater kept the study warm for hours, and was just what we needed during the extremely cold and snowy winter that was to come.

Moobli disliked the noise of my hammering and stayed outside for most of the day. In the evening, as instructed, I opened Margot's parcel. It contained a lovely thick bed, which she had painstakingly made from woollen remnants, and a card that read –

'Happy birthday, Moobli!'

Good heavens, it was Moobli's fourth birthday and I had forgotten all about it! He loved his new bed, and whenever we travelled away after that the bed had to come with us. I gave him a little 'party' that night, fed him choice fresh meat and made a big fuss of him. Even Liane came through the window to join in, though she seemed to have forgotten that she was a boxer.

A few days later a team from BBC Television Scotland arrived to make a short film about my way of life and the wildcats. I boated them over in rough storms, which gave them a real insight into what our sort of life could be like. They said that the best sequences were those with Liane and Moobli in shot! I did not see the film, for although I had intended to ask Dave Sturrock to allow me to watch it on his set, ferocious great waves smashed on the shore all day and I could not get out. When we finally crashed up the loch five days later, I was delighted to be approached by three local men in the village who said how much they had liked the programme. One declared it had been the best thing on television for months, another thought I had said some beautiful and relevant things about the Highlands and its rare wildlife. A man who knew of the incident with the trees told me that if ever I heard criticism from any local quarter I should ignore it, for many of them were behind me and my work. As I had always believed myself to be regarded locally as something of a crank, I went home in a rare buoyant mood.

After winching the boat out of the stormy water, however, I found that the gale had smashed down my little windmill generator. It took half a day to patch it up again. There was no end to the labour of merely surviving in this wilderness.

14 · Mark of Intelligence

On a supply trip in January Moobli helped me to extricate the Land Rover from a snowdrift. I had parked it on a snow-covered grassy path just off the road while I went to check some cliffs for eagle eyries. When I got back and started it up, one of the rear wheels dug itself in and began to spin. Four-wheel drive did nothing to move the vehicle. I wedged the accelerator open just enough to keep the wheels turning when I was not in the driver's seat, got out and started to push. I could just about move it a fraction before it sank back into its slushy ruts, and needed some extra help. Seizing one of his thick sticks, I held it out to Moobli and urged him to grab one end and pull – a game we often played. He could pull like a little bulldozer, and with him jerk-heaving the stick, which I held in my right hand, while I pushed the vehicle with my left shoulder, we just managed to get it free. I then had to leap in fast, put the gears into neutral and unwedge the accelerator before the Land Rover took off at speed down the road by itself.

All through late winter and early spring we made many wildlife treks on which we often saw the eagles, especially the huge female I called Atalanta and her eaglet, which was always on its own now. Through Moobli's scenting help I tracked one fox in and out of snow for nearly a mile to its den. I also learned more lore about foxes and badgers; that foxes would make small screw-twists when digging down for beetles, worms, grubs or pupae, and that

142

they would cache old bones of dead deer in rock clefts, probably intending to eat the marrow later. Moobli located badger trails from the 500 ft high sett that led to a new one which had been made below a rock slab 125 yards to the south east. There were large and fairly small prints mixed up in the trails and the latrine pits outside the new sett contained smaller droppings than those outside the higher main old one, which now had new 'white grass' bedding hauled into the tunnels. It seemed that some time in the winter the older badgers had taken their cubs to the new sett and helped to excavate it for them while they were preparing for a new family in the old sett.

Over the next few days I found two deer and one sheep carcass from which a great deal of meat had been taken, overnight in each case. The skins had been neatly flensed off and rolled back, the ribs chewed right down, and the spines severed. This looked typically the work of a large species of cat. At the time I was having correspondence with people in Caithness and Sutherland where it was believed a cougar or European lynx was running wild, for several sheep had been found with their skins neatly flensed off. From my cougar experiences in Canada, I was working out on maps of sightings and kill positions where, if true, the animal might strike next. I deduced that it would probably be in the Forsinard area. I was agreeably surprised when I later received a letter that the next kill had indeed been found not far from where I had predicted. Unfortunately, no snipers or live traps had been posted to protect the sheep flocks in the area, as I had recommended. I wondered if someone had released a cougar or lynx in the hills near us!

It was Moobli who solved the mystery, at least as far as the carcasses in our area were concerned. We went up to the nearest, finding it had been almost completely consumed. He scented around and twenty-five yards uphill found rows of shallow dung pits that could only have been dug by badgers, all filled with loose oily-black droppings. This indicated the meals had contained little but raw meat. Moobli then set off on a scent trail, and I was surprised when he led me to the old badger sett at 500 feet half a mile away. Around it were new deep latrine pits, all filled with the same loose droppings. (In an interesting experiment at the Highland Wildlife Park, Kingussie, Dr Raymond Hewson and Dr H. H. Kolb fed sheep carcasses to both foxes and badgers and found that badgers bit through the spine and ribs, and also pulled off the fleeces without tearing off a great deal of wool, which the foxes certainly had done.) With their powerful forefeet, badgers would find it easy to pull and roll back the skins to get at the meat with their teeth. I also found that a pair working together could drag even a hind carcass many yards by constant pulling at skin, meat and bones.

I devoted one sunny day to chain-sawing up two large old dead larches which had fallen across the secondary burn in the east wood, and carrying back the 'bolts' and bigger branches to the woodshed. It was hard and heavy work, and I wished I had a helper. Then, as I dropped one load into the shed and came out again, I was astonished to hear loud puffings as Moobli came into sight carrying in his teeth a branch four feet long and four inches thick. He was having difficulty negotiating it round tall rocks and between bushes, but he quickly learned that if he turned his head sideways he could do so more easily, despite the strain it put on his neck. I found his action, his obvious desire to help, most endearing.

'Good boy!' I said. 'Help with the firewood. Fetch the firewood!'

After that the command, 'Help with the firewood!' always had him working like a Trojan. He was proud to be part of the action instead of just sitting nearby and watching me work, which was boring for him. At times he carried in a fifth as much firewood as I did.

I had always believed it best to train, or rather educate a dog while it was still very young, but it was now clear that Moobli was at his most intelligent in early maturity, and also still malleable. One evening in March, with nothing to do while our food cooked, I thought I would see how quickly he could learn something new. After only four commands, with appropriate hand taps on it beside me, I had him 'Up on the Table' and sitting down, and shaking hands there. It took ten minutes for him to understand 'Fetch the tin!', which involved him going to the pile of dog food tins by the workshop door, scraping one out with his paws, picking it up in his teeth and bringing it to me. After a while I even got him to hold it up for me to take, rather than dropping it on the floor at my feet.

In the study he quickly learned 'Fetch the cloth', which enabled me to stay at my desk if I wanted to mop up spilled tea or dust its surface. By concentrating mentally myself on the object I wanted him to bring and by saying a sharp 'Na!' if he picked up the wrong

The Wildernesse woods and the first 4-mile reach of our journey down the 18-mile loch.

Wildernesse in its bluebell splendour.

Moobli was playing. The fox was not.

Gentle Moobli could not take the vixen's attacks seriously, dodging them with ease.

Moobli would bury legs of dead deer and then locate them by scent days later. As I made the egg count on the gulls' islet I heard a snorting sound. Moobli had swum over, and was glowering down like a bear.

The owl showed no fear of Moobli, even when he sniffed up close.

Fully mature at five years old, he was now at his most intelligent. He fetched tools for me, and even worked out how to balance a sledge hammer and bring it to me in his teeth. He would carry heavy logs back to the woodshed without being asked.

item, I later taught him to fetch his green food bowl, white water bowl, or his own towel, so that I could dry him. After the first few attempts, none of these commands were ever again forgotten. When I was cutting firewood, or driving in fence posts outside, I taught him to bring the axe, and even the heavy sledgehammer, though it took him a while to work out that these did not balance like a stick but had to be picked up close to their heavy metal heads. He would also carry plastic oil containers behind me when I took the chain saw into the woods.

Between early March and mid-May, Liane came into oestrus no less than three times and rubbed herself over grass tufts, rolled on the ground and made loud churring growls, as if in frustration. Sometimes I saw her by Moobli on half bent legs, tail up and her backside quivering sideways as if she was trying to 'stand' for him. The big dog stood there, mouth open in a soppy grin, thoroughly enjoying her sudden matiness but probably without any idea of what was causing it. Twice she disappeared, the second time for a worrying four days. Whether she had been seeing Sylvesturr in the long wood down the loch I did not know, but we found no traces of the old tom in our woods after April 6, and she did not become pregnant. Indeed we never saw sign of him again anywhere.

This year provided the busiest summer season I had ever known. After many weary treks I knew of twenty-six eagle eyries, six of which were occupied by chicks. One of these Moobli helped me to locate. Reaching it involved a tough return hike, climbing up and down a total of 12,000 feet, that culminated in a high buttress on the other side of which lay the cliff face where I thought an eyrie might be found. I was too frightened to stand at the edge and look over the dizzying sheer drop, and eventually decided to go round and down so as to come at it from a different direction. Just then, Moobli got a strong scent, fearlessly approached the edge and peered over. I did not want to be beaten by a dog! Steeling myself, and with one foot braced well back, I leaned out over the cliff. There was the nest, containing a ptarmigan, two headless rabbits, and a well-fledged eaglet! Clearly Moobli had smelled the carrion in the nest. Here was the first of Atalanta's chicks I had ever found in one of her eyries, and I made sure Moobli had a tasty reward on our return home.

145

This eyrie was really too far away to work on a regular basis, especially without a helper, so that year I put my hide near a breeding eyrie on a high inland cliff to the west. Even so, quite apart from the boat trips, I had to drive and hike further than last season. The hide also had to be set up on a far more precarious ledge than last year's, but that was not the only reason for Moobli enduring six nights in the Land Rover as I completed my longer watches. At home I was also looking after the first of four young vixens, all of which had been caught by the foot in illegal gin traps, and could not leave the dog alone with her there.

I called this young fox Aspen, and during the process of taming her I let her run about outside on a long lead attached to a collar. She was a lovely chubby little creature with lustrous dark auburn fur and a white tip to her tail. Naturally, I had to be sure that Moobli accepted her. After keeping her for a few days in the kitchen, I took her into the study on her lead, and then brought in Moobli too.

'Good boy. Don't hurt!'

Good as gold, he sat down and then went forward gently to sniff her. She glared at him and made a weak spit, snapping her jaws. Moobli just whined, a hurt look in his eyes, and withdrew his head. I brought her into the study again the next evening, and after she had finished trying to dig up the carpet with her forepaws, I re-introduced Moobli, who this time lay down. Furtively she approached him and sniffed the whole length of his body. It was then she seemed to decide he was not just a big fox but a *dog*, and all her wild predator instincts emerged. She tried to attack him, barked at his head and attempted to nip his feet and jaws. Moobli swiftly withdrew his feet and dodged her easily, his mouth open in a grin as if he was enjoying the little fracas. Sure now that he would not harm her, I began to leave her outside on her long lead so that she could play and run about with more freedom.

Whereas Moobli soon accepted Aspen, Liane did not. One morning I saw her come round the cottage and launch a brief attack on the vixen, bowling her over. We dashed out, Moobli first, and scared the wildcat back to the woodshed. Luckily the vixen was quite unhurt. After that Aspen seemed to think Moobli had protected her for she often went up to him and let him lick her. They began playing games together, with Moobli running up and down as she snapped at him, boxing her gently with his paws and easily dodging her playful bites. He wagged his tail and cocked his head at her with a cheerful quizzical look during these games, as if he was happy to have her to play with as well as boring old me. Sometimes he let her climb all over him.

Unfortunately this all ended when Aspen escaped with her lead and collar still attached. For two days I had awful visions of her starving to death somewhere, her lead caught up in bushes. Moobli seemed quite unable to track her. On the third day, however, I was relieved when he found both collar and line empty, snagged up among pine tree roots in the west wood. He then tracked her to a rocky den which my first brood of wildcats had used three years before. I set meat and the live trap out for her. She must have taken some of the food but did not enter the trap. Extraordinary though it may sound, I was able to keep track of her over the months and indeed years that followed, and discovered that Aspen became the mate of a big fox that I saw many times near the cottage and had several litters by him in the wild. But that is another story, which I told in full in my book *Out of the Wild*.

It was after seeing Moobli's tolerance of Aspen that I took on three other vixens, all with quite different characters. The smallest was scared of me but quickly accepted Moobli; she would run to him for protection whenever I went out. The middle-sized vixen was scared of us both, always running to the end of her line when we went near. The big sandy-coloured vixen would allow me to pick her up without protest and I could stroke and cuddle her at will, but she hated Moobli right from the start! If he ever nosed close to her with friendly interest, she would arch her back like a cat, making '*kek*' spits, or a deep '*urm*' sound at the back of her throat. Even when he was just walking by, she would launch herself straight at him, trying to bite his muzzle or feet.

This would not do, and a proper order had to be established between them. On July 3 I decided to let them work it out. I was sure Moobli would not hurt a much smaller dog-like animal, especially a female, despite the vixen constantly throwing herself at him and snapping at his head. His tolerance was amazing. He fended her off with his paws, dodged her with reflexes a boxer would envy. He pushed her away with shoulder bunts, so that she just bounced off him, or momentarily pinned her down with a giant paw. Not once did he try to retaliate or bite, yet one powerful chop of his jaws would have ended her life. The vixen's courage and stamina were astonishing; she refused to give up or to accept him as 'boss dog'. In the end I had to order him away before she dropped from exhaustion or a heart attack.

While I spent a night in the eagle hide on July 5, I kept the largest and the smallest vixens (the most friendly towards each other) in the kitchen, and put the third in the old wildcat pens. When I returned next evening, all the foxes were fine but the kitchen was smelly from fox droppings. I opened the window, which was extremely stiff, just an inch and set its latch. Next morning the housebound pair had escaped. The stronger vixen must have lifted the heavy brass catch and forced the window open. I was sure I would never see either again, but here Moobli really came into his own. Outside, he found scent below the window and set off to track them.

He ran zigzagging through the east wood, over the burn at its narrowest part and into the six feet high bracken that covered most of the four acres around the next bay. I could hardly get through it at speed, but I could see by the way it was shifting ahead of me that Moobli was on a good trail. I came out on the far side near a huge tangled cairn of large mossy boulders, and saw by the waving bracken that Moobli was working his way towards me. The next thing I knew was the smaller vixen tearing out of the bracken and past me a mere two yards away. I made a dive at her but missed, and she shot into a low hole under the rocks. Moobli tracked her out of the bracken, passed the hole, but turned back immediately, scenting her down there and whining with excitement. How marvellous he was now, on a none too fresh scent. I stuffed up the other holes with rocks, and then went back to the cottage for the old box-cage live trap. I set it as cunningly as I knew how near the burn. It was hopeless to think of attempting to track the larger long-legged vixen, who was probably a mile away by now.

Next day Moobli tracked the old scent back to the hole, over which was now stretched a cobweb. He then tracked back through the bracken, crossed the burn lower down and showed me that one or both foxes had been all over the east wood during the night. The trap, however, was untouched. I carried it further down in the wood and re-set it. I put a heavier collar on the remaining vixen in the pens and made a new lead out of old boat rope. I certainly did not want to lose her now that the others had gone. I went early next day to check the trap, which was again empty; even the bits of 'tempter' meat near it had not been taken. Moobli crossed the burn and went up the high twenty-foot bank into the bracken. I whistled, sure he was wasting his time, but decided to make one more brief search. The cobweb was still over the hole; the foxes must be miles away by now, I thought.

Just then I saw the tops of the bracken moving not far away. Moobli was there, but he seemed to be turning round and round, looking at something. As I hurried over, he darted forward and I saw that he was holding the smaller vixen by the scruff of the neck! He had tracked her down after a long scenting search, and what was more, had caught her. He let go as I came up, and she tried to run off, but he bowled her over with a big paw. She snapped at him, but he held her there, up against the bracken stalks. I grabbed her thick brush, lifted her up as she snapped again and gripped her by the back of the neck. And that was that.

I put my other hand under her backside for support and carried her home in victory. Good old Moobli! I made a fuss of him and gave him a small treat of milk, raw mince and a few chocolate drops. The errant fox gobbled down food too before I put her out with the vixen in the pens on their collars and ropes. Within minutes the two were playing as if neither had ever been away.

I was repairing and varnishing my long oars in bright sunshine the next afternoon when Moobli whined for me to throw his sticks. I slung one into the east wood, and off he went. I ambled away to take a look at Liane, who had just caught a vole near the woodshed, and was bringing it round to the front of the house. Moobli was nowhere to be seen. I whistled, then heard the pounding of his feet and a faint thrashing noise coming from the east wood. By golly, he's got something there, I thought. I cantered over ponderously. He was in high bracken near the burn, thrashing to and fro, as he had when he caught the small vixen. Heavens, had he now caught the other? I went close, and there was the larger fox making '*Urm*' growls and '*Kek*' spits in the bracken as Moobli held her at bay. How could I catch her? Her hatred and fear of Moobli made her far more fierce than the little fox had been. She still had on her collar. Hoping that Moobli would not bite me, I made a quick grab for it and hauled the vixen up, gripping her round the neck before she could bite, and carried her back home. She was thin and obviously had found little to eat in her four days away. I put a sheep's heart and two slices of bread and dripping in the pens, and the big fox ate it all avidly once Moobli was back indoors.

What an incredible performance Moobli had put up. To scent

149

out, round up and catch two foxes like that, when they had been away two and four days respectively, seemed quite extraordinary. And he had done it all without hurting them. A dog has to be very fast on its feet to catch a fox in the open and hold it at bay, and despite his great size, he was certainly that.

'Son,' I said. 'We are together until death, mine or yours.'

The adventures with the foxes continued, and it would be nice to report that they ended up running free about the place, without collars and as tame as little dogs. Alas, as I wrote in *Out of the Wild*, it did not turn out that way. The biggest fox escaped from the pens and returned nine days later, thin and injured by wild foxes. I tended the wound, but it must have been worse than I thought for she died of blood poisoning two days later.

In mid-August I hurried down to London to have my eagle films developed and to do biological library research for a future book, and again stayed in the Regent's Park flat, which had a large balcony. I made a portable pen and took the two remaining foxes with me. I left a huge supply of food in the shed for Liane, although she was now catching much of her own prey. One evening, when I was running with Moobli, a police Alsatian came out of the shadows, and attacked him. A short and frightening fight ensued, which mountain-muscled Moobli won, and the attacker ran back to his owner. I expected trouble then, but all the police handler did was tell off his own dog! On our last day in London one of the foxes slipped her collar and escaped into the wilds of Regent's Park. The last fox bit through her lead and escaped into the woods beside Loch Lomond on the way home – and that was the end of the fox project fiasco.

A far worse shock awaited our return home: Liane was missing. Moobli and I made many weary searches but we did not find her, and I never saw her again. After being with us for more than two and a quarter years, her absence was most depressing. While racing after Moobli on one of these searches, I turned my right foot sideways on a tussock with great impact. The pain was excruciating, and the ligaments were so badly torn I could not move the boat for more than a week. Even after hospital treatment I had to hobble on a stick for several weeks.

On the way back from the hospital I collected a tawny owl which had been found injured in the road by local people. With several children in the family to care for, they could not look after the owl any longer and thought I should keep him until he was strong enough to be released.

The owl was squat and chunky, and I called him Wallie. Although his right eye had been damaged by a car, it was healing well, and I soon had him installed on a perch in the kitchen. To my surprise Wallie showed no fear at all of Moobli and just gazed down at him from his perch with a calm contemplative air. When he flew round the kitchen, however, Moobli did not like the sound of his beating wings and stole away to flump down on his day-time bed in the hall. Sometimes, when the dog was eating, Wallie flew down to the upended pine block I used for chopping Moobli's meat and watched him gulping down the food with goggle-eyed stares from his huge dark eyes. Moobli seem disconcerted by such attention and gingerly sniffed up close to the owl.

Wallie would sit for hours on my shoulder while I was typing at my desk, snuggling up close for warmth and nibbling gently at my ear in a most affectionate way.

Returning from a trip abroad in Spain, during which time Moobli and Wallie had enjoyed the company of Margot in Worthing, I received the most astonishing demonstration of the Alsatian's intelligence. I launched the boat over the pine roots and tied it with just one knot, then went back to the Land Rover for the gear to load into it. While I was stacking items by the vehicle the wind began to blow hard from the north. I went back down to the boat and found that the rope had come undone. The boat was twenty yards offshore and drifting away with Wallie in it. In that late autumn weather I had no wish to strip and swim for it. I yelled to Moobli –

'Fetch the boat! Go on. Fetch the boat!'

He knew the word 'fetch' and what 'boat' meant, and plunged straight into the water. At first he just circled round it, but finally worked out the meaning of my frantic shouts and signals. He kept swimming up to the boat and kicking it forward with his front feet as he did so, until I could plunge in up to where my left trouser leg joined the right and grab it.

After his stay in town, Moobli showed signs of weakness in his left rear leg, though it improved with exercise on the hills, and he was soon back to his old fit self. On his runs along the loch shore, he would stop if ewes were in his path and wait until they moved uphill before continuing his run below them.

In late March two large rams entered the garden from the unfenced side of the west wood and insisted on guzzling down the shoots of wild primroses, wood sorrel, wood anemone, celandines, and the new shoots of the front pasture grass, which I encouraged by hacking down the bracken for the deer. We tried to drive them out, but they usually went only as far as a high rocky promontory overlooking the burn gorge and there turned at bay. The larger ram showed fight, stamped its feet and drove its horns at Moobli, who dodged them easily. He did not like the rams on his territory any more than I did, and bared his teeth. Not wanting either the ram or the dog to be knocked over the precipice, I called him off. The rams took little notice of our attempts to herd them out and just sauntered back to eat the plant species I was studying once we were back indoors.

By the tenth day they were confident that we could do them no harm, and the big ram not only stood its ground but charged Moobli, who knew he was not allowed to approach sheep and ran off. I got mad then and ordered him in. He looked at me in disbelief before running hesitantly towards the ram, which was bigger than him. Twice the ram butted him with its great horns and sent him sprawling. Moobli got up, a spark of battle coming into his eye. He woofed on a high perplexed note and went in again, quickly working out the ram's battle style. Seizing the thick woolly back of its neck in his teeth, he gave repeated tugs and soon had it off its feet. The ram shot up and lunged, but Moobli dodged and again seized its neck after jumping right on top of it and holding on with all four legs. Again the ram went down, and I knew that if this went on any longer it would lose its life. I called Moobli off, grabbed the woolly beast by its great twisted horn, shook it and told it to push off! After that the rams left and did not return.

So much for the theory that a big ram could knock a dog about and so cure it of any tendency to chase sheep, as I had been assured by the farmer when Moobli was a pup. Moobli had been so well trained that this incident gave him no ideas that afterwards he could go near sheep whenever he wished. I had *ordered* him in on this occasion, and that was as far as it went.

15 · *Down from the Heights*

All through early spring we tramped the hills checking eagle eyries. We had to negotiate many hard snow sheets before reaching Atalanta's furthest eyrie, which was not being used. We were at 2,000 feet on the sunless northern slopes of Guardian mountain when I lost my footing and slid towards a precipice on my backside. Only frantic kicking and digging in with my heels stopped my descent. I marvelled at the way in which Moobli managed his great hairy hulk across these slides. The rough pads on his huge feet found friction on the rough icy surfaces in a way that no human footwear could without crampons.

On June 9 I started working eagles intensively from a hide on a sea cliff. Of the three occupied eyries I knew that season, it was the best for photography. I gave Moobli a three mile run beside the boat, and another two miles behind the truck, so that he would be content to sleep in the Land Rover while I spent the night in the hide. When I got back to him next afternoon, he had heard me coming and was standing on his bed in the Land Rover, gazing out with a grin, his tail wagging. How patient he was, and he had made no mess in over 25 hours. I let him out for a short run as I drove home. He did not stop even to urinate for half a mile. Old iron tanks!

I gave him similar runs before and after my next five overnight visits to the hide. Never did he show the slightest resentment of the runs or the long patient waits. When my bush hat blew off into a muddy creek below a bridge, away he went to retrieve it. Without his loyal stoic companionship I felt that I would not be able to tolerate this isolated life much longer, certainly not the arduous treks, for of course he always came with me when I went to check other eyries in the 300 square miles I included in my eagle study area.

One day I took him with me to check the eyrie on the high inland cliff at 1,200 feet which I had observed the previous year. My right knee had been giving me some pain due, I was told, to osteoarthritis, and the weak ankle had also produced ominous twinges. With my left foot braced back I put the right as close as I dared to the sheer drop, looked over and saw that the eyrie was black, empty and unused. As I turned back, my right foot slipped. I threw myself to the left as it slid over the cliff and just managed to grab tussocks with both hands to arrest what would have been a fatal fall. Both my legs were over the cliff and I could find no foothold to give me leverage necessary to push up, and the tussocks were not firm enough to allow me to use any great force to haul myself up by arms alone. Moobli was standing close, looking down at me, as though not fully appreciating my plight. Terror made me icy calm.

'Moobli!' I gasped. 'Come here. Pull!'

I lifted my right elbow slightly.

'Pull!' he understood at once, and came forward to grab my thick camouflage jacket at the elbow with his teeth. He heaved so hard with his powerful legs and clamped jaws that I hardly needed to use my own arm muscles to haul myself back over the lip. It was probably the second time he had saved my life. I might have managed it on my own, then again I might not. As I lay beside him for a few moments, tears sprang to my eyes for love of the dog as much as for relief at my escape.

After a hard trek on June 23, to check our highest eyrie at 1,600 feet, Moobli located a new badger sett. It was 200 feet above one I already knew, which was empty. Without his nose I would have presumed the badgers gone. That afternoon the big Alsatian, treading carefully, sniffed about above a rainpool and then stopped still with his nose down. I parted the long grasses and there in a deep grass cup were four whitish eggs with thick brown speckles – the nest of a skylark, rare in my area.

Four days later I spent the worst night I had ever endured in an eagle hide. Rain swished down, the sleeping bag became a sodden lump and rivulets of icy water ran on to my face and into my ears through tiny holes in the thin sheet of plastic which I tried to hold over me. Although I took fine shots of the adults flying to and from the nest next morning, I had failed in the dark and the cold to fix a new film on to the spool correctly and it did not go through the camera. All I got for the miseries of that awful night was a misty picture of the eaglet and its mother standing forlornly like scrawny vultures in the rain. My knees cracked and ached under the weight of two heavy packs on the long descent out, but how glad I was again of Moobli's enthusiastic greeting when I reached the Land Rover.

As he ran along the loch shore on our way home I saw him swerve and then pause to sniff at something white. I pulled the boat in to see what he had found. It was a dead fulmar, a most unusual discovery. These strange birds have tubular nostrils and can eject foul smelling liquid from their beaks at intruders to their nests. Fulmars are normally birds of the open sea which seldom go to land except to breed, yet this one had died on the shores of a fresh-water loch nine miles from the sea. Its body measured 1ft 6ins long and the wing span 3ft 8ins. I noticed that its wings were nowhere wider than 4¾ ins, and their main outer halves were slim and sharp like a falcon's, yet the fulmar is one of the world's great soarers and gliders. This bird was also very thin: maybe it had been migrating between west and east coast and had died of starvation. I sent it for analysis to the government laboratory at East Craigs, Edinburgh. Dr A. D. Ruthven replied that the bird was in poor condition, its liver was very pale in colour and its stomach contained only a few beetle cases. While liver tissue showed higher residues of DDE, PCB and mercury than were found in many seabirds, they should not in themselves have caused the fulmar's death.

After that sleepless and miserably wet night on the eagle ledge I had hardly the strength left with which to haul the boat beyond the reach of the rising loch. On the slope up to the cottage my knees hurt even more, and I found myself walking with a stoop under the packs, moving like an arthritic old man. To soothe the pains in the pelvic region and lower back, I put a pan of water on the stove for a primitive swab down. I longed for the luxury of electricity and a wallow in a good hot bath!

Two days later I took Moobli on the longest unplanned trek we had ever made. We set off to check Atalanta's farthest eyrie, and were poised at 1,600 feet above the first of two deep glens still to be negotiated, when I noticed Moobli, who had been faithfully

155

following behind, was no longer with me. Damn him! Had he gone off on a deer trail? He had not disobeyed like this for a long time. A little further on I spotted a big wild dog fox taking a nap in a dark peat hag. I made two careful belly stalks, and took photos of it sleeping. I eventually got to within thirty yards of it, and was just setting the camera on a rock for a really close picture when it leaped to its feet in alarm and shot away. Moobli had come back, tracking me down by scent, and was standing on the close skyline.

The far eagle eyrie had been built up slightly but was not in use. I wondered whether Atalanta had another somewhere in that deep yawning glen, and took Moobli westwards for a further two miles of steep tortuous terrain until we were nearly at the summit of a 2,700 foot mountain. But there were no new eyries. We turned south, down to the glen bottom, searching unsuccessfully the faces of the steep 2,000 foot 'wall' on the way back. By the time we reached home we had covered 16 miles and about 15,000 feet of ups and downs. My right knee had begun to hurt again, though not badly. Moobli seemed all in, and flumped down on his bed with a groan. He had limped slightly on his rear left leg over the last mile, yet his paw showed no sign of a thorn or any other injury.

I paid another visit to the hide on July 3, then took it easy for a few rainy days, cutting from a dead pine and digging in new garden fence posts and hacking back the bracken that still invaded the front pasture.

On July 11 I took Moobli round Eagle Rock mountain for a last look at the four eyries I knew there. On this trek he more than made up for his lapse on the fox stalk. I had just finished photographing a young cuckoo at close range, which was being fed by four meadow pipits, when he nosed out the carcass of a red deer calf that had fallen into a deep runnel. I would not have found it alone, nor have realised that such runnels (caused by water flowing underground) could be such a treacherous cause of death in a calf's first few hours of life.

Coming back over some high peat bogs, the wind behind us, I came upon a well-defined animal trail, indented among the grasses. It led on to some hard brown peat where no tracks showed. I walked over it, in and out of a few short but deep hags, and picked up the trail again in the thick grasses on the other side. I was sure it had been made by foxes, though it seemed a dangerously clear trail for them to leave. Suddenly, as I came to a flat area, a light sandy-coloured

156

fox got up and ran off. After a few yards, it stopped and looked
back. The camera was in the pack! I could see it was a cub, though
almost fully grown, and it soon confirmed by sight that it had seen
a man and a dog, and shot away again. After spending months with
our four young vixens, surely Moobli would not hurt or kill a fox?
I wondered if he could catch up to it and hold it at bay, so that I
could take a picture.

I gave the command, 'Go on! Track the foxy!'

Moobli shot away, his great weight floundering slightly in the
peat bogs before he vanished. Tired as I was, I tried to run after
them, hampered by the pack and keeping my right foot twisted
outwards so as to avoid cracking the ankle again. In a few seconds
Moobli re-appeared, scenting the air, then dashed away again
downhill. I was caught in the maze of peat hags and had to jump
from turfy islet to islet. By the time I reached the lip of firm ground
ahead there was no sign of the fox, or of Moobli. High *'rowl'* fox
barks floated up from somewhere below and to the left. I climbed
two little knolls, but still could not see either animal. Lower still I
was stopped by some dwarf trees growing on cliffs. I heard the fox
barks again, and there they were – Moobli had the fox at bay among
some heather about half a mile down the hill.

Before I could put the long lens on the camera I saw Moobli
dart forward, haul the fox out, and then start to carry it by the
neck up through the cluttered scrub of birch and rowan between
us. As I worked my way down the side of the cliffs I lost sight of
them and gave encouraging whistles. I then caught another glimpse
of Moobli, still carrying the fox by the back of the neck. He was
actually retrieving it. Because of the trees, it was not possible to get
a picture. As I came into the open I heard two more *'rowl'* barks.
Moobli's panting breath came from behind some boulders, and as
I rounded them I saw the fox legging it down the hill two hundred
yards away, as fast as it could run. Either it had managed to escape
or, hearing my urgent whistles, Moobli had let it go, thinking he
ought to obey them and get back to me. Of course, I did not scold
him for letting the fox go. I should not have whistled. Instead, I
praised him for what had been a marvellous performance.

There was now no sign of the limp in his rear leg after his hard
chase. Maybe he had just sprained it on the earlier rugged trek. It
was easy enough to do on that steep, rocky, tussocky ground.

In late July I set off up the steep hill to the north east to photo-

157

graph red deer calves with their mothers. We were only half a mile
from home when he scented something and wanted to hurry on.
I hissed him back and then saw, less than a quarter-mile ahead, two
young foxes slinking along. After careful stalking I managed to get
good pictures of one of the full grown cubs lying on a bank and
catching grasshoppers with its paws cupped like a cat's. A little
later we caught a glimpse of the big dog fox, which was clearly
running with the cubs.

We carried on, hoping to see the foxes again, and Moobli soon
got their scent and hurried off on the trail as I stumbled after him
through bracken which disguised the trunks of fallen trees. It was
impossible to move fast in such rough and almost sheer rocky
terrain. After a quarter of a mile Moobli headed back to me, having
lost the scent. I was sure the foxes must have doubled back down and
then run downwind so that they were harder for him to follow.

We laboured up to the peak at nearly 1,800 feet and I spied the
surrounding hills with the binoculars. There was not a deer to be
seen. Oh well, I had the fox photos and was feeling pleased with
myself, for I had taken nine good pictures of foxes in the wild that
year, the most ever.

We struck back down through the lochside woods to the shore.
Halfway home, I climbed the slopes to the 500-foot level, hoping to
run across the foxes we had seen earlier. And sure enough, we did.
I managed to keep up with Moobli for about three hundred yards
through the manacles of bracken that often hid bramble leaders
which tore my hands when I grabbed at the foliage to prevent a
stumble. Moobli went down to the left, on to an open tussocky
path of dark green flowing grasses, where he got a strong whiff
and pranced before running over a small ridge out of sight. He
was on the scent all right. I clambered to the edge of the ridge and
looked over. Nothing moved anywhere; it was as if the ground had
swallowed him up.

After a long silence I struck down diagonally, hoping to leave
my scent on the wind so that Moobli could follow it back home.
He had not returned after an hour, which was most unusual at his
age. I began to have awful visions – the big heavy dog might have
jumped a crevasse, or a cliff, and broken a leg, or even his neck, or
back. The place felt suddenly lonely. I had lived the lone wilderness
life for over thirteen years: if he was dead, I would not stay here
alone much longer. I left the camera pack in the cottage and wearily

set off in the drizzle back up the wooded hill to try to find him.

I had covered half a mile of the steep terrain when I heard a snuffling noise behind me. Moobli must have returned to the cottage, found I was not there, and tracked me down along my fresh scent. He came up with an odd and anxious expression on his face, as if he wanted to tell me something. He scraped at my trousers with his paw.

'Good boy. Go on!'

He led me towards the shore, then stopped on a ridge just above a tangle of big boulders over which lay an uprooted birch tree. He wagged his bushy tail, panting with that tongue-lolling smile of his, as he looked to a hole below the rocks and then back to me. There was a great deal of scraped-out earth before the hole, and even from three yards away I caught the pungent ammonia scent of the foxes that were down there. Because I did not want to drive them out on to land where they might be hunted by the local hound pack, I refrained from setting the camera nearby to take pictures.

It was in mid-July that I lost the maturing owl, Wallie. Though I had become extremely fond of him, my intention had always been to train him to hunt and to release him in his natural habitat. It worried me that he did not hoot until a few days before the fishing line on which I allowed him training flights outdoors snapped and he took off into an ash tree by the loch shore. Despite his exceptional tameness, he did not return, though I sometimes saw him in the wild.

The owl which now occupied the kitchen perch had an altogether more prickly disposition, and for that reason I called her Holly. She had been shot through the left wing and found in a London park. The RSPCA hospital in Putney, which had asked if I would give her a home, instructed me to remove the plastic splint from her wing after a week or so. The wing was slow to mend, and when a little pus began to show under the splint, it had to come off. As she was much tamer than when she had first arrived, I took her out into the sun and set her on Wallie's hazel bow perch, where she let me snip off the splint without any trouble.

Holly did not seem able to fly well, so I left her on the perch and went down into the front pasture. When I looked back minutes later I was startled to see her sail on to the bird table, up on to the porch roof, then take advantage of a gust of wind to fly high into a birch tree beside the cottage. An attempt to reach her with my ancient ladder ended when a rung broke off at ten feet and I fell to the ground, fortunately without injury. By dusk she was forty feet up an oak tree. She could not possibly hunt in the wild and look after herself with her weak wing.

Next morning I set out with Moobli on what seemed the hopeless task of finding her, for there had been gales overnight and she was no longer in the oak. As we searched the woods, I was too busy glassing up and down every tree to notice where Moobli was going. After nearly an hour he came running up, whining, as if he wanted me to throw his sticks. He knew the word 'owly' well by now, so I said –

'Track the owly. Go on. Track the owly!'

Off he went again, and this time I watched him. He trotted through the east wood towards the shore, swerving to scramble over the dry rocky bed of the secondary burn, and up into the wood again. There he paused, his nose pointing to a mossy rock near the main burn, his tail wagging slowly. And there, to my surprise and joy, standing on the rock, was the dark form of Holly! I crept close, repeating her name as she regarded me imperturbably with her sloe-black eyes. Afraid that she might fly up into the canopy again, I made a swift grab with both hands and caught her.

Back in the kitchen she grabbed a piece of meat from my hands and ate it ravenously. She had a remarkable facility for changing her shape, elongating her body in sleep and arranging her plumage to look like tree stumps and twigs. She was much noisier and more inquisitive than Wallie had been, and I grew so fond of her that by mid-October I decided to speed up the tethered flights to strengthen her wing so that I could free her before I became too attached to her.

With the stag shooting season coming to an end, Moobli was at his best on some fine rutting treks that we undertook at this time, alerting me to deer I could not see and keeping right behind my moving form like a silent ghostly shadow. In just one afternoon I took pictures of a tired stag roaring while it was lying down, of a stag chasing a hind with its tongue out as it tried to lick her rear, of another running round his harem with loud piston-like thumpings of his feet on the turf, and of yet another, caked in black peat, picking a fight with a smaller beast though neither had hinds with them.

Always when I stalked up to a rock or a ridge, I removed the long lensed camera from the pack and then left the pack for Moobli to sit by. This not only helped him learn to guard an object of mine but gave him a fixed point at which to wait. The trouble was that I might make a dozen or more crawling stalks in an afternoon and have to go back 70 yards each time to retrieve the pack, then carry it forward the same distance before we carried on. That meant covering about a mile more of the rough terrain than was necessary. Why didn't I get Moobli to bring the pack to me after I had taken pictures? It was worth a try.

Having taken one set of photos, I looked back at him.

'Moobli, fetch the ball. Fetch the pack!' I urged him.

He got up and came forward, sniffling the ground for a stick to bring, a puzzled expression crossing his face when he failed to find one.

'Na!' I said, patting the camera and then my back. 'Fetch the pack! The pack!'

As he returned towards the pack, I kept encouraging him every time he went near it, and at last he seemed to get the idea. He grabbed the pack with his teeth and brought it a few steps as I said 'Good boy'. Then, as if feeling guilty at touching this precious object with his teeth, he dropped it and came padding towards me, ears down, tail wagging, wondering what I really wanted. I gave him the command again, said 'Yes. Good boy!' when he sniffed the pack, and then he brought it all the way to me. After two more attempts on later stalks, he never again forgot this command, and he saved me a great deal of extra walking.

When we reached home, a huge flock of nearly 200 migrating red-wings were dashing about everywhere, filling the woods with their cheerful '*chup*' and '*quip*' calls, denuding the rowan trees of their scarlet berries. A female sparrowhawk soared and swerved almost on to her back as she entered the west wood. The trees came to life as the redwings fled, swimming through the sky, their red underwings flashing. Maybe she kept them on the move and, like a lone wolf, was staying with them until she found a suitable territory.

Over the loch a grey skirt of mist drifted in across the forest of conifers. I looked at Moobli and pointed.

'It's *raining*!' I said. To my great surprise, he shook himself.

It was turning into an even wetter autumn than usual. Several times I had to rescue the boats from the rapidly rising level of the loch, and many of my best photos were acquiring a ruinous damp bloom under the glass of their mounts. Gloomy days of torrential rain and hail followed each other, but I got down to work again on the most ambitious book I had ever attempted – an evocation of the whole range of Highland wildlife through the seasons, which I had decided to call *A Last Wild Place*.

When I took Moobli up through the steep wooded terrain to the east to stalk young stags during a brief interval in the downpour on October 28 he was much less sure-footed than usual. The ground was very wet and slippery and I had to cling to the grasses and small rowans and ash saplings to prevent myself from slithering over some giddying cliff edges, one of which fell away sheer for 900 feet. Even the dog kept slipping backwards, and once he almost fell. At times he looked unusually anxious, as if he could not understand his sudden weakness. Surely he was not growing old at the age of six? Then it occurred to me that already he would be past his prime and entering middle age, and yet had never had (bar one unfortunate brief encounter) any opportunity to fulfil his natural instincts with a female of his kind; he had never mated.

I decided to write to Molly Thomson, the Sussex breeder, to ask if she could find him a suitable bitch. A few days later Moobli slipped on wet grass while I was throwing sticks for him and fell heavily on to his rear with two loud yipes of pain. When he got up, he ran with a limp, which eventually wore off with more exercise. Molly Thomson was glad to have news of him. In her letter she said that she had read my wildcat book and that he certainly looked happy with his animal friends in its photographs – 'but I do not know anyone who would use him at stud as his ear carriage is not good, and this would be hereditary. I have found out where it came from in my breeding and have had a campaign on to eliminate it, and have really improved the breeding a lot since.'

There followed three weeks of heavily overcast and drizzly days, so that it was like living in a dark tunnel, the area round the cottage a quagmire. I worked steadily at my new book and took Moobli for short exercise treks in the few brief periods of finer weather. His rear legs improved and remained quite normal.

In late December, I attempted to leave on a journey south to help sort out my father's affairs but found that we were besieged in Wildernesse by the appalling weather. After carrying everything down to the lochside, the wind and rain increased. I tied it all down under plastic tarpaulins, hoping for a lull. With darkness descending by 3p.m., the gales were even worse and were now accompanied by thunder and lightning. I carried everything back to the cottage – six trips down and six trips up again with heavy loads. I tried once more next day, but the storms were now up to Force 10; it was impossible to negotiate the seething loch with the old small boat fully laden. At 52, I could no longer hold the bigger heavy boat against such driving waves while loading it up, not to mention launching it far enough out from the shore to get the engine going before it smashed back against the rocks. I finally made it out the next day, having consumed the last slice of bread in the house, but the engine broke down and I had to pole the last four miles with a tree branch. For the first time I seriously considered abandoning the wilderness life.

16 · Adrift Between Earth and Paradise

Moobli moved well enough on our many treks during the winter and early spring. He tracked a fox so truly for two miles that we caught up with it and saw it being mobbed by hooded crows. I took him with me at night to photograph badgers at the 500-foot sett. The big boar badger dug a dung pit, performed in it, rooted for worms, and behaved as if the camera flashes were just natural lightning. Even when the boar twice worked his way towards us, and Moobli, alert and up on all fours, could clearly see and scent it, he showed great restraint. Not until the badger shot out of the far hole and galloped downhill over the tussocks did he give a deep barking '*wough*', but it did not matter then. He was a great help in guiding me back to the cottage in the pitch dark.

Then suddenly, on March 19, when chasing up the steep north hill after sticks, he began to run oddly again. His rear legs seemed stiff and he held them close together, at times almost losing his balance. At supper, I usually held his bowl out straight and he would leap up to pull my arm towards the floor with his forepaws: that evening he could not jump up far enough to hook his claws on to my arm, and his back legs sank beneath him. There was a very small cut on his left rear foot, which I dressed. It was not enough to handicap him seriously. I had heard that big dogs, such as Alsatians, were prone to suffer from hip dysplasia, but surely that could not be the cause after all the hard exercise he had had? On a supply trip next day I let him run only half a mile and, while he was slower than usual, he seemed to move without difficulty.

He was not able to retrieve his sticks normally on the following morning, constantly over-running before picking them up. Again he could not reach my arm at night when I held out his bowl, and once more his legs sank beneath him. Seriously worried now about Moobli's legs, I wrote to Trevor Farrell, the fine London vet who had treated Moobli after he had injured himself on the park paling three years previously, saying that I wanted to bring him in for an examination when I came south to see my new publisher the following week.

The big dog's legs appeared to recover before then, and on April 6 he could again reach my arm with his paws. Three days later I took him on a six-mile eagle trek and he travelled well enough, though his legs looked oddly weak to me. I myself did not move as fast as usual either, for the pains in my knees had returned. Indeed we were both, it seemed, turning into old crocks.

After three sedentary days in London, during which he was either on the bed in the Land Rover or in the hotel room, I took Moobli up to his usual place on Hampstead Heath for some mild exercise. It would not do him any good to have no exercise at all. I have always felt this way about myself too, and a few months earlier had started a weight training programme to try to increase the strength in my arms and back. Hauling the boat and carrying the big engine were both getting more taxing with every passing month. I also wanted to build up strength in my legs so that I could still carry packs up the Hill, which also seemed to be getting steeper! Gradually I worked up to pressing a bar-bell of 130lbs and using dumb-bells weighing 24lbs (not onerous weights) and was surprised to find that, even at 53, I could put on good new muscle. Unless there was something seriously wrong with Moobli's legs, it made sense to keep him strong too.

As always, he was eager to chase the sticks when we reached the Heath. I threw them down the short hill, but saw that he sometimes skidded on his backside when he chased after them. His rear left leg was dragging slightly as we walked back to the hotel. He was still limping a little when I took him to Dr Farrell's surgery in Acton early on the morning of April 16. He would have

165

to be totally anaesthetised so that a series of X-rays could be taken when he was relaxed. I left him there looking sad but resigned. I was sure he remembered the place from his previous visit. I telephoned during the day and was told all had gone well and I could pick him up again after 5 p.m. I struggled through the rush hour traffic and found Moobli still wobbly from the anaesthetic, falling over at the rear, his eyes doped and dark. I had to lift him on to the bed in the Land Rover.

After consulting the X-ray photos, Trevor Farrell said that Moobli did not have hip dysplasia, but there was an odd deformed growth on the tibia bone of his left rear leg where it joined the femur. This could have been caused by an injury, but was now complicated by arthritis. (I remembered the gash I thought had been caused by an otter years ago: now it seemed possible that Moobli had hit his leg on a sharp rock on that run home instead.) The vet said the growth probably impinged on the joint as Moobli walked and ran, occasionally trapping the tendon and causing him pain. It was not operable. He gave me some pills which would alleviate the condition and help to dissolve the growth. Moobli should have no hard exercise for ten days. When we got back to Scotland, I could try exercising him in slowly increasing amounts, and if the condition became worse I could telephone for more advice, but he thought the dog would adjust to it.

It was when I suggested that there also seemed to be a general weakness in Moobli's whole rear end that Dr Farrell came up with a more dire prognosis. He said that this could be due to spinal nerve degeneration, to which Alsatians were prone. It would take more time for this to show, however.

I rested Moobli for a couple of days but he grew bored, so I took him for a walk up to the Heath, then let him trot behind me as I ran back, a gentle 'run' for a big dog. He still limped a little, but he certainly felt no pain, nor did his foot drag. He was marvellous about taking his tablets. I thought I would have to crunch them up into his food, but once he *knew* I wanted him to take them, all I had to do was hold one out in my fingers and he would take it gently in his front teeth, cheerfully crunching it up and swallowing it. He had plenty of rest in the Land Rover over the next few days while I was completing biological research at London Zoo or having talks with my publisher. One night I went to my publisher's home for dinner and found he also had an old arthritic dog, a Highland terrier called

Montrose (nicknamed Mintrice) who took some delight in bossing placid giant Moobli about. We were discussing arthritis generally when I happened to mention the pain I had felt in my knees on eagle treks. My publisher's son, a qualified doctor, immediately gave me an impromptu examination and announced that I had osteo-arthritis too! He said it was also incurable.

On May 2, our last day south, I took Moobli up to the Heath again and threw his sticks for him. On the walk back he trailed behind and looked hang-dog. When we reached our vehicle I noticed that one of the long middle toes on his left rear foot was bleeding. He had worn two claws down to stumps by dragging them over the town pavements. I rang Trevor Farrell, who said I could either buy him special leather dog-boots or make them myself from leather or canvas. A number of people I had met recently suggested cures for Moobli's arthritis, including pearl garlic tablets and cider vinegar in his food. Dr Farrell laughed but said that any 'old wives' remedy' was always worth trying.

As we boated home I allowed Moobli a very short run along the shore. He had somehow adjusted to lifting his feet a little higher for there was no bleeding when I inspected his toes at Wildernesse.

After a week of gardening and repairing the boat bay, I went to the village to post urgent mail. Moobli had certainly rested, only accompanying me on slow morning walks round the woods, and as he did not limp any more, I gave him a half-mile run to the first bay. To begin with, he ran normally, but then slowed right down When finally he climbed into the boat, he looked like a grey old mole, though still he was not limping. Three days later I took him for a six-mile trek through the lochside woods and found hooded crows and buzzard nests, photographed a roe buck with velvet streaming from its little antlers, and he scented out a new otter holt. This time he moved easily, and even begged me to throw sticks on our return, though his uphill strides were still short. He may have been an old boy but he could still get around a good deal faster than I could. Perhaps the tablets or the pearl garlic were doing him good. (He hated cider vinegar in his food, so I stopped giving him that remedy.)

I took him up to the badger sett on May 13, but the wind veered round behind, blowing our scent before us. Whether it was this that stopped any badger emerging, or the fact that Moobli kept shaking midges out of his great ears, which sounded as loud as the flapping ears of an elephant I was not sure!

167

Through the rest of May and early June, we made the most of a record dry and sunny spell and I took him for many treks. He performed well, limping a little only towards the end of each – as indeed did I from the recurring knee pains. We went right over the big corrie, photographing dippers in the burns, golden plovers, fox tracks in peat hags, and a pregnant hind, to which Moobli alerted me. It moved brokenly, as if on disjointed legs, then flopped down in the shade between two large rocks. When we came to a small high black lochan, Moobli wanted to plunge in to cool off. After checking there were no red-throated divers nesting on it, I allowed him to swim about, huffing loudly and thoroughly enjoying himself.

We hiked through the steep easterly woods on May 25, and Moobli scented a fox cub with a white tip to its tail. It vanished before I could get the camera out. We tried to track it upwards, and were at 500 feet when Moobli sniffed the air again and I heard a faint crashing in the bracken higher up. It turned out to be a small badger, foraging in daylight. Moobli started forward as I gave the command he well knew – 'Don't hurt it' – in the hope that he might be able to turn it so that I could take a picture. I knew he would not hurt it, for foxes and badgers were potential playmates to him. He soon caught up with the badger and romped alongside, but it was scared and snapped at him as it ran into a sett beneath some boulders. Shortly afterwards it came out and took another look at Moobli, who was wagging his tail in a friendly way, before diving back down again. Imagine my surprise a few days later when I discovered that the badger had started coming to our woods regularly at night, digging for worms, grubs and pupae. Maybe it had deduced that we, or rather Moobli, were friendly for we saw it several times at dusk.

Moobli's leg seemed almost as strong as in his prime by June 6. He could even jump up to my arm again and pull it down with his forepaws to get at his supper bowl. He had also finished his spring moult and, with virtually no gap, had started his summer one. It seemed to be a five month process! I noticed an odd bony ridge that had developed along the top of his skull and bony arches over his eyebrows. I wondered if I had fed him too much calcium in his puppy diet.

Five days later we set off to try to find red deer calves high in the hills, and on the way to check the new badger sett. We found it empty, with cobwebs over the holes. I felt sure the badger had moved to a new home nearer the cottage.

As we toiled up the slopes high above the big corrie, a large auburn dog fox, with dark grey moulting patches in its coat, shot up a few yards ahead and loped slowly up the steep hill. To my surprise, Moobli chased after it without my command. I was about to yell when I saw him jerk, as if he had pulled his bad leg. When he set off again he was limping. He had no chance now of catching up the fox, which gave us a disdainful glance before vanishing over the crest. I was angry at Moobli's rare lapse but was too worried about his leg to do more than mildly tell him off.

We found three recently born red deer calves in the next two hours, each lying still in grasses, hoping it could not be seen. I had difficulty restraining Moobli, who wanted to sniff and play about with them. We moved round each one, leaving plenty of scent in the hope that the big fox would not cross our trail and find them. On the way back along the rugged west side of the mountain I found a fourth calf, also lying down. This one was bigger, about four or five days old. I changed lenses, but as I turned round it got up and shot away. Already it could run like the wind. It went down the hill like a springbok, every so often leaping into the air with all four feet hanging down. *Dammit*, Moobli had again gone off without command! But then I realised that with his great weight and his gammy leg he could not hope to catch up.

To my great surprise he did, running and often stumbling down 500 feet until he was level with the calf. I yelled, knowing he would obey. When I got down the almost sheer slope, the calf was quite unhurt as the dog held it down with one foot! Moobli was looking as pleased as punch, with an expression that said – 'There, I have proved yet again I am still a great hunter, and that I never hurt anything I catch!'

I could not find it in my heart to reprimand him. After taking some pictures, I picked up the calf to sex it (it was a hind), and it screeched so loudly I quickly let it go. It ran along the hill and disappeared over a small ridge.

On the last descent of the tussocky steeps Moobli again began to limp slightly. Back home he fell asleep before his supper and did not eat until nearly 9p.m. That extraordinary day was but the prelude to the unexpected events which followed.

Next morning he seemed fine again, and more than made up for his lapse in chasing after the fox. We were heading along the shore edge of the east wood when Moobli made a brief '*huff*' snort

169

and darted forward two paces. As he pointed, a chocolate brown animal with a long tail dashed from a stump and rapidly climbed a thick larch tree. It was a rare pine marten, the first I had seen at Wildernesse. Heart thudding, I took some photos, then instructed Moobli to stay by the trunk to keep the marten up the tree while I rushed home for my longest telephoto lens. After crossing the burn, I took better pictures of the marten staring down at us like a miniature bear. That was the start of many adventures with the marten, and later with his mate and youngsters. In time, they became tame enough to run about the place like little dogs, and would even take food from my fingers at the study window.

Meanwhile, the small badger began coming round the cottage every night, demolishing some of the food I put out for the martens. I noticed that it was weak on its feet and seemed to have wounds on its neck. It turned out to be a female, and I called her Bessie. I bathed her in the kitchen sink, dressed her wounds and looked after her indoors until they healed. (I told the whole story of the martens and the badger in *Out of the Wild*.) Once he knew I was encouraging her, and the martens, Moobli never tried to chase them or to run down their scent trails. He was marvellous with Bessie, and sat and watched, with his great ears forward, as the badger regarded us solemnly, her head resting on the side of her hay-filled den box. Only once did he whine as the badger climbed out in front of us and began to eat from the feast I had laid out. Moobli showed no alarm nor the slightest sign of jealousy, even though he had to sleep on his bed in the hall while the badger was recovering. After she went free, he tracked her to a new sett she had made under some boulders three-quarters of a mile to the north of the cottage.

As if all this was not enough, I had discovered that Atalanta's new and much nearer eyrie contained not one but two chicks, which were well fledged by mid-June. I had never observed eagles at a nest containing twin chicks before. When I heard that there were others who knew of the nest, I was determined that it would be watched closely. I applied for the necessary licences and hiked up to the 1,200 foot site with Moobli on June 22 and plucked long heather to obscure my hide. He showed no sign of his limp and he bounded along the loch shore afterwards, full of beans.

It was then that I noticed a line of what looked like very large rounded bags stacked up on the forestry track on the opposite shore. What were they? Waste of some kind, to be dumped in the loch?

I boated over, climbed the cliff, and found they were just bags of phosphate fertiliser which a helicopter would soon be drifting over the compartments of conifers. As I climbed back down to the boat I was startled by a rustling, crashing sound in the bushes above the shore. It was Moobli! He had not only trekked to the eyrie face with me and run nearly a mile beside the boat, he had also swum the loch! By rights, he should be tired for days now.

On June 24 I left Moobli in the house and made the strenuous hike to the twin chick eyrie with the new hide, which I had in place in record time, after making sure there were no eagles in the sky. Minutes after slipping into it, I saw Atalanta as she swept over the hide with a great rush of wings and into the eyrie to feed the chicks. This was the incredible start of the most profound experiences watching eagles at the nest that I had ever enjoyed.

I made in all six treks to and from the hide, including one body-wracking stay of 37 hours, while Moobli endured these long vigils alone in the cottage. I would find the old trooper calmly and glumly looking out at me through the window when I returned, for like any other good dog he knew I was coming long before he heard my footsteps. As the eaglets took their first flights on July 5, I felt uplifted, as though I had been specially privileged to witness every secret enlightenment Highland wildlife had to offer. When finally I carried down the hide, wet and heavy, I felt no twinges in my knee. I had become really fit again.

Moobli came with me to locate the two flown eaglets and to ensure that they were still being fed by their parents. In case they were not, I took with me a traffic-killed rabbit in my camera pack. I climbed up the almost sheer hill west of the eyrie on July 9 and found that Moobli could not follow; he had to make a curving shallower traverse to the west before he could join me. He could now run well along the shore, but his legs were not strong enough for a climb that once meant nothing to him. We found the male eaglet back in the nest. The search for the larger female proved more difficult. Hearing squeaks from below a ridge half a mile away, we began to descend and rounded a small bluff. Immediately Moobli got an odd scent and looked up to the right, an amazed expression on his face. I followed his gaze and there, perched on a grassy ledge, only a few yards away, was the female eaglet. She watched us calmly, without a trace of fear, as if we were familiar objects. So close were we that I had to walk away a short distance to focus her in the camera. Moobli did not bark at the sight of the huge bird. I left the rabbit on the grass.

Through the rest of the summer and the autumn we went on many treks, and often saw all four eagles. On the day of the autumn equinox we were at over 2,000 feet on Guardian mountain, the sun blazing, gales roaring in our ears as I photographed several herds of hinds and calves, their red-brown coats lit up like flames. Moobli loved the height, the vast perspectives, the wind exciting him, and as he stood high, braced, with panting lolling tongue, the wind blew rosettes in his hair. What a wonderful tracker and friend he had been over the years. The long crowns of mollinia were waving in fluid motion in the wind. It looked as if herds of little animals whose heads we could not see were racing through them, fleeing pell mell, hurling themselves along in heedless flight. There is a wild poetry in this wild running of the grass.

We had a hard walk back against the blasting air and Moobli again began to limp. Although he often moved normally, sometimes he seemed to have periods of reversion, and would begin to hobble before reaching home. There was no question of my making him stay at home all the time, though occasionally I told him it was for his own good. It was better for his legs to have exercise, providing he *wanted* it.

I spent a few fine days painting the iron roof, though I was less agile when scrambling about on it in gym shoes with a paintpot and brush than I used to be. Moobli had very little exercise at this time and I noticed on November 5 that he would sometimes hop along, keeping his rear feet together. When I ran round the front pasture, making him chase me, his legs would loosen up again and function properly.

The hail and rain-filled gales seemed worse than usual at the end of the year. Having run out of meat for Moobli and other essentials, I decided to brave the loch on December 30. It was the worst trip of my life. I could hardly kick the bucking, heavy boat out against the crashing waves, but luckily the engine fired before it turned broadside and smashed up on to the rocks. Crashing up and down in a wild frenzy, soaked by spray, we endured an hour and a half on the churning water in order to reach the Land Rover in the pine wood.

172

To make matters worse, the Unilever fish farm, which had been set up as an experiment earlier in the year, now had so many tanks in my anchorage bay that I could not head in *with* the waves, sling out the bow anchor in a trough and then drift in before pulling the boat back out to the anchor. I approached broadside to avoid the tanks and immediately shipped water over the gunwhale. The boat had to be bailed out as it tossed about before we could get in at all. The irregular bangings up and down on the trip had unnerved Moobli, who was shivering when finally we got ashore.

It was worse on our return. In the near darkness I could not see clearly, and the oncoming waves filled the stern before I could haul the boat out on to a runway, never mind the easily winched up trolley. I stood in the boat as it heaved up and down, frantically baling out with a bucket the pounding waters which immediately filled it up again. I had just got the upper hand, and was hauling it out a bit further so that I could lock the winchwire to the bow, when I felt a jagged convulsive pain across my chest, as if an iron hand had tightened on my heart. For a few seconds I could not breathe, then I felt oddly dizzy. There was no let-up in the fiendish battering elements as I thought I was about to have a heart-attack. I felt very frightened, and moved more slowly after that, but managed to get the boat out of harm's way.

Once indoors my emotions turned to anger. I could just die like this before I had got my work done! Why was it all so damned difficult, battling with the loch, wrestling with the boats, growing my own vegetables, making my own meals, carrying and chopping logs to keep warm, performing scores of chores which would be quite unnecessary in so-called civilised life, trekking thousands of hard miles to get my work, much of it original, published at all?

On New Year's Eve, gales carrying hail and snow roared across the landscape, gusting up to 90 miles an hour. At midnight I went out into the spruce glade but made no resolutions, felt no great emotion, except a sort of creeping despair. After 14½ years in remote and inhospitable places I thought I had loneliness beaten, but it waits in the dark corners, like damp and cold, to creep into your bones and your soul, and will eventually destroy you or drive you mad. I knew in my heart that I could not sustain this harsh life style much longer in winter.

Next morning I woke after hearing a loud thump, followed by regular dull thuds. The gales had blown the big boat right

off its trolley and it was awash. Filled with water, it was banging
in the waves against the rocks and roots of alder trees that lined the
shore. The loch had risen nearly three feet overnight. Waist deep in
the icy ferment, I reached down to untie the boat from the trolley
which was two feet under water, and struggled to haul it out again.
Its stern was holed at last, and I had to wait several more days until
a brief calm spell enabled me to patch it up again with fibre glass. As
I worked, badly pulling a back muscle, I saw Moobli sitting in his
'proud' position, head well up and regarding me with placid dignity,
his eyes full of love and devotion. I realised I loved him as he loved
me; he was all I had left now, him and my dear old father fretting
his time away in a Worthing Nursing Home. I began to think that I
ought to head south and look after them both in a civilised place, do
my writing in comfort, and just use Wildernesse as a trekking base
in spring, summer and autumn. If many Highland roads had not
been blocked with drifted snow, I might have left there and then.

But the mood passed, for I was now seeing a great deal of
Atalanta's family, and a new female buzzard had come to the area.
One evening at dusk I saw Moobli looking up to the north east and
followed his gaze as he watched a stag across the burn. It seemed
to be thrashing the end of a beech tree branch with its antlers, but
then I saw that it was using the antlers, twisting them sideways, to
haul the branch down so as to eat the tips of the twigs. I had never
seen that before. In the west wood, the small herd of hinds, calves
and yearlings barely bothered to get out of our way, as if knowing
we would not harm them. Moobli appeared to get a fox scent and
I let him pursue it. I lost sight of him in the trees, and then spotted
him running up out of the wood and turning east, a weak yearling
deer in front of him. I was sure that, with his bad leg, he would
not catch it up, and even if he did he would only round it up so
that I could catch it and try to feed it. To my surprise he kept pace
– no trace of a limp now – as the deer turned downhill (a sure sign
of weakness) and they vanished from view. I hurried over as best I
could through the snowy tussocks and found the deer down by the
rear fence, Moobli standing guard over it. I lifted up the yearling (a
young stag) and walked it over to the empty wildcat pens where I
set out hay, green garden vegetable leaves and carrots for it to eat.
The next morning it was dead. I skinned it for a rug, removed its
haunches as meat for Moobli and myself, then hauled the remains
up the hill for the eagles.

A period of torrential rain followed in February. It was like living in a marsh with a constant shower faucet overhead. Then came a two-day snow blizzard. I looked out of the window one morning while working on my book and saw that Moobli looked oddly ill. He was standing with head lowered, holding his left rear leg off the ground. He put the leg down again as I went out to him, and seemed to move normally, though with a slight limp. When I threw his sticks the next day, he fell down several times at the rear while swerving after them.

It occurred to me that if Moobli's leg continued to be bad, or even to get worse, he would no longer need, or be able, to make his old exercise runs along the loch shore. After eight years I too had had enough of the tedious and often extremely dangerous 13-mile return boat trip to fetch supplies. I decided to approach the Forestry Commission and succeeded in getting permission to park the Land Rover on a rough track on the opposite shore in sight of my cottage. The switch was worth every penny of the £23 a year I was charged.

The move took all day. I crossed to the far side of the loch in the big boat and then putted in the small one to the pine wood to collect the Land Rover and drive it the 26 miles to its new position (which I could just see from my study window) before taking the big boat to the pine wood in order to tow the small one home. Yet even with a crossing of less than a mile, which would save a good deal of time, there were still drawbacks to the new place. For one thing, I would have to manhandle supplies, including heavy calor gas canisters, down a steep, tussocky and marshy slope 80 feet to the shore. To reach the nearest village entailed negotiating a 1,200 ft pass, which was sometimes blocked by snow in winter.

The first person to make use of the new crossing was my publisher, Roland Gant, who braved the rough gale on February 26 to bring me the proofs of a book I had written about the three years I lived on the sea island of Shona, just north of the Ardnamurchan peninsula, before finding Wildernesse. How strangely its title, *Between Earth and Paradise*, contrasted with my present mood, I thought as I gazed at the sheets of typesetting that awaited my correction – and there were doubts about the future. I had been asked to set aside *A Last Wild Place* unfinished and instead to attempt a book about eagles, the first draft of which I had just completed without a contract for its publication. I was becoming hard up, and had begun to eke out my meagre earnings with wildlife articles for a Glasgow newspaper.

Tinny hootings and flashing car lights in the dusk had signalled Roland's arrival on the opposite bank and somehow I managed to launch the boat and get across to bring him back to Wildernesse. When our business was finished, I took him on a trek to the twin-chick eyrie, and before long Atalanta's mate swept over and performed some spectacular territorial dives as if for his benefit. Moobli came with us, and seemed to be moving well. Roland thought he could see a definite deterioration since our dinner together the previous spring, a greater weakness in the rear legs. I knew then that soon I should have the Alsatian examined again by a qualified vet.

Meanwhile, Moobli continued to have good and bad days. One morning, when I was power-sawing firewood logs in the east wood, a small branch jammed in the saw and irritably I tore it off and hurled it away over the burn, which was swollen by heavy rain. Moobli must have thought I had thrown it for him to retrieve, for he dashed away and plunged into the torrent, using his strong front legs to fight his way across. I was amazed, for with my two good legs I would not have tackled that rush of deep water. Once he had the branch in his mouth, the stimulus of chasing after it removed, Moobli seemed afraid to re-cross the burn. I encouraged him to walk down the far side to where it widened out into much shallower water. There he crossed easily and dropped the branch at my feet. Foolhardy or not, I admired his bravery. It seemed that while he was concentrating on something which interested him, he could control the weakness, but it reasserted itself in his unconscious moments.

Moobli caught the snowballs I threw at him and crunched them up – a great game for him! Dislodging one of his thrown sticks, he showed the fearsome armoury he never used except at my command. An almost freezing raging torrent in winter did nothing to deter him.

Taking a breather after completing the first third of the killer trek.

Tolerant of all sick wild creatures, he even let the badger take over his kitchen.

On the heights the autumn gales blew rosettes in his hair.

Just before his seventh birthday, he looked perplexed at failing to clear the porch logs.

After four months the developing weakness in his rear legs seemed to disappear when he rounded up a weak deer calf for me to feed.

In March he was still keen to flounder across the burn to retrieve his sticks.

17 · Things Sent to Try Us

A letter arrived out of the blue from the artist Shirley Bellwood. She was a cat and wildlife enthusiast who had seen a photograph of me with the wildcat Liane in my wildcat book and wondered if I would sit for a portrait which she wanted to hang in that year's Royal Portrait Society exhibition. She wanted to include two vignettes of Liane to make it an unusual picture. She had painted many well-known figures and asked me to sit for her in the high, light 'eyrie' studio in her beautiful seventeenth-century house of Tudor origin in Chertsey. The invitation was irresistible, and the opportunity presented itself when I arranged to drive south late in March to sign the eagle book contract and take Moobli for another visit to the vet, Trevor Farrell.

Shirley was a tall and striking Yorkshire woman of my own age with an unsuccessful marriage behind her. We soon found that we had many views in common, and she put me completely at ease while she made her preliminary sketches. I took her out to dinner on that first evening and camped overnight near Chertsey Green. Next day she completed a portrait in coloured chalk, and both that and the more elaborate drawing were accepted for exhibition. I little knew then that she was to become a close friend and play such a central part in Moobli's future.

When I took the Alsatian to the Acton surgery, Trevor Farrell watched him walk and try to run. After examining him, he turned

177

to me and spoke the words that I had been dreading.

'It *is* spinal nerve degeneration,' he said. 'The messages are not coming through from the brain properly, and his co-ordination at the rear is going. It's this as well as the problems caused by the tibia growth. I could put him on a course of injections or tablets but, frankly, there is nothing one can do. He may have another year. Once he starts soiling himself, loses control of his urination, you will probably have to put him down.'

I found my eyes beginning to fill and hurriedly took the dog out and put him into the Land Rover. Hell, what a nightmare, I thought. In my distress I had not paid the bill and went back. There would be no charge, I was told.

Geoffrey Kinns did his best to lift me out of my state of gloom and, with our cameras, we took Moobli for a gentle stroll round Kew Gardens. I was amazed by the plethora of wildlife on the waters there – mallards, moorhens, coots, long-tailed ducks, shovellers, golden-eyes, mandarins, black swans, Canada geese and even a snow goose. I reflected on how much easier it all was than trying to photograph the wary divers, or anything at all, on the far less tranquil and emptier waters of our home loch.

I stayed the last weekend with my father in Worthing, taking him to meet friends and for drives in the Sussex countryside. He wanted to put his money with mine and buy a house in the area, where I could look after him and Moobli too. His fees at the Home had shot up and his capital was dwindling at an alarming rate. I began to think that this might be the best solution; it seemed ironic that my love of nature had begun in Sussex at the age of ten and looked like ending there. I told my father I wanted to complete one more season in the Highlands and would make a final decision before the end of the year.

All this time I exercised Moobli gently to keep up the strength in his legs, but he chased after sticks half-heartedly, as if he knew that he would not get better. I bought him some special leather boots from a pet shop and drove him back to Scotland in a despond-ent frame of mind.

After boating across the loch, I found that someone had broken into the cottage. Tinned food and milk were taken and a rear win-dow left open. A £1 note was left with a scrawled message: 'Sorry, but our provisions ran out one day ago.' It showed all too well how vulnerable my isolated home was whenever I left it.

For a short while Moobli's happiness at being back on his home ground seemed to give his legs a new lease of life. We trekked up to eyries 27 and 28 on April 5, but neither were being used, even though Moobli scented out several dead deer, one of which had died on a bed of primroses within half a square mile of the nest sites. Enough winter food for an army of carrion eaters.

A week later he came with me on a short high trek to the north east, where we saw a pair of kestrels mobbing and diving on the female eaglet, emitting high pitched '*vee vee vee*' screams as they did so. We rested a while at 1,000 feet and saw the female kestrel land on her nest on a ledge in a sheer rock face. Moobli climbed poorly that day, struggling over small obstacles he could once leap with ease.

To add to worry about the dog and uncertainty as to my own future, I detected a distinct air of hostility locally when I boated out on supply trips. Here and there my usual greetings were met with little more than grunts. I still patronised a small shop at the end of the loch, a long way past a village nearer to my new parking spot, because the young couple who ran it were having a difficult time making ends meet, and on three occasions there I found my Land Rover hemmed in by local cars and farm vehicles. The drivers stood about inside, chatting while they ordered single items like a bottle of lemonade or a bar of chocolate. I was told that the fish farm at my old boat anchorage was expanding to twenty-four tanks, as if to say, 'don't come back'. A man who had recently published a map of good fishing places on the loch, a map which ended at Wildernesse and indicated there was an excellent beat for salmon trolling up and down outside my cottage, explained that it had been compiled from information left by a well-known fisherman and printed as a tribute to him. The fisherman had been dead for many years. On return journeys (never on outward ones) men with sheep burst out of the woods in front of the Land Rover, as if deliberately holding up my progress. Was I beginning to suffer from paranoia, or a persecution complex, on top of everything else?

When I was asked for contributions to a new local community magazine, I said that I could not cope with any more regular writing commitments as I had just started the weekly column for a Scottish Sunday newspaper. I explained that I was barely making a living from writing books, and offered instead six of my books as prizes for the best nature essays sent in by local schoolchildren for the magazine. This was described in such a way as to make it appear that I had foisted the books on the editor, as if I were trying to barge into the venture from outside.

It was impossible to avoid reading ominous signs and portents into other curious things that occurred at this time. For two weeks a small band of unmarked sheep persistently broke into the garden, chewing up my front pasture and the newly sprouting wild flowers. I herded them out as best I could without much help from Moobli, who was hampered by his bad leg. I also began, suddenly and repeatedly, to be woken at dawn by ravens flying about, passing my window and landing in trees on the shore and in the east wood, croaking loudly. I recalled Gavin Maxwell's fear of ravens, how he had called his last book *Raven, Seek Thy Brother*, which (according to legend) one is supposed to say to offset the evil that the sight of these birds in early morning is said to foretell. It seemed too great a coincidence when the next issue of the local magazine carried an item about the legends surrounding ravens, one of which was that if you saw a raven before breakfast it meant someone in the family was going to die! I held no fear of ravens myself; to me they had always been among the great clowns of nature. Indeed, I had often been able to imitate their croaks and to call them out of the sky so that they flew close over our heads. All these incidents could more easily have been coincidence than malice, but I could not get the latter possibility out of my mind. I was bothered enough to wonder if some local faction wanted me out of Wildernesse, now that I had improved the place – whether for commercial or some other vindictive reasons I could not guess.

When I next met the local police constable, whom I knew quite well, I mentioned the incidents to him but stressed that I was not making an official complaint. He agreed it was all very odd and said he would make discreet enquiries. He assured me that some prominent local folk he knew respected my work, liked my new newspaper column, and thought I was doing a lot of good for the Highlands in general. This cheered me up considerably, but I was still on edge, and what with Moobli's leg troubles, they did little to enhance my general mood. I decided to keep cool and attempt to find out what lay behind it all, then act. I also increased my weight training programme.

Shortly after that my Shona book was published, and it attracted many good reviews. I was also asked to take part in a number of interviews for newspapers and on radio and television. Whether there was a connection or not, to this day I do not know, but the strange incidents ceased then as suddenly as they had started.

Moobli had begun at times to set down his rear left leg in front of his right, so that when he walked forward his right foot tripped over it. I examined his legs but could find nothing outwardly wrong, and there were no crackings in the joints. It had to be what the vet had said, a slow degeneration in the spinal nervous system. He lay down for long periods, head on the grass, his brows furrowed, as if trying to understand what was happening. On April 19 I took him for a short two-mile trek through the steep eastern woods, looking for owl, buzzard and sparrowhawk nests. I climbed one long steep gully to inspect a promising tree covered with ivy, Moobli could not manage to follow. He tried all ways,and almost fell off one short precipice. All the power in his rear legs had gone. He looked unhappy too, as if he knew that he was almost finished. I went back down and took him home on a lower easier route.

After a restful week gardening and polishing my eagle book, I set out to take another look at Atalanta's nearest eyries. I was about to insist that Moobli should stay behind when he climbed into the boat before me. If he *wanted* to go on a trek, it seemed better to let him try than to leave him lying down all day, so that his legs atrophied faster. Although we covered twelve hard miles, and he limped at times, he went quite well and was eager to see and scent ahead. He nosed out a sheep with a broken back wedged between some rocks, her rear legs splayed out behind her. I thought of ending her misery, but as she was not my ewe, I carried her 200 yards to a long fertile patch where she began hauling herself along on her front legs alone, cropping away madly at the grass. The eyries were not being used. I arrived home suffering in my new boots more than Moobli, for he had not dragged his foot at all.

On our next two supply trips I put him off for short quarter-mile 'runs', but he just walked, even so covering the distance faster than a man could! There was a sore on one toe of his bad foot where it had been dragged over rocks. It would soon be time to make him wear the special leather boots I had bought for him. I had tied them on once before but within minutes he had ripped them off with his teeth.

He still wanted to chase his sticks, but by mid-May I had to be careful how and where I threw them. A hedge sparrow had made a nest in the brambles in front of the cottage and was sitting on seven bright blue eggs. The nest was made almost entirely of Moobli's moulted hairs.

It was on my birthday a week later that I realised Moobli's trekking days were coming to an end. Margot was visiting us for a few days and we set off for the nearest eyries, and to look for possible new ones. Again Moobli insisted on coming. He kept up well on the first half of the trek, and we saw Atalanta. On the way back Moobli nosed out the paralysed ewe, now just a skeleton, a full mile and a half from where we had left her.

It was just below the twin-chick eyrie that Moobli's left rear leg suddenly collapsed completely. He hopped along on the right for a quarter of a mile, but then that leg gave way too and he was reduced to towing his hindquarters along by the power of his front legs alone. We still had over a mile to go to reach the boat, and fortunately it was nearly all downhill.

He panted, his tongue out, but did not whine, nor attempt to give up. We helped him over the beds of two rocky burns and when he got stuck between deep tussocks. I tried to carry him for a while but he was too heavy and soon yelped, perhaps with pain due to the awkward way in which I had to hold him, or because it compressed his breathing. I put him down and he struggled on gamely, all the way down to the shore. We then lifted him into the boat. His trekking days seemed finished. Two days later I took Margot on the hard trek to check the eagles' farthest eyrie. Moobli was back on his feet but still wobbly at the rear, and for the first time I had to make him stay behind. He looked very sad as I held his paw and tried to explain before we set off.

For a week after Margot left I worked in the garden, painted the cottage, took Moobli for gentle walks round the woods, and wrote articles for my new column, aiming for a stockpile of six. June 7 was a gorgeous sunny day. I shoved the typewriter aside and decided to go on a trek. Moobli's legs seemed well recovered once more, and he was anxious not to be left behind again. If he conked out on the Hill, he could always wait for me to return along the same route. We headed through the long eastern woods, checked a couple of badger setts (which were empty) and came to the wide river valley more than two miles from the cottage. I took a picture of a whinchat perched on the upper twigs of a bog myrtle bush, singing its ringing fractured song, then started to head up the western slopes above the river. After a further quarter-mile I sat on a rock and glassed the great jagged peaks at the end of the valley.

Suddenly, high above them, Atalanta came into view, sailing along like a great flying board. I watched her for ten minutes, my arms aching as she made hunting circles, glided to new areas and circled again. Finally she went into a fast glide down into her nesting glen which lay at the end of the long 'killer trek'. I was now almost sure she had an eyrie this year on the south side of it which I had yet to find.

I decided to head up above that glen, to about 2,000 feet, and keep watch in the hope that she or her mate would fly into the eyrie and so show me where it was. It would save me, and certainly Moobli, who could no longer handle the almost sheer rocky mountain wall, a great deal of work. I swayed about on the steep ground, heart pounding. When I stopped for a rest I began to wish I had not left home. I then picked my way from the jagged rocky bed of the burn up into an area of tussocks where my head came level with a small deer calf lying in the grasses. I did not touch it. There was no hind in sight, nor had I seen any all that day. Moobli came up, anxious to sniff at the calf. It looked at us trustingly with its large long-lashed eyes, then turned away.

As we headed higher, zigzagging to the south so that we could traverse the almost sheer ground at the top of the glen, I saw a hind lying in a contorted position on her front with one rear leg stuck out oddly to the side. There was blood coming from her vaginal area, which looked swollen. Was she still alive? I touched her: she was dead but her body was still warm. I turned her over and found that her neck was loose. One open eye was as bright as in life. Then I saw some whitish fluid behind her which looked like afterbirth. She was sure to be the mother of the calf that was lying 25 yards away. This was most unusual, for when giving birth red deer rarely suffer the problems that can afflict domestic sheep. Had she just been able to give a breeched birth?

I called to Moobli, who was not moving as well as he had been. We headed up another 300 feet, with the wind blowing from the valley towards us, and hid under a screening overhang to see if any hind went near the calf. We stayed there for an hour without a hind coming in sight, and then went back to the calf which, I now realised, had only recently been born for its coat was still wet in places. It looked weak and trembled when I touched it. I was sure it had been born to the dead hind. I lifted its rear and saw that it was a stag calf.

I had never taken a young calf from the Hill. I knew that, while they often appear to have been abandoned, the mother always comes back to give milk, even after grazing half a mile away. This would not happen here. I did not want to raise a stag calf for it would grow up without any fear of humans, perhaps become aggressive when mature, and if let loose in the hills would soon be shot because it would not flee from man. I walked 40 yards away to think. Moobli did not want to leave the calf, and began licking it all over as if *he* were its parent. I called him to me, and he came reluctantly.

The calf got up and staggered after him, then collapsed in some tussocks, looking at us with huge eyes, its long velvety ears twitching. I went back and again it struggled to its feet and came towards me, sniffing at my trousers and opening its mouth as if looking for a teat. It could hardly stand and its long graceful legs were quivering. Moobli whined and licked it again. I suddenly thought that the calf might make a good playmate for him, now that his trekking days were virtually over. Oh, dear god, what should I do? One thing was sure – it would die where it was if I left it. We had seen several fox scats in the valley. That settled it. I could always give it to a wildlife park, or even a deer farm, if it became difficult to handle when older. I estimated it to be less than a day old and just hoped that it had been able to get some suck from its mother before she died, though this seemed unlikely. If such a calf has not had any milk from its mother it will not have taken in the colostrum which is in that milk and enables its digestive system to cope with artificial milks fed to it by man. I had no choice but to try and rear it.

I took everything out of my pack and put the calf gently on some grass inside it. Carrying the camera gear in my hands, I set off for home as fast as I could. I had fresh cartons of Ostermilk and glucose in the cottage, and a lamb feeder bottle, and I wanted to get something inside the calf as soon as possible. To save Moobli's legs, and mine, I went round the side of the steep mountain rather than taking the shorter route over the tops, stopping on the last shoulder of the hill because Moobli had fallen behind. I saw him some way off, hobbling over a small ridge. When I had gone another half-mile he was no longer in sight. The calf was making shrill bleats from

time to time. I set it down in the pack and went back for Moobli.
I found him panting hard as he lay in the heat, his rear legs having
given way again completely. I lifted him up, but he could not move,
and sank down again.

'All right, Moobs,' I said, 'take a rest. You know the way, you
have my scent, come when you can. I have to get this calf home
quickly to feed it.'

He seemed to understand and licked my hand. I left him there
and stumbled home, carrying the calf as well as the camera gear. My
knees ached again, but the lethargy of the earlier trek had gone.

I sterilised the feeder bottle with boiling water, mixed the milk
powder and glucose, warmed it up and fed it to the calf. It no
longer came towards me, and it refused to swallow. I carried it
to the more natural surroundings outside, but it walked away and
tried to hide in some bracken. I left it for a while, then lifted it out
and left it standing. As I walked away, the only moving thing in
the landscape, it instinctively followed. Finally it nuzzled round my
legs. I hid the teat just behind my knee. When its mouth found it,
I held its head gently as it sucked strongly until it had imbibed two
thirds of the bottle. Then I carried it back into the kitchen and made
a bed from an old sweater and a deer skin, on to which it sank down
and went to sleep.

Now the problem was Moobli. I went out twice, scanning the
high hills and all the ridges and hollows that I had negotiated so
fast, but there was no sign of him. As dusk began to fall, I realised
he would not make it home tonight, and I felt guilty, for I was just
too tired to go back all that way for him there and then. Anyway,
a summer night on the Hill would not kill him. I would retrace my
steps tomorrow and find him.

Then I thought – My god, what if I don't? What if I miss him
among all those myriad shelves, rock faces and gullies? I can't scent
him as he can me. If his legs do not recover at all, he could die of
starvation up there.

Feeling utterly miserable, I gave the calf a second feed at 9.30
p.m. and prepared something to eat myself, although I did not feel
hungry. Ten minutes later I went out of the kitchen again.

Moobli was there, on his mat in the hall! He moaned and made
crying sounds as I bent down to him, as if he thought I had forsaken
him. He was all in and soaked through. He must somehow have
got down the hill to the water and then swum most of the way

home. Despite his disability, he could still swim well, using only his powerful front legs. Even so, he had several bleeding bare spots on the tops of his toes as a result of dragging his rear end over the rough ground. From now on he would have to wear his boots, whether he liked it or not. I gave him a really good meal and was glad to see that he ate it all. Then I cossetted and cuddled him, explaining that I would only have left him for one night and would have gone back to find him at dawn next day. I am not sure that he believed me, for he still gave the occasional moan, his eyes dark and dull with reproach. I let him spend the night in my bedroom after giving the calf another feed at 11.48 p.m.

Next morning Moobli could stand again and even limp along for a few paces, but his whole rear end kept twisting to the left, and the foot on that leg kept dragging. I put his boots on and told him to leave them alone. After an hour he had pulled them off again. I knew that he could never resume a normal life yet I resolved to keep him going as long as possible. I swore I would never have him put down by a vet in some town surgery. If it ever came to it, I would put him down myself, from love, and with love, with a single shot.

In my boyhood I had worked for years in the fields and woods with a fine old Sussex gamekeeper called Jim Adkins. Jim had owned many gun dogs, but his favourite had been a wonderful golden retriever bitch called Sally. When her time had come, and she was suffering and could no longer walk, Jim took her out and shot her. I had never understood that as a boy. Now I did.

The deer calf was full of life for most of the day, drank lustily and ran between Moobli and myself; sometimes it curled up in the warmth of the Alsatian's body and went to sleep. Moobli loved it, and seemed to forget his bad legs when it sniffed his muzzle, and he often nuzzled it and licked its coat. When it was hungry, the calf emitted shrill 'eep' bleats and ran to me for a feed. It was a sweet and delightful creature, and I was glad we had not just left it to die. Yet it suffered from diarrhoea from the time we found it. Even towards evening its defecations were soft and yellow.

On June 9 I went to feed the calf at 7 a.m. and was horrified to find it in the death throes on the kitchen carpet, jerking its head upwards with open mouth. It had clearly not had any suck from its mother and had not therefore taken in the colostrum it needed to adjust even to gentle Ostermilk. Moobli whined when he saw its dead body, scraped at it with a front paw as if trying to bring it back

186

to life. I buried the poor mite under the beautiful canopy of silver firs in the west wood.

It was a drizzly day, and I tried to overcome my depressed mood by writing two articles for my column. Moobli just lay glumly, his eyes dull, staring into space. By the evening he still could not walk. The only progress he could make was by hauling himself forward with his front paws, sliding his rear along on his left buttock. I felt then that if he did not improve this time I would have to take him south and look after him in an easier place. Within three days, however, Moobli could hobble jerkily along, well enough to follow me slowly round the woods each morning.

One evening, after trekking round the western seascape of the eagle territory I was covering, I stopped for a drink in a hotel bar with another eagle enthusiast and there met a vet from Lanarkshire called Marshall Watson. When he heard about my dog's problem, he agreed to take a look at him there and then. I took advantage of this kind offer and brought Moobli into the bar. After watching him move and a brief hand examination of his rear region, Dr Watson said there was nothing that could be done. It was not possible to operate because the blocking molecules that paralyse the spinal nerves continue to be produced. He said that when the time came he would be glad to help. The dog could be given a pill to sedate him, then an injection which would send him into a peaceful sleep from which he would not wake up. I thanked him and took Moobli back to the Land Rover, still cherishing the hope that he would prove to be an exception to the rule, and somehow in our healthy active lifestyle would get better.

By late June Moobli had recovered enough to urge me to throw his sticks, but after only two or three runs his left leg again began to drag. Yet in all other respects he was alert, healthy, and seemed quite happy. I still fed him pearl garlic capsules, which I did not have to mix into his food. He took them from my fingers, chomped them up and swallowed their garlicky juice with alacrity. I also began to massage his spine and hips vigorously twice a day. A week of this brought about some improvement, for when I let him come on a short trek to 1,200 feet overlooking the big corrie, he made it there and back with little trouble. Alas, it proved to be just one of his short remission periods.

After a few quiet days, when I was studying the rare butterflies and moths using the flowers in the front pasture and the honeysuckle

I had encouraged, I took him on a trek through the long woods to the west. He conked out after less than a mile and just sat down. He waited until I returned, then gamely hauled himself down with his front paws through the high clinging bracken to the boat. His boots saved the tops of his toes from further injury. He wore these boots for our gentle ambles round the woods each morning quite stoically, but if I left them on during the day he still pulled them off with his teeth. Probably his increasing immobility made him bored; he had little else to do.

In early July he began to lose control of his bowels, and this remained a problem for the rest of his life. Sometimes he defecated on his bed in the hall. He was a big dog and his droppings were correspondingly large. Fortunately they were usually solid, easily removed with newspaper, and a little wiping down with a damp cloth was all that was then needed. The aroma was less than pleasant. At first I was irritated, for I felt he could at least ask to be let out, and I cuffed him. Sometimes, when he had not performed, I opened the door to let him outside, where often he would stay for an hour or more before returning to let go another smelly deposit in the house. It was infuriating. Twice, after being outside for most of the morning, he hobbled into my study to lie down, pump his tail and let out a great sausage. He looked round at it with puzzlement, as if it were not his own. I realised then that with his increasing spinal paralysis he probably could not feel it coming. He just could not help it. It was bad for me and even worse for him. Usually he managed to move forward an inch or two so that he did not soil himself, and that was the only saving grace of the whole business. Poor old boy, I thought, he probably has not long to go now.

On hearing that a new vet had taken up practice in the nearest town, some 40 miles to the east, I took Moobli to his surgery. Dr Chris Evans examined him and confirmed that he was indeed suffering from spinal nerve degeneration. Nothing could be done, but he gave me a supply of tablets which would alleviate, though not cure, the condition. They certainly helped, for Moobli picked up enough to hobble round the woods each day without falling down.

In July I heard that my father was miserable because the matron had stopped him smoking, as he tended to fall asleep with a lighted cigarette and could have set fire to the place. To smoke now, he had to go outside and sit on a bench. His letters were entreating me either to look after him myself or to take him back to Spain, where he had lived in happy retirement until he fell ill after his wife (my stepmother) died. Before going south to see him, I converted what had been my workshop into a bedroom, thinking that, if he was now fit enough, I might bring him back to Scotland. The walls of Wildernesse were made of thick whinstone and the floors of solid concrete: he could smoke his head off in there! And with his income added to my own, I could perhaps afford a generator, so that we could have electric light and he could have his beloved television.

I made an appointment for Moobli to have a full examination at the RSPCA animal clinic in West London. It was not that I disbelieved the other three vets; I was just exploring every possible avenue to find a cure. Meanwhile, I took him for short walks on Kew Green, but the heat made his limp worse and he sometimes fell on his backside. People asked if he had been hit by a car; some freely offered their opinions that I was being selfish in keeping him going and that he should be put down at once.

On August 4 we arrived at the RSPCA hospital in Putney where I was introduced to a kindly and greatly experienced vet, Dr Tony Self, who said he would give Moobli a full examination under a general anaesthetic and try to find out exactly what was wrong. Gail, his nurse, was a devoted reader of my books, and it was she who had given me the wounded owl Holly.

I took Gail and Geoffrey Kinns to Richmond Park for lunch, and we walked about taking photos of bigger and better stags than survived in the hills around Wildernesse. I was too worried about Moobli to enjoy the outing and returned in the late afternoon to the Putney clinic.

189

18 · *Decline*

Tony Self held the huge X–Ray photographs against a lighted screen and pointed out the effect of osteo-arthritis in Moobli's left rear leg where all the cartilage had gone from the top of the tibia. There was also spondylosis of the spine in the thoracic cavity, with bony growths to be seen sprouting from one vertebra, though these were not causing trouble yet. Spinal nerve degeneration was caused by four vertebrae becoming fused due to calcification of the cushioning discs, one or two of which might have disappeared altogether. This was not the result of years in the cold and wet climate of the Highlands, Dr Self hastened to tell me, but was an inherited condition which could not be operated upon.

I waited for the verdict and felt a flood of relief when he said that there was certainly no need to have Moobli put down yet. Because of the paralysis, he would feel no pain in his bad leg unless he injured himself seriously. I was to give him a four-month course of anabolic steroid injections, and was handed the plastic syringes, needles and capsules there and then. I pretended that I had often given injections before, though in fact instinctively I recoiled from doing so. Under Gail's watchful eye, I administered the first in the thick muscle flesh of Moobli's buttock, and he appeared to feel nothing whatever. I thanked Dr Self, made a donation to hospital funds, helped Moobli into the Land Rover and drove away, exultant at my dear dog's new lease of life.

190

Before returning home I spent a few more days with my father and took him round the Sussex countryside. His attempt to cross a field for a better view of the Chanctonbury ring ended after fifty yards when his legs began to shake. We both realised then that he would not survive long in the spartan conditions at Wildernesse. I searched for a property where I could look after him and Moobli, but prices had risen sharply and I left with the promise that I would get him out of the Home when next I came south.

Moobli's legs seemed to improve for a while, the steroids helping to build up muscle. On August 20 I heard crows and ravens calling and went out to see Atalanta lurching along to the east. The corvids were flying along beside her, just close enough to ruin her hunting with their racket. I hiked up the burn for a better look. Moobli began scenting the north-east wind and moving anxiously, oblivious to his bad leg. Had he found the pine marten which had been leaving twisted scats near the cottage? As I stole quietly nearer I saw that it was a fox feeding from a dead hind that had been washed downstream in recent heavy rains. She looked up as I froze, stared straight at me, and then resumed feeding. I shrank back to get my camera, but Moobli did not follow. I hissed for him to come down, but as he moved he fell over at the rear, snapped a twig, and the fox slipped away through the bracken. Poor Moobli was not much use at stalking now.

Three days later I set off for a trek up into the big corrie. Moobli conked out on the first steep hillside half a mile above the cottage, and when I came down again he was just sitting there, admiring the view. He had done well to get that far, I thought. He struggled home behind me, puffing and wheezing, and arrived a few minutes after me, avid for his supper. At least his boots had saved his dragging toes from injury.

It was so hot on August 27 that I swam in the cold loch in snorkel, wetsuit and flippers. Moobli came with me and seemed to swim as well as ever, even towing me towards the shore with his tail. I could see underwater through the glass of the snorkel mask that his rear legs were kicking normally, yet when he left the water they appeared weak, and he hopped along using his stronger rear right leg.

He started to lose bowel control again. He let go on the study carpet at the end of our morning walk round the woods one day, and rushed from his hall bed into the kitchen on another, defecating near the cooker instead of heading out through the open door. Perhaps he had felt it coming at the last second and had instinctively come to me for help. I tried feeding him earlier, then walking him round in the hope that he would perform before we settled down for the night, but always he seemed to time his defecations for the early morning. It began to happen so often, and without any warning, that eventually I decided he would have to spend the night in the woodshed. I moved his bed there, fed and watered him, and spent some time explaining to him that his shits were too big and smelly for me to carry on allowing them to soil the carpets. He looked forlornly at the meagre surroundings of the shed, as if knowing his status as my beloved companion was being eroded through no fault of his own.

I shut the top batwing door as I left to keep the midges out. After that I always cuddled him there at night, telling him I still loved him. Even so, I sometimes found him in the porch in the early morning, and he still headed into the cottage when he needed a latrine.

One morning, after he had messed his bed in the shed, I cleaned it up, thinking that would be that, and let him into the cottage where, within seconds, he let another load go on the floor. Without thinking, I yelled at him and made him go outside. When I went out later he was gone. I donned a shower suit and set off along the shore to look for him, certain that he would have made off downhill, but there was still no sign of him after half a mile. Was he trying to leave me? Surely he could not have gone farther than this? I returned, calling urgently and whistling. There was a stir in the bracken below the west wood. He was lying there, ears back, the picture of dejection, as if not knowing what to do or where to go. I felt overwhelmed by the whole situation. Old age and infirmity seemed the inevitable tragedy that followed the triumph of one's youth and prime. It happened in nature. It happened to man. It would happen to me.

I brought Moobli back into the study and dried him off with a towel. After that I tethered him in the shed each night with a 15ft rope so that he could still get off his bed and go outside to perform. By mid-September he seemed to have accepted the new situation for at dusk he headed towards the shed of his own accord.

When I set off on the first stag trek of the season he wanted to come too, so I let him try. He got over the burn all right, but collapsed after 400 yards as we headed up through the steep

By mid-April he could no longer climb a small cliff in the woods. When his legs collapsed on a long trek in late May, he gamely hauled himself down to the shore on his front legs alone.

Forced to rest, he lay in the sun brushing the midges from his eyes.

Two weeks later he had recovered and insisted on the long high trek which proved his last, when he scented out a newly born calf whose mother had died. I carried the calf home where Moobli befriended it.

Wearing the leather boots that prevented damage to his dragging feet.

Shirley Bellwood with Sandy in the walled garden where Moobli
recovered enough for a last wild summer.

After seeking his company in the woodshed, the deer calf lay sprawled
across his paralysed legs.

Unable to take any exercise except the occasional swim, Moobli loved to watch the chaffinches taking scraps from his bowl.

The great heart of the once mighty gentle Moobli had been stilled at last.

eastern woods against a north-east wind. Well, he could wait as he did before, or hobble back to the cottage. I told him I would not be long and set off up to a 1,800-foot peak and then along the high eastern rim of the big corrie. I took many good pictures, and after eight hard miles I returned to the cottage. Moobli was nowhere to be seen. I prepared supper, and still he had not returned. Wearily I set off to look for him, wondering whether he had fallen into a bog, or worse. After a mile I heard a whine above me, and there he was, sliding down on his left backside as fast as his front paws would pull him. He had covered a mile and got up to 300 feet. He whined and moaned with relief as I fussed and petted him. Then I noticed his gut was full. He had located a dead hind and had eaten well! My fears that he would starve to death if I did not find him were groundless. Even in his semi-paralysed state he could still look after himself.

A week later he wanted to come on another stag trek but this time I told him to stay. I was heading up the side of the burn when I saw that he was hobbling along behind, then he started scenting the air. I had just come opposite the hind carcass which I had dragged out of the burn to stop it polluting my water supply, when I saw an auburn brown animal like a hare retreat behind a rock. I kept still and it came out again. It was a fox that darted forward, seized a large mouthful of something white, withdrew behind the rock where she dropped whatever it was and then started licking it up. I moved behind a tree and took the camera from the pack, but the fox must have got our scent for she leaped on to the bank, gave me a broadside look, then dashed off through the bracken. When I crossed the burn I found she had been eating maggots! The carcass was teeming with them. She had been grabbing mouthfuls of the juicy squirmy things, no doubt holding her breath, then withdrawing back behind the rock, below the wind carrying the fetid stench, to chomp them up. She was performing a useful service too, helping keep down the future blowfly population. One never stops learning, I thought.

Moobli came up to 400 feet then conked out again, near a prominent deer crossing in the burn. Never mind, I would pick him up on the way back, if he did not get back to the cottage of his own accord. On my return there was no sign of Moobli at the deer crossing. I searched for a while, calling and whistling, scanning the terrain with binoculars. He must be at home, I thought. With dusk falling, I abandoned the search.

He was not at the cottage. I bathed down and made our suppers, sure he would be back in an hour or two. By 10 p.m. he was still absent and I became worried. How far had he gone? He had proved with the fox earlier that there was still nothing wrong with his scenting ability. Had he tried to follow my entire scent trail for over nine miles? If so he could now be in trouble. Well, it was a calm moonlit night, not cold, and while he had not eaten in 24 hours there were plenty of burns and water runnels up there from which he could at least drink. Towards midnight a strange thought crossed my mind. Could he be trying to die a sort of honorable death up there on the lonely Hill? Surely, such a concept was ludicrous for any animal. And yet, having looked into his dark troubled eyes recently, I was not so sure. I put his food and water bowl out by the porch and went to bed.

All through the night I kept waking up, worrying about him. At dawn I looked into the hall, for I had left the door open, but he was not there. I went outside – both his water and food bowls were full and untouched. An icy hand gripped my heart; I could hardly breathe and felt physically sick. I looked through the window in the workshop.

Moobli was on his bed in the shed and he looked shattered. Maybe he had only had the strength to reach his bed before collapsing. I took his food round and he climbed groggily to his feet, swaying, but he ate it all. He could not use his rear left leg at all now, and I saw that his spine was sticking out, the whole rear end beginning to waste away through lack of normal use. The steroids had slowed down the deterioration but, as expected, they could not halt the disease. I let him rest until lunch time, when he padded round to the study on his front legs as I held up his rear end. He whined now and then, and kept looking round at his weak legs. He messed the floor again, but now I could feel only compassion.

During the next few days he improved slightly and tried to come with me on our usual walks round the woods. At times he would go all the way, at others he sat after a few yards, scenting the air to detect where I was, or made a short cut for home when we had reached only the far edge of the west wood. He still wanted to chase after his sticks but all co-ordination in his rear legs had gone, and the right rear leg was giving way too. He dragged himself along with just his powerful front legs, and did not scrape his back toes while long lush grasses of summer still covered the front pasture. I found a perfectly round stone in the burn which he preferred to his sticks; yet I did not *make* him chase after it. If I left him outside for long, he would pick up the stone in his teeth and stare through the window at me, willing me to go out and bowl it down over the pasture so that he could run after it.

After days of torrential rain had made the ground a quagmire in mid–October, I took him to the large inland town on a supply trip. He could hardly get up the 80-foot slippery, marshy slope to the Land Rover. He messed the bed again during the drive and it took a long time to clean up. I began to feel I should do what several people had urged and have him put to sleep. I screwed up my courage and drove him round to Dr Chris Evans's surgery. I felt at my last ebb. As we waited outside, and I saw people going in and out with their pets, Moobli looked at me with huge dark eyes, as if guessing what I might be about to do. I leaned over to where he lay on the bed, looked into his eyes and asked the question in my mind: 'Do you want to go, Moobli, do you want to die?'

One huge paw came up and touched my left elbow, his sad eyes seeming to say, 'Do what you will.' His look was one of complete devotion, trusting me to do what was right. I broke up quietly and the tears began to flow. I started the engine and drove away, knowing that I could not do it. We had been through too much together for me to give up so easily.

At the village post office I found awaiting collection a letter from Nikki Ridley, a reader who owned a small farm in the Lake District, and whom we had twice visited on trips south, enclosing some green–lip mussel extract from Australia and a supply of devil's claw tablets. She had heard these were good for arthritis, and gave me the address of a veterinary surgeon called Dr Trevor Turner, who was a specialist in Alsatians and had a practice at Northolt in Middlesex. I immediately wrote a long letter to Dr Turner and began feeding the new cures to Moobli along with the pearl garlic. Besides administering weekly injections, I began to massage his spine and rear end regularly with embrocation. Maybe I was clutching at straws, but anything new that might help keep the dog going seemed worth trying.

Once again Moobli began to show signs of improvement, enough to get most of the way round the woods in the mornings. When I bowled his roundstone, I took to chasing after it too. This galvanised him, and he dashed down over the grasses at

195

such speed on his front legs that he usually reached it before I did.

I made him stay behind when next I went on a stag trek, and was glad that I did for I was deluged by sleet storms and had to take shelter. When I returned Moobli was on his mat in the porch, and a sore on one toe told me had tried to follow for some distance. Unless I put him on a long rope I realised he would never give up trying. I was afraid that he would get lost or injure himself if he followed me again. I found him shivering in the woodshed one cold morning, and wrapped him in two of my old sweaters each night after that, and these kept him warm.

In late October I received a reply from Trevor Turner analysing Moobli's trouble:

I was sad to read of Moobli's problems. Reading your letter it appears very obvious to me that the basic condition is so-called CDRM, chronic degenerative radicular myelopathy. This is a condition of nerve degeneration which affects mainly the German Shepherd although it is seen in other large breeds, Boxers, Danes etc. As you know, Shepherds are also prone to arthritic change as they grow older and the two conditions together contribute to so-called 'Alsatian Disease' where they become wobbly at the back end and gradually lose the use of their hindlegs.

Unfortunately although a lot of work is proceeding in the various veterinary schools, there is no cure for this condition at present and although I am reluctant to put it to you so baldly, I feel it is better I tell you rather than build up your hopes and waste your time bringing Moobli to see me, for I feel that reading the very full case history that you have sent to me that there is really little more that can be done.

Anabolic steroids (Nandrolin etc.) certainly help, as do corticosteroids and analgesics. I treat very similarly to the way he has been treated up to now, using injections of Nandrolin plus tablets of either Phenylbutazone (Butazolidin) or Predleucotropin, which is another analgesic combined with cortisone to reduce some of the inflammation. The condition is usually quite painless except when the animal falls awkwardly or does the splits when obviously some pain is caused by the arthritic bone.

196

In certain cases in the past I have used injections of Vasolastine which is an enzymic preparation reputed to help nerve healing but again the treatment is palliative rather than curative. Good nursing helps a tremendous lot. Since the condition is slowly progressive, rather like multiple sclerosis in humans, massage, particularly with a vibro massager does help to prevent muscle wastage as use of the hind limbs is lost.

A problem you will be particularly aware of is the gradual loss of control of nerve function of the bladder and bowel and this is probably more distressing to a house-trained animal than any other sign associated with the condition. Thus it is important to keep him on a diet that does not produce diarrhoea. Bran in the diet often helps in this respect and at the same time, bed him on Vet Bed or one of the other synthetic acrylic materials available today, so that any urine soaks through and does not cause wetting of the fur and possible bedsores.

More than this, there is little one can do. Provided the animal is reasonably happy and not too distressed with his reduction in ability to move, there is no reason why one should not go on. Also, spontaneous temporary remission (just like M.S.) does occur and under these circumstances I am never in too much of a hurry to suggest euthanasia. However, once the animal is no longer enjoying life, and you, as the owner, are the best judge of this, knowing the animal's habits better than anyone else; then I feel that euthanasia is the only kind thing to do, otherwise one ends up hanging on to an animal for one's own sake rather than for the good of the patient.

I am sorry to write to you so frankly, but felt that you would prefer it this way. If I can be of further assistance please do not hesitate to contact me, but I feel it would upset Moobli too much to bring him such a long way and do not think it would be to any good purpose.

Yours sincerely,
Trevor Turner

I read the letter again and found my eyes swimming with tears. Here, beautifully put, was the plain truth. It was also a veritable sentence of death. I sat for a long time with my head in my hands, giving way to my emotions, knowing that no medical knowledge in the world could help Moobli now. I stole into the workshop and shone a torch through into the woodshed. Moobli had never liked the arms of one sweater being pulled over his front legs, and he had pulled it off completely with his teeth. It was a cold night and he lay all crouched up in a ball.

I felt a great surge of self-disgust. What on earth was my dear dog doing out in that awful shed anyway? What the hell did it matter if he made a mess on the floor of the cottage? I brought him back indoors, made up his bed in the hall and spread newspapers in the study. I resolved to love him, comfort him and keep him warm, no matter what, until the end. 'Good nursing helps a tremendous lot', Dr Turner had written. Well he would have that.

I wrote thanking Dr Turner for his kindness and help, and mentioned the dog's continuing determination to come with me on treks.

Acknowledging the contribution to the hospital's research fund, he replied –

> I do hope Moobli remains happy in himself for as long as possible. All of us here feel for you, we have experienced similar problems with our own pets and all you can do is *know* when the time comes.

Strangely enough, Moobli enjoyed another period of remission. For the next few days he was able to accompany me round the woods with only an occasional rest. This encouraged me to increase the vigour of his spinal massages. I did possess a vibro massager but without electricity it was useless. His right rear leg had recovered almost its normal strength. I learned that I could alleviate the weight on his back legs by holding up his thick bushy tail, not hard enough to strain the vertebrae between tail and spine but strongly enough to give him a little lift so that his rear legs would clear the ground more easily. He did not object to this at all, and after a while the root of the tail adjusted and became thicker and stronger.

On a fine sunny day at the end of October I set off on a stag trek, mainly for the exercise. Moobli wanted to come too, so I helped him over the burn, which was running fast after recent rains, and he managed a quarter mile. When he stopped for a rest I told him to lie down and wait for my return, which he did. It was bitterly cold up on the tops and a sleet shower soaked my clothes. It felt good to be once again part of this vast open landscape but my mind was not really on the natural world around me. I fell down and accidentally smashed the aperture vanes in the 640 mm lens. When I returned to collect him, Moobli was nowhere to be seen.

He was not at the cottage either. I put some bath water on the gas and went out to scan the hills with binoculars. I soon located him. There, at 700 feet and a mile away, was his great tan chest gleaming in the light of the sinking sun. I yelled, whistled and waved, and saw him look towards me, his huge ears pricked up. Then he started sliding down through the tussocks. It would take him an hour to reach the burn, and after bathing I would go out and help him over it.

Moobli was sitting by the front door when I went out half an hour later. How he had got over the swollen burn I did not know, but it had been an heroic effort on his part.

It proved to be his last trek. He went quite well round the woods for three more days before the right leg began to give way again and he was back to slow hobbling. I gave him a little party on his eighth birthday and fed him well. At 8 p.m. his tail quivered and out came a sausage turd on to the newspaper. He just looked up in a friendly way as though he simply could not feel it coming. When I set off for a trek on November 8, he followed for the first hundred yards, then shuffled back home. He knew in himself now that his trekking days were over.

It was desperately lonely up in the hills, especially when I realised that never again would I have his company out there, that never again would he alert me to wildlife I could not see. Perhaps it was time for me to quit the wilderness life. On the way home I came to a decision.

19 · A Last Wild Summer

I winched up the big boat, locked it to the gateposts and carried everything I valued or might need through the rest of the winter – cases of diaries, wildlife notes, the half-written script of *A Last Wild Place*, camera gear, photographs, books, records, bedding and other items – down to the shore where I loaded the small boat to the gunwhales. There was scarcely room left for Moobli and me. A late November gale started to blow just before we set off and it was a dangerous crossing. No clear plan was formed in my mind. Somehow I would find a way in which to get my father out of that Home and take care of him, and Moobli, through the winter months. I would camp with the dog in the Land Rover until we had found somewhere to live.

Most of my friends urged me to let Moobli go soon. Margot said it would be the kindest thing to do. I could have him cremated and scatter the ashes at Wildernesse. Geoffrey thought I had already kept him going too long. Gail was sure it was time I faced the heart-breaking decision; she could book him in for euthanasia at the RSPCA hospital in Putney in a few days' time. If I did not want to have him cremated, he could be buried in her garden in Epsom.

My heart rebelled against the whole idea: Moobli was quite happy in himself and certainly was not feeling any pain. He had even regained some measure of control since leaving Scotland and seldom soiled his bed in the Land Rover. Sedate walks in the park and across trim fields were a far cry from the rugged life at Wildernesse but, apart from slithering about on the light dusting of snow, he seemed to enjoy my constant company.

I telephoned Dr Turner and asked him to give the dog an examination, and he invited me to bring him in the very next day to the Mandeville Veterinary Hospital in Northolt. I took Moobli into the surgery holding up his rear end with a towel slung under his belly. Dr Turner was sympathetic, but with a grave face he confirmed what all my friends had said – that Moobli was finished and should be put down now. He would do it right away if I wished, and the dog would feel nothing. As I caught his eye, Moobli gave a sharp whine, as if saying 'No', and retreated into a corner. I could not bear it! I could not face the decision there and then. Hastily stammering my thanks, I took the dog out and drove him away.

It was my father who produced the brainwave. Why didn't I take him and Moobli back to Spain, at least for the winter?

'He has not long to go anyway, no matter how well you look after him, and perhaps the sun will do him good.'

I could scarcely believe that the idea had never crossed my mind! Such an obvious solution had certainly not occurred to me. If Moobli improved in the Spanish sunshine, and he was still happy at the end of three months, I could stay on longer, continue the study I had begun of Spanish wildlife . . .

I told my father we would do precisely that.

In the next few days I part-exchanged my old petrol-guzzling Land Rover for an almost new VW camper with modern equipment such as a refrigerator, sink, water tank, wardrobe, storage cupboards and five beds. It would be the ideal vehicle in which to take Moobli and my father to Spain. I booked our passage on the ferry from Plymouth to Santander and paid the small additional fare for the Alsatian. I then completed all the documentation. Shirley Bellwood let me leave some of my and my father's belongings in her house. Everything was arranged.

It was when I telephoned the Spanish Embassy in London to find out what injections a dog would need before entering Spain that I received the terrible shock. In addition to the necessary vaccinations, Moobli would need a certificate of good health from a qualified vet, stating that he was free from any disease. It would be impossible to obtain such a document. I felt shattered as I put down the phone.

When I told my father, he simply said quietly, 'I am afraid you will have to face it, Michael.'

Were they all right after all? Had I hung on to Moobli so long because I simply could not bear to lose him? Was I thinking of myself rather than the dog? In the last few days his legs had got worse and now he could hardly walk at all. I could not sleep for worry, and agonised about it all the next day. Then, steeling myself, I telephoned Gail and told her to book Moobli into the Putney hospital for (I did not mince my words) 'execution' in two days' time.

Next evening Shirley Bellwood phoned while I was with my father. I blurted out the news about the good health certificate required by the Spanish authorities and that Moobli was booked in to be put down on the morrow. She was horrified.

'You simply can't have that wonderful, noble animal put down,' she said. 'He's no *ordinary* dog. I will look after him while you're away. He will be happy in this big house, and he doesn't even have to be taken out. He can have the run of my large walled garden.'

I was overcome with relief. We talked a little more before I put down the phone and hurried into the bathroom to burst into tears.

On the last day of December I drove Moobli to the home of his saviour in Chertsey. Shirley had cleared the enclosed rear porch and we put his bed down in one corner of it. When the door was open, he had a short clear way over smooth rounded flagstones to reach the garden, with its large lawn and a wild area of trees at the far end. The enclosing walls kept Moobli from any risk of hobbling out into the light traffic of a cul-de-sac. I gave Shirley some money towards his keep and brought in his bowls, food, pills, collar and lead, and a few items to store in her wine cellar.

'I'll do my best to make Moobli happy,' she assured me. 'I hope I can keep him going so that you can take him back to Wildernesse and give him one last summer there.'

As I tried to explain to Moobli what was happening he turned to Shirley with a pathetic look. I left promising to call her later to hear how the dog was settling down, and drove back to Worthing feeling very lonely in the empty van. I would probably have gone crazy if Moobli had been put down that day. Shirley said later over the phone that she was beginning to worry about the responsibility of it all, though Moobli seemed happy enough. I set her mind at rest as best I could.

'He's a tough working mountain dog,' I said. 'He is also a stoical character, and if you just feed him, throw a ball for him now and again each day, he will be all right. If he dies, it certainly won't be your responsibility. I can't thank you enough for what you are doing.'

She promised to write often and let me know how Moobli was getting on.

For two months my father was happier in the small rented villa near his beloved Puerto de Mazarron in the south east of Spain than he had been for years. Many of his old friends came by, and we visited them. It was strange to find how much I enjoyed the socialising after years alone in the wilds. Regular letters from Shirley told us that Moobli had made friends with her 'wild' cat Sandy and explored the garden. Warm nights were spent not in the porch but with her and Sandy in the luxury of her drawing room. A few sheets of newspaper tucked under him took care of accidents, but usually she had a good idea of their timing and got him outside. I kept my wildlife column going for the Scottish newspaper, although it felt strange to be sitting in sunny Spain recalling the harsh reality of life in the Scottish Highlands.

As the weeks went by, however, I began to feel trapped. I could not leave my father alone for more than a couple of hours, and whenever I asked him if he wanted to return to Worthing, his face darkened and with a vigorous shake of the head he said loudly 'No!'

Eventually, through friends, I found a former nurse, a woman he liked who had been recently widowed, to look after him in her apartment. I took off into some wooded mountains for three weeks to make sure that they settled down together. That short adventure convinced me that, when Moobli was gone, I would return to investigate more thoroughly the rich wildlife of Spain, where wolf, brown bear and the rare lynx are still to be found roaming wild. I returned to the Puerto for the last time in early March, when the nurse and my father said they were very happy together. He most certainly did not wish to return to England, and as I bade them goodbye, I was glad that I had succeeded in taking my father to what he thought of as home.

I meandered slowly north through Spain, making several mountain treks from the van, and had more than a glimpse of the possibilities for a most exciting book in the future.

Moobli recognised me immediately upon my return to Chertsey. He whined with pleasure and buried his great head between my legs. Shirley had looked after him well for he was plump, his coat thick and shiny. His front half had become so developed from hauling himself around on his forelegs that he looked like a lion. His rear quarters, however, were wasted away and he could not walk at all unless his tail was held up. Shirley guessed the first thought that would cross my mind for she said –

'I really would like it if you took Moobli home and let him die where he belongs, in Scotland. I would be far happier if you did that, gave him a few more good times at Wildernesse, than if you had him put down right now after all my good work.'

How could I possibly do otherwise? It was quite clear to me that Moobli was (his paralysis apart) in fine health and perfectly happy with life. When I threw his ball in the garden, and held up his tail, he pulled so hard and fast with his thick-muscled front legs that he almost had me over. He seemed to want to show me just how strong he still was after adjusting to his handicap. He was, when all is said, in much the same position as a human wheelchair patient, and we do not put them down.

That evening I took Shirley out for a Chinese meal and camped in the van for the night beneath the trees on the far side of the green. Next morning we loaded up everything and then 'tailed' Moobli into the van. He panted happily on the high bed and, after a sad goodbye to Shirley, we set off on the long drive back to Wildernesse. I was determined that he would enjoy one last contented summer.

Nature had almost completely taken over Wildernesse by the time we returned. One wooden boat runway had been washed away, the windmill generator was down, and the waterpipe, swept from its moorings, was hanging over the falls like a disembodied snake skin. Inside, a copper pipe had been burst by ice and a green mould covered everything, including my bed. But the roof was intact, and Moobli was happy to be back, though it soon became clear that his life would be confined to the area round the cottage.

He tried to drag himself after me when I set off on an eagle trek on March 28. I could not risk him getting lost now, so tied him to the porch logs with a long rope. When I returned he was on his bed in the porch. He had chewed off his third pair of leather boots. So badly damaged were they that I made him new ones from a canvas mail bag. He cheered up considerably when I fed him with fresh venison which I had cut from a newly dead deer.

Slowly he became adjusted to a more restricted life. He was as eager as ever to chase after his roundstone as I puffed along behind holding up his tail near the root. Sheep began raiding the front pasture again, but he could not help to herd them out now. Instead he gave a '*huff*' bark when he saw them, so alerting me to their presence. He was still being useful.

I made the first attempt at what I came to call the 'killer trek' to Atalanta's farthest eyrie on April 11. The misery of having to do it alone was alleviated only when I found her sitting on eggs. I felt hardly any pain in my knees, and thought that maybe Spanish sunshine had finally driven away my bouts of arthritis.

Moobli gave me a fright when I boated out five days later on a supply trip. Because he could no longer get up the steep slope to the van on the opposite shore, I left him behind without securing him on the long rope that I was sure made him feel like a prisoner. Although I instructed him to 'stay', I saw, looking back from the far bank, that he had hauled himself down to the shore and was launching himself into the water. God, he will drown, I thought. I was about to jump into the boat again as he swam out when I saw him turn back and drag himself up on to the bank. He was too sensible to try it again. Though, as I was to learn, his power in the water on good days was almost undiminished.

In the village I asked the keeper Allan Peters, who was a first class shot, if he would deliver the *coup de grace* with a single rifle shot when the time came.

'Never!' Allan said stoutly. 'That dog is unique. When you make that decision, you'll be strictly on your own. As far as I'm concerned, you'll have to get the vet over.'

Most people who knew Moobli half as well as Allan loved him

too. As I landed the boat, I saw his great bear head rise from the daffodils by the cottage. This time his boots were intact, and as I removed them I hugged him close, knowing that I loved him too much to end his life while he remained tolerably happy.

In fine weather I fed him outside, and afterwards he would lay down, head on paws, his brow furrowed as if he were still trying to figure out what was causing his paralysis. Colourful squabbling little chaffinches would hop about nearby for the scraps left in his bowl not daring to go too close. From the kitchen window I often saw him shift his paws and head further away from the bowl so as to let them in to feed. He watched them closely, with his huge brown eyes gently switching from one bird to another. They might have been *his* little birds, *his* personal squad of entertainers.

When it grew warmer in late April, I gave myself and the cottage carpets a break and put Moobli's bed back in the woodshed. I always made a fuss of him when I took him there last thing at night, and fed him a few tasty titbits before turning in myself. I tidied up the place and hung a blue blanket over the ladders and the logs to reduce its stark appearance, and wrapped him snugly in an old green sleeping bag. Usually he had kicked it off by morning, but his feet were still as warm as toast. He might not be able to control his motions but there was nothing wrong with his circulation.

He clearly took the move as a humiliation. One morning, after he had messed himself, I took him to the burn to clean him up. Later, when it began to drizzle, I found him not on his mat in the porch but back in the shed, asleep. He woke as I went in, looking very sad, and put up his paw to shake.

When howling gales and hail storms replaced the fine weather I hurried out early to make sure he was all right. To my astonishment, a weak red deer calf struggled to its feet from where it had been lying next to the dog and tottered off on wobbly legs towards the west wood. As it disappeared behind some bramble bushes, Moobli dragged himself out, anxious to see where the calf had gone. Clearly the young deer had sought shelter from the hail and had not been put off by the proximity of the huge gentle dog. It may even have sought his company. Moobli had disappeared by the time I returned from my walk round the woods, and eventually I found him a hundred yards away beneath the cherry trees, with the calf lying over his rear legs. Although it was now in its death throes, Moobli had certainly not harmed it for there was not a hair out of place. It must

206

have fallen on top of him, and he was licking its eye and cheek with utmost tenderness. He sat near the calf for a long time after it died, whining, as if in sorrow at the loss of another playmate. How could I ever face putting down this gentle creature?

It was after losing my keys on a trip to the islet where rare black throated divers nested that I decided to give Moobli a treat and helped him into the boat when I went back to look for them. He was so glad to be part of my life again! He sat on the deck with that tongue-lolling smile, gazing at the passing shore along which he had once run with such powerful careless abandon. We were a quarter of a mile from home when he began to stare eagerly over the side. He could not run, or even walk now: I just said one word –

'Swim?'

In answer, he put first one paw and then the other up on the gunwhale. As he looked at me expectantly, I lifted him over. He went in with a splosh, disappeared for a second, then came to the surface looking as if I had been trying to drown him and struck out for the shore as strongly as ever. Neither of his rear legs were kicking at all and they dragged uselessly behind him. I puttered along beside him, urging him on, ready to haul him out quickly if he got into trouble. He needed no help and, after scrambling ashore, urged me to throw out a stick!

Moobli became quite manic about swimming, the one joy left in his life, and longed for me to throw sticks into the loch. He seemed proud to show me he could still do something active. After two or three swims, he waited patiently for me to lift his tail, then pulled hard on his front legs back to the cottage for a towelling and to dry off in the sun. The exercise set him up for the day. Finding him plagued by midges in the porch after one exhausting trek, I tailed him down to the shore. So eager was he that he pulled me along faster than I cared to run. I intended to let him go when we reached the rocky steps below the gateposts, but I was tired and my responses were too slow. My foot hit a step and down I went, banging my right knee on a rock. I yelled with the pain, sure the knee was broken. I also fell hard on Moobli, and might have killed him, or been badly bitten. Instead he gave a brief yipe and then had a shit! While I limped back to the cottage in consuming pain, Moobli got on with his swim. For two days my swollen knee felt as if a dagger was lodged between shin- and thigh-bones, but it did not keep me long from eagle trekking.

My fears that the golden eagle survey, set in motion that spring by the Nature Conservancy Council, would result in the takeover of most of my old eyries turned out to be well founded. Of the 31 eagle eyries which I had located and listed in confidence for the Royal Society for the Protection of Birds, and which they had passed on to the N.C.C. without a word to me, I was left to cover only the two pairs on my side of the loch. Of course I was angered by the snub, but I tried to take the situation philosophically for I had chided the N.C.C. a year earlier for not doing enough for rare species such as eagles, as well as wildcats, otters and pine martens. Eventually things worked out to my advantage when the N.C.C. field observer Jeff Watson and I became friends. Jeff found an eyrie that even I did not know about, one on which I could look down from an ideal hide site, and he helped me to set up the hide there.

It was an even more rewarding season than two years earlier, when I had watched Atalanta's twin-chick eyrie, for the parent birds spent a great deal of time in this nest. The crowning moment came on July 25 when I was showing off the newly fledged eaglet to the wildlife journalist Brian Jackman for a feature he was writing for the Sunday Times. I described it in my book *On Wing and Wild Water* as one of the finest sights I had ever witnessed in the wild, though readers of that book would scarcely imagine Moobli's unwanted but patient vigil at home. I wrote –

> The male (eagle) rose effortlessly into the air until he was beside the eaglet, then both hung in the air like a pair of giant black bats. The male seemed to be trying to teach the youngster a certain manoeuvre. After bending his wings back he spread out the front alula feathers, which are designed to smooth the air flow over the wings to prevent the bird stalling at slow speeds, spread his twelve tail feathers out like a fan and with his talons extended, descended very slowly to land on the ptarmigan. As he performed all this, the eaglet copied his every movement, then landed beside him. It was superb to watch.
>
> Then both birds launched themselves into the void, rose into the air, hung there again like great dark kites and repeated exactly the same manoeuvre, parachuting down with talons stretched out below them. This time the male landed beside the ptarmigan while the eaglet landed on the other side. It appeared that this was not what the male had intended, for he

was clearly teaching the eaglet how to hunt, how to kill. Once more he rose into the air, watched by the eaglet on the ground, and again descended slowly, hitting into the ptarmigan with great force. Then he hopped gawkily to one side. The eaglet now appeared to understand what was required. Again it rose into the air, hung momentarily, came down faster, landed on the ptarmigan and began to feed. The male watched for a few moments more, then sprang from the rock (and) went into a jet glide. . .

We finished taking down the hide and tramped back to the boat. It was the last of 17 treks to and from hides that I had made between May 15 and July 25, including three to the far end of the killer trek. As so often, bored Moobli was at the gateposts to greet us as I landed the boat. There was no need to keep him tethered or cooped up in the van, for there was no risk now of him straying far enough to get lost, and he roamed as freely in the cottage area as his two front legs would allow.

Meanwhile, my father had died in his sleep in Spain on May 24. In that hot country, the law requires that humans are buried within twenty-four hours of death. After the initial shock of the message I received in the village post office two days later, I felt glad that I had been able to take him back home to Spain where he had enjoyed five happy months before being laid to rest there, as he wished, next to his wife. I said my goodbyes to him in my own way in the peaceful oak and spruce glade.

My world seemed to be shrinking. Both my parents had gone, two of my best friends in Canada had recently died, so had my boyhood mentor, Jim Adkins. And it was clear that Moobli had not long to go.

I had discussed the most humane ways of ending Moobli's suffering, if it should come to that, with Shirley Bellwood when she visited us for a week at the end of June. I took her for a couple of treks to see the eagles and an eaglet in the nest, and to the islet where the black throated divers nurtured their single chick. She stayed behind with Moobli when I made an overnight visit to the eagle hide, and this made him very happy for he remembered her well. It was obvious to her, as it was increasingly to me, that he would not

209

last out another winter for he could control neither of his disposal functions. There was no movement at all in his rear legs now, and every two days they had to be bandaged, with canvas boots tied on over the bandages, to prevent him wounding his toes as he dragged his feet along behind him. We hit upon the idea of an overdose of sleeping pill in his food. But how, I agonised, could I judge the correct amount, or bear to feed him the murderous dose?

Often I had to wash his woollen bed in the loch. He tore to shreds the top of the sleeping bag I gave him to lie on while his woollen bed was drying out. I solved this problem for a while by making my own version of a vet bed with leak sheets made from canvas mailbags over a layer of soft water repellent plastic chips. I could no longer leave him in the cottage when I went out, so I made a special shelter from thick plastic sheeting and pronged hazel poles under which he could lie on his bed on the soft grasses near the porch. He took to the shelter at once. It kept him dry when it rained, and he preferred it to the dreary surroundings in the woodshed.

At the end of July it became necessary to make the trip south that I had been putting off. There was my father's estate to sort out and research to be done, not to mention the interviews for magazines and radio with which my publisher wanted to launch *Golden Eagle Years*. I doubted that Moobli could cope with the trip, and he seemed to know what was going through my mind. As I sat at my desk contemplating the possibilities, he began to give high yiping barks from his vet bed beside me. In some uncanny extra-sensory way he seemed to know precisely what I was thinking. He had never made such sounds before. Could he read my mind? It was a nightmare, and I swiftly reassured him. After that I disciplined myself never to entertain such thoughts in his presence – though I even felt uncomfortable about whether distance made any difference at all to the unknown perceptions of a dog.

During the next few days all such thoughts receded to the back of my mind, for once again he began to improve. He became even more manic about his swims, as if desperately trying to show me that he still enjoyed life. From my desk I watched him through the window gently picking raspberries from the wild canes and chewing them up with relish. He regained control of his urine, though it was probably just one of those brief remissions. Dammit, I thought, I will not give up on him yet but take him south with me.

I spent all day ferrying gear across to the van and hauling the big boat out of the water by hand, for the loch level was so low that the winch wire would not reach it. I tried to use a block and tackle, but the rope was so chewed up by mice that it kept breaking. Twice I went flying on to my back in the shale. I took Moobli across in the small boat and searched for a spot on the opposite shore where the forestry track came close to the water's edge, for the 80ft slope up to the van was so steep in places that I could not carry him up it. After loading up the van I hauled the boat out of the water and turned it upside down, keeping a close eye on the dog. When he had finished performing in the long grass, I helped him up on to the carpeted floor of the camper, over which I had spread newspapers. He was so happy at the prospect of going driving with me again that he panted with excitement and thumped the floor with one paw. It was heart-rending to see the root of his bushy tail twitching slightly as he tried to wag it.

Somehow he seemed to have been able to pick himself up for the occasion, and during the next ten days, as I dashed about my business, he did not once make a mess inside the vehicle. I chose our camping spots carefully, so that he could sleep outside at night on his bed on top of soft grasses. It did not rain so there was no cause to put up his tent shelter.

Not until we reached Crianlarich on the way back did we see any sign of real Highland weather, and from there on it was rain and gales all the way home. As the small white dot of Wildernesse emerged through the grey curtain of mist, I felt for the first time that after that wonderful season had finished we were returning to a lonely jail of my own making. I waited for a lull in the rainstorms before launching the boat, but even half-loaded it was a rough crossing, and the little boat yawed alarmingly in the waves and the shrieking wind.

The rain deluged down in earnest as I was carrying up the last load to the cottage. To escape a soaking, Moobli had hauled himself not into the open cottage but into the woodshed at the back. It was as if he felt himself no longer fit to be with me indoors.

For the next ten days the howling gales and incessant rain continued unabated. The level of the loch rose seven feet, coming up so fast in one night that both boats were completely submerged. It took almost a day of hard baling and sweaty hauling to rescue them. The small boat's keel was smashed in on a rock, and only by making a foot-long aluminium splint and fibre-glassing it on could I effect a temporary repair.

The weather depressed Moobli, and once again he lost control and could not keep clean. He could not swim in the raging loch, and his only joy during lulls in the rain was to chase after his round-stone through the sodden grass as I held up his tail. For the rest of the time, he lay bored on his bed in the hall while I worked at my unwanted book.

August 26 bestowed upon us one sunny period of two whole hours and Moobli had his best day for a long time. The sun seemed to revive him as he chased his stone with enthusiasm and enjoyed a swim. When the heavy rains gave way to showers, he went for a week without fouling his beds in the hall or the woodshed. As I tidied up the cottage one morning I heard the throb of a boat engine, followed by a loud shout.

'Wake up!'

My ex-logger friend, Geordie Tocher, had arrived on a quite unexpected two-day visit. We had enjoyed many wild adventures together in Canada and here he was, in a hired boat, looking me up on his first trip to Britain. Moobli thoroughly enjoyed the company, and even came with us to dinner at a luxury castle hotel. Geordie carried his front and I carried his rear up the steep slithery 80ft slope, and we boated home in total darkness. When I tried to judge where Wildernesse was from the almost undiscernible line of the hills, I made a mistake and could see nothing of the boat bay, or anything familiar, in the dim light of the torch. We got Moobli over the side and I said—

'Home, Moobli!'

Immediately he turned to the right, and sure enough we entered the boat bay fifty yards away. The dog had saved us maybe hours of searching.

September 2 was another fine day, and Moobli again seemed much more lively than of late. Once more he lost control of his bowels but did not foul his bed. He chased after his stone but I did not take him for a swim in the much colder loch. Three days later, after renewing the bandages and canvas boots, I noticed that the root of his tail was strangely hot. I thought it was probably some local infection but could see nothing amiss through the dense covering of fur. He was very thirsty and drank a lot of water. I also

212

noticed that he showed far less interest in his stone, and after chasing it twice did not want to do it any more.

I did not realise it then but this was to signal the beginning of the end for the poor old trooper.

20 · The Time Comes

When I went into the woodshed next morning I was shocked to see that Moobli's tail was red raw along one side and all the hair had been removed. Oddly, he did not seem to be in pain. I helped him round to the kitchen, washed and disinfected his tail and bandaged it all up. I returned to the shed to renew the papers round his bed and saw a large vole standing where his tail had been. It looked sick and was trembling slightly. I was sure then that voles, and perhaps even shrews, which are carnivorous, had been chewing at his tail overnight and due to the paralysis, Moobli had not felt them doing it.

In rage, I smashed the vole to death with a piece of wood.

Next day more hair was missing and his tail looked worse where the bandages had begun to stick to the flesh. All had to be washed, dried, and smeared with antibiotic cream again. He had also messed his bed, and for once he had not even tried to inch away from it. I realised then how great was the risk of infection. If I could not keep that at bay, the final decision would have to be made. I found another vole and a pygmy shrew in the shed, killed them, then went on my lonely walk round the woods in a daze in the rain. Although *A Last Wild Place* was almost finished, I still had not received a contract for it, and when I returned to the house I felt so miserable that I was unable to work on it. My only foreseeable income was a £500 advance due on publication of my eagle book in a few days time – not enough to see me through the lonely winter without dipping into my small savings.

Moobli no longer had the pleasure of dragging himself after his roundstone ball, for the grasses would tear at his raw tail. And even if south-west gales had not been whipping the loch into a foam, I could not let him swim either for it was important that his tail be kept as dry as possible to help the healing process. The mood around Wildernesse seemed even more depressed when above the wind I heard the ghostly wailings of the black throated divers, a sound they make not only upon arrival in the spring but also when preparing to desert the loch to winter on the sea.

When the rain ceased and the sun emerged for a while, I slung a towel under Moobli's belly and helped him down to a soft grassy patch in the front pasture. Later through the window I saw him licking, chewing and tugging furiously at something with his teeth. Thinking he was pulling off his rear boots, I shouted for him to stop. I was appalled to see when I went down to him that he had chewed all the new dressing and some old scabs from his tail, which was now nearly all red and raw. There were tufts of hair on the grass and he had also swallowed some. Clearly it had not been voles or shrews chewing at him but he himself that had torn out all the hair. What on earth could be the reason for it? Frustration at his immobility?

Much of the rest of the day was spent applying dressing which he resolutely pulled off again. At night I soaked a long silk shirt-sleeve with antiseptics, strapped it on and talked to him for a while, telling him not to pull it off. He ate with apparent gusto almost twice his normal rations, in which I was now putting mange medicine and vitamins. I wondered if he was being brave or merely stoic, or because of his paralysis simply could not feel the pain that the state of his tail should now be giving him. Before going to bed I pulled a warm sweater over his front, helping his legs through the arms like a baby as he licked my face.

In the morning I was thankful that the shirt-sleeve was still in place but the furry base of his tail now seemed swollen and again felt hot. I decided to give the whole area a hot bath with water, soda and a strong antiseptic liquid, rubbing well in. To my horror, white maggots began to wriggle out of his fur and fall to the ground. It was like a nightmare. Greenbottle flies must have laid eggs on the base of his tail and now about 30 maggots were infested in the fur,

215

scraping at his skin, though as far as I could see they had not yet burrowed into the flesh. It was clearly the ticklish agony they had been causing that had made Moobli tear his tail hair out; for in his paralysed state he could not reach to exactly where they were with his teeth. I killed the lot and gave the whole area another sousing with the strong solution.

Although his tail seemed to be healing over the next two days, it was a constant struggle to keep it and him clean. Once a heavy rain shower made him drag himself over some rough gravel to get indoors. Off came the third shirt-sleeve and part of the tail was again rubbed raw. On my next supply trip I rang the vet, Dr Chris Evans, to ask his advice but did not speak to him for he was operating on a cat. I told the receptionist that, if or when the time came, I would like Dr Evans to meet me in the village where I picked up my mail so that I could boat him over to Moobli. I wanted him to die between the two little woods and below the hills where, until recently, he had spent his marvellous outdoor life. She said it was asking rather a lot to expect an extremely busy vet to make an 80-mile trip, involving two ferry crossings that would take most of a day, just to put one dog down. It would also cost me a good deal of money. It would be better to bring Moobli in to the town surgery. I said I did not care about the money, if only the vet could spare the time.

Just then Dr Evans came on the line. When he heard about the maggots, on top of the paralysis, he reckoned that Moobli certainly had 'Fly Strike', and if it was well advanced there would be little hope of avoiding fatal infection. I should cut away his fur close to the skin in a large area round his rear end and then treat the infected area with antiseptics, to make *sure* all the maggots had gone.

I still hoped Moobli's tail would continue to heal and that there could thus be a stay of execution. As if to show I might be right, the old trooper appeared at the gate as I pulled into the boat bay, glad to see me return. He had somehow got down from the cottage without pulling the protective sleeve from his tail or injuring it further. I was hugging him when I heard faint hootings and saw flashing lights near my van across the loch. I re-launched the boat and crossed to the waiting postman who handed me a telegram from my publishers. They had arranged for me to be interviewed about my eagle book on an important books programme on Scottish TV in Edinburgh on September 17, and also by a leading national newspaper the following morning. What was more, they wanted me in London

216

a week later to do five more media interviews around the actual day of publication. I could not refuse to support the book and the sense of impending doom grew stronger. Moobli would not come to any harm in the cottage overnight while I dashed to Edinburgh and back, but he surely would not improve enough to endure the long trip to London.

That evening I obeyed the vet's instructions and close-cut with scissors an eight-inch swathe of thick fur from around his rear end. To my further horror and disgust, I found three more instances of 'Fly Strike'. Infestations of younger, smaller maggots were embedded in his skin yet he did not appear to have felt these at all. I removed and killed them then doctored the whole area. As he surveyed his bald rump he seemed more upset by the indignity of its ugly appearance than anything else.

Over the next few days it was clear the 'Fly Strike' was under control for although his bald rump and tail were scabby they were both healing well. He now showed little desire to leave the cottage. Perhaps he knew that if he went outside the flies would get to him again. After a high lone trek, during which I took the best deer hind photos for years, I returned to find him lying morosely on the kitchen carpet. He did not even lift his head when I went in. Trying to cheer him up, I slung a towel under his belly and walked him on his front legs down the path. He managed that all right but when we turned to come back he seemed weaker, and he paused for a few seconds before putting one leg in front of the other.

I rose early on September 17, feeling tortured that I would have to leave him alone all day and night, but I had no choice. I fed him double meals, left plenty of food and drink around him in the kitchen and hall, made him as comfortable as possible and tried to explain I would be back as soon as possible the next day. As I washed and cleaned him he put his huge paw into my hand and there was a look in his sad eyes as if he were trying to express more than mere thanks. Somehow I got through the Edinburgh interviews, the TV one taking all afternoon because of some recording problem. After an almost sleepless night in a dreary hotel full of noisy American sailors who had just arrived in port, and doing the newspaper interview, I did not boat back to Wildernesse until dusk next day.

As I opened the door I heard Moobli whining and flopping about. He made a strange baying noise as I entered, a sound that seemed to carry a sense of betrayal, as if he had thought I would never return.

217

He had messed himself, and his stomach seemed blown by the total lack of exercise. I put the towel round him and took him out and after making a big fuss of him, apologising for leaving him so long, he seemed all right again. He certainly ate with apparent relish the big raw steak I had bought for him. I cleaned him up well and made him a new bed from one of my blankets.

It was bright and sunny for a change next morning. I helped him down to the lush grasses of the front pasture, bathed him clean again, and left him there lying on his right side, hoping he would enjoy the warmth of the sun. After a few minutes I heard him whining. I went out and found he was trying to right himself, to get on to his stomach, but he could not do so. He was kicking his legs like a dying deer, his eyes showing the same desperate whites. His whinings were not just from frustration but from bewilderment, and fear too. I knew then, as I righted him, that I could not delay the fateful decision much longer. He *was* beginning to suffer now, certainly mentally. I helped him back to the cottage. That night came the first hailstorm of the approaching winter.

By noon the following day, however, he seemed to have perked up a bit, to have recovered some of his strength. When I went in to carry his bedding down to the loch, to give it a good wash, he seemed to guess what I was going to do. And when I said the word 'Swim?', his ears pricked up and he tried to thump the floor with a front paw, though it was more of a scratch at the carpet than a thump. As I helped him down the path with the towel I noticed that his steps were short and slow, lacking their old pulling power. I was sure he would not actually go for a swim.

When we reached the loch's edge, he lay a few moments panting to recover his breath. He looked this way and that, out over the waters which had once been his element, then hauled himself in and started to swim. He did not go far and after a few yards he stopped, as if he had run out of strength. Alarmed that he might drown, I plunged in but he turned and swam slowly back. He regained the beach but could not haul himself out. As I helped him up, his front legs were both trembling. I had to half carry him back to the cottage.

Two mornings later I was woken up by whinings from the kitchen. Somehow he had manoeuvred himself against the wall, and was on his back, unable to push away from the wall and right himself. There was now a bedsore on his rear left haunch, the side on which he always lay, caused by his uncontrolled urinations. As I helped him back to his bed his sad eyes told me all I needed to know. He knew he was finished, and the pleading look in them tore my heart.

The words of Dr Trevor Turner came back to me then – '...all you can do is *know* when the time comes.'

That time was now. I made the final decision, for it was clear that he *was* suffering. I boated out and rang Chris Evans who said he would be in the village the very next day. He would meet me there at 4.30p.m. As I put down the phone I felt like a traitor. I told myself, I still had time to change my mind. Even so, I bought Moobli a large piece of steak for supper. When I got back I saw that the last segment of his bald tail had a greenish look, as if gangrene was setting in. There could be no change of mind now. I made a fuss of him, fed him a superb meal, and taking the best and most costly hand-knitted woollen blanket from my bed, made him comfortable.

That night I had a nightmare about him and could hardly face what had to be done next day. It was dark, raining heavily, and a grey mist hung low over the hills. I staggered round the woods as if I was still in the nightmare, feeling a boiling rage that my wonderful dog had been permitted less than nine years of life. I used the strength of that rage to dig his grave up on the little north hill above the cottage, a spot where he had loved to sit in the sun and look at the sublime view. The ground was hard, filled with rocks, and I smashed away at it, blinded by tears, until the spade broke and I had to finish off the grave with a shovel. I then carried the broken spade down to the shore and, with a great hammer-throwing heave, consigned it to the loch.

During a lull in the rain I took Moobli outside but he whined oddly and fought to get back into the kitchen. For the rest of the morning he was strangely calm. His eyes were darker than usual but kept looking into mine with deep devotion and trust, as if he knew something momentous was about to happen. I hugged and talked to him for a long time, trying to explain that we were going to have to say goodbye for a short while.

I met Chris Evans in the village and after shaking hands he asked to see Moobli. I realised there had been a misunderstanding for clearly he expected to put Moobli to sleep in my van. I told him that the dog was not in the van but back at Wildernesse, twelve miles over the hills and across the loch. I told him I had explained to his receptionist that I wanted Moobli put to sleep in the beautiful surroundings where he had spent most of his life, but for some reason Dr Evans had not received that message. I also explained that to carry so heavy a dog up the steep slope to the van would have caused him even more suffering. At first the vet was displeased. He said he was extremely busy in the area that day with calvings expected all over the place. But as he saw my agitation, the natural kindness that makes anyone want to be a vet in the first place took over. He relaxed, shrugged his shoulders and said –

'Come on, then. I'll do it for you anyway, and do the best I can for Moobli.'

He went to his car to fetch some scissors, a syringe, a phial of Pentobarbitone and a thick rubber band. I said nervously that Moobli was a very large dog, had a powerful heart, and I wanted to be sure that he went out at once. For answer, Dr Evans held up the phial and said it was one with which he put a horse to sleep.

On the way back I drove fast, trying to save him some time, but he quickly put his hand on my shoulder and told me to take it easy; we would get there just as fast. When we had boated over, I got the key from the shed and opened the front door. To my surprise Moobli now seemed anxious to get outside. He hauled himself strongly out through the front door on his front legs and made towards Dr Evans as if he knew this man had come to treat him in some way. Now the heavy rain clouds had cleared, the sun was high in the sky, while above the east wood hung a double rainbow. Wildernesse had never looked more beautiful.

Dr Evans looked at the bald tail and rump, the paralysed rear legs and winced.

'It's time?' I said.

'It is past time,' said Dr Evans sadly. 'It has to be done. It is kinder for him.'

'Very well. Let's get on with it.'

It was not a sense of tragedy, nor even sadness, that I felt but a sort of subconscious compulsion to be cheerful; as if my mind had forced itself to click into a self-protective slot, to treat death not as the end of life but a new beginning. I brought out the brightly coloured new blanket, got Moobli on to it and cradled his great head with my left arm. Dr Evans snipped some hair away from his right foreleg and told me to hold the two ends of the rubber band tightly so that main vein stood up.

After his last look at the sunlit shimmering loch and the trees of the woods where he and I had lived so wonderful yet hard a life, Moobli's eyes gazed lovingly into mine. I told him that he would have peace at last and no more suffering. I told him that I loved him, loved him more than any creature I had ever known, man or animal, and would revere him for ever. I said I would join him before too long and that he was to stake out a territory in the Happy Hunting Ground, and work out where the deer were, and the wildcats and the foxes, and to try and find another eagle eyrie, as he had done for me.

I watched the needle go in and Dr Evans' thumb pressing. Only a few millimetres of fluid in the syringe had gone down when Moobli whined and gave a little kick. I had the terrible feeling he knew at the last moment that this was not a cure but a death dose. It was while I was telling him again that he was my darling dog, my beloved one, that he gave a great sigh, the air rushed from his lungs, his eyes slipped backwards, his head fell against my arm and his body went limp. I heard myself give a gasping sob but I did not cry. I seemed to be beyond emotion. Suddenly the whole area went dark, and I saw that a small black cloud had briefly obscured the sun.

I stood up and looked down in stupefaction, horror, terror almost, at his still form, his eyes wide open as if in disbelief, hardly able to take in my mind that the great heart of the once mighty gentle Moobli had been stilled at last. Again the desperate cheerfulness took over and I found myself telling the vet that I wanted to take a photo of Moobli dead. It was a personal thing and I hoped he would not think me callous. Oh no, he said, he understood. He had seen hard Highland men break down at such moments. I got the camera and took two pictures of Moobli stretched out, so big even in death that he made the double blanket look like a towel.

I left him lying there in the sun, boated Dr Evans over the loch, drove him back to his car in the village and paid his reasonable bill. He told me I should get back fast, before *rigor mortis* set in, or it would be difficult to bury him. It was dusk when I returned and walked up the path. Moobli's eyes were still bright, reflecting a greenish light, and his limbs remained supple. For one awful moment I thought that he might still be alive, that his heart was still beating. I put my ear close to his chest for a long time but heard no movement, and his body was going cold. I gave way to emotion then. Tearfully, I wrapped his body in the thick blanket

221

that would be his shroud and used the brief extra strength of sorrowful anger to carry him up the north hill to the grave.

I spread half the blanket over the bottom, lowered him down and laid him in his favourite lying position – back feet tucked under his haunches, front paws out, his head resting between them – then covered him with the rest of the blanket. The sky was clear now, and a quarter-moon eerily lit up the scene. He was facing south, the cottage, and the supernal view, the one he would never see again. I placed in his collar and lead and said a brief prayer, but I could not restrain my sobs as I shovelled the earth over him, stamped it down, then set the grass sods over the grave.

That night I drank a lot of whisky.

In the morning I packed my few valuable belongings, boated out in cold misty drizzle and drove south to London. I was sure then that I would leave Wildernesse for good. With Moobli's death a whole era had ended. There was an emptiness about the place. A great spirit had been removed.

Epilogue

My grief lasted a full two years and it was exactly five years to the anniversary of his death before I could face writing about it. Sometimes when I visited his grave, I found myself on my back, staring blindly at the sky and retching, with real pain in my heart and gut. At others I heard a strange keening sound wailing from my throat. Before I set out mechanically plodding on lonely treks in the mountains I went to his grave to ask his spirit to come with me, and some nights I prayed for his ghost to appear. Never once did I feel his presence. It was as if he had never been.

For a long time I could not adjust to the knowledge that I had lost my aide-de-camp in the wilds, my adjutant, befriender of the wildcats, brilliant tracker of all forms of wildlife, my best pal, and twice the saver of my life. There was guilt in my grief too. Perhaps I had not looked after him as well as I might have done. I often knelt on the wet soil by his grave longing to have my time with him over again, to stroke just once more that beautiful head. The thought that he was rotting down there in the earth was almost unbearable.

I intended to leave Wildernesse and even tried to sell the rest of the lease, but after experiencing storms on the loch, potential buyers cried off. The truth was I really had nowhere else to go. Without money from a sale, I could not afford to move back to civilisation. Unable for almost another year to find a publisher for my book, I felt trapped in a sort of living grave below Moobli's. That was replaced by a dogged determination to complete my studies on rare Scottish wildlife. When I found my favourite eagle on eggs in a nest that others knew about, keeping a close eye on her successful rearing of her chick was reason enough to stay longer. After that I began filming the wildlife around me. For four more years I soldiered on alone at Wildernesse, so completing over twenty years alone in remote wild places.

In the first months many people told me that the best way to assuage grief was to replace Moobli with another dog. To me the idea was total anathema. I could not 'replace' Moobli in any such way. He was not just a family pet. He had been my only and constant companion through both idyllic and harsh times for nearly nine years. I had spent more time in his company than with any other animal or human in my whole life, including my parents, for my mother died when I was four and my father, a travelling salesman, had been seldom at home. To this day, five years after his death, I still miss my beloved old comrade. I have never felt the urge to get another dog. Maybe I will one day, and of course it will be a totally different character and perhaps just as lovable, but for me there will never be another Moobli.